THE
GREAT
LEGEND

D0324839

THE GREAT LEGEND

by Rex Stout

CARROLL & GRAF PUBLISHERS, INC.
NEW YORK

First Carroll & Graf edition 1997

Carroll & Graf Publishers, Inc.
260 Fifth Avenue
New York, NY 10001

ISBN 0-7867-0443-8

Manufactured in the United States of America

CHAPTER I

"YOU ARE KESTEN!"

I SHALL BEGIN BY WRITING DOWN MY NAME. AN ATTEMPT at concealment would be futile, and, even if successful, would serve no good end. You who are already acquainted with my history will find herein my justification; strangers will meet with new friends, beautiful women, and heroes.

I am Idaeus, brother of Phegeus, son of Dares.

I expect to live through many peaceful years in these groves of Mount Ida; but never, while breath is in me, shall I forget that bloody day in the field beside the winding Simoïs, which now flows past the ruins of great Troy.

Achilles, the champion of the Greeks, sulked in his tent. Ulysses and Ajax did not appear; rumor had it that they conferred in the tent of Agamemnon, the commander-in-chief. We of Troy made ourselves easy, after an early visit to the temple of Apollo. Everything was quiet.

A little before the middle hour of day I had gone, together with my friend Cisseis and my brother Phegeus, to join the crowd which filled the public square at the entrance to the Scæan Gates. Old Antenor, on his way to the Towers, had halted to talk with us. Nothing was expected of the warriors that day, and our conversation had veered to some trivial topic of the town. The throng of old men, women, and children hung about disconsolately, wavering between anxiety and expectation.

Suddenly there was a commotion among the guard of soldiers at the gate. The motley crowd pressed forward curiously. The captain of the guard roared a command to make way for someone. The next instant the massive iron doors swung open and a royal messenger plunged through the entrance on horseback. He was covered with sweat and dust, and spots of blood were on his clothing. The horse was white with foam.

The messenger pulled on the reins for a single moment to say to the captain of the guard:

"It is Diomed. He had taken the field in his chariot. He is mowing down the Trojans as a storm does the corn of Thrace!"

Then he spurred forward, bellowing hoarsely:

"Make way! To the palace!"

His words had been heard by all, and instantly a thousand voices were upraised in clamor. Clenched fists were lifted to heaven; shouts of despair and dismay were heard on every side. The captain of the guard despatched three messengers to different parts of the city in search of Hector. Phegeus, who was standing next to me, turned and said with a sigh:

"My brother, I do fear that great Jove frowns on Troy."

I shrugged my shoulders. Let religious devotees like Phegeus tremble at the frown of Jove. As for Diomed, I had never had a very high opinion of him, thinking him, indeed, the weakest of all the Greek princes.

I said as much, aloud, to Phegeus, and was overheard by old Antenor, who turned to me with a stern face.

"Boy," he said—I was then only twenty-two years old—"boy, it is not well to scoff at a great hero, though he be of the Greeks."

I made no retort, but maintained a respectful silence, for Antenor was really quite a decent old chap. But when a bystander chimed in, singing the praises of Diomed and expressing a fear that he would drive the Trojans from the field, I could contain myself no longer.

"How!" I exclaimed. "Afraid of Diomed? Who is this Diomed? To hear all this talk, one might think that he really amounted to something. Would that I were at spear distance from him at this moment!"

I spoke louder than I intended, and was overheard by many who stood near, as well as old Antenor. He, turning, muttered, "Braggart!" quite audibly, and I observed a smile on the faces of several of the others.

My blood leaped to my head. Impulsively I turned to Phegeus and asked:

"Brother, will you drive?"

He nodded, understanding me.

Ten minutes later we had brought forth our chariot and made ready to hasten to the field.

All was confusion; we were surrounded by a crowd of all sorts of people, wagging their prophetic tongues and lending eager hands to our assistance. I overheard one fellow making a wager at five to one that neither Phegeus nor myself would return alive, whereat I smiled scornfully. Cisseis, I remember, smiled at me quite naturally, but I fancied that there was a queer look in his eyes as he turned them on my brother.

Phegeus, always eager for a combat, leaped onto the driver's seat; I sprang into the quadriga. Through the open gates of Troy we rushed toward the field, our ears filled with the shouts of those we passed. The cry was, "Behold Phegeus and Idaeus!"

There was an unmistakable note of scorn in their voices as they uttered my name, but little I cared for that. My irreligion was known all over Troy, and irreligion was anything but popular in the ninth year of the great siege.

The dust of the conflict filled our nostrils and obstructed our sight almost as we passed the outer wall of the city. At first all was confusion; but as soon as we had made our way through the rear ranks things were plain enough. To the right and left the combat raged; in the center was a large open space, guarded, it appeared, by a detachment of Trojans. Answering to my call, Phegeus guided our chariot thither.

We approached them, and passed; as we did so I heard their voices raised in a great cry of warning:

"Beware of Diomed! The strength of Pallas is in his arm!"

I grinned disdainfully and bade Phegeus drive on.

At a distance off to the left there suddenly appeared a great cloud of dust. It was a chariot, advancing like a whirlwind. On all sides was heard the cry:

"Diomed!"

A little more, and the forms of his horses, his driver, and himself were easily distinguished. Phegeus urged our horses forward; I grasped my lance and held it aloft, ready. I considered it most unlikely that he should find the mark at his first attempt; for the rest, I depended on the speed of our horses, which my father had brought from Thrace and which were unsurpassed in all Troy. We were now quite close to the chariot of the Greek.

Suddenly, to my surprise I saw his horses pulled backward on their haunches. As the pace of his chariot slackened the warrior leaped to the ground. He was encased in shining armor and held in one hand his shield; in the other was a javelin. At the same time Phegeus pulled on his reins, stopping abreast of the other chariot, and brandished a lance with his free hand.

The Greek was advancing on foot. "Trojans you are, and brave," he cried; "then know that I am Diomed, son of Tydeus!"

His intention was plain enough; he meant that I should descend from my chariot to meet him afoot. Thank the gods I was not such a fool! If he chose the part of rashness, so much the worse for him. I crouched behind the bulwark of my chariot, ready to attack him the instant he hurled his javelin.

But hot-headed Phegeus spoiled my pretty plan. That day would certainly have been the last for Diomed if it had not been for my brother's impetuosity. Raising himself high from his seat and uplifting his lance, he let it fly straight at the breast of Diomed.

The Greek caught the lance squarely on his shield. He staggered, and turned; then, recovering himself instantly, he drew back his javelin, aiming, I thought, at me. I dropped to the floor of the chariot. There was a whirring through the air, a cry—my brother's voice—and I looked up in time to see Phegeus tumble headlong to the ground with the javelin buried in his breast.

It had been hurled with such force that the point stuck out through his back just between the shoulder-blades; I saw it, red and dripping, as he fell.

I maintain that what I did then was the part of wisdom; those who censure me may advise fools, being themselves fools. The horses, deprived of a guiding hand, were beyond control; the chariot was useless.

I leaped to the ground. In two bounds I was at the side of Phegeus. His staring eyes and still form told me in a glance that my brother was dead.

Turning, I saw that Diomed had caught up another javelin and was coming toward me. Stopping only to hurl my lance at him in blind fury, I wheeled about and took to my heels. After me came the roaring voice of Diomed, and the javelin flew past my head. I did not wait to catch the words.

It has been said since—everyone has heard the story—that Jove covered my retreat in a cloud of smoke. You may guess what I think of so silly a tale. There was indeed a cloud, but it was of dust, and was raised by the thundering feet of Trojans struck amazed at my brother's death and my own enforced flight. Depend on the Trojans to run like sheep when any little thing goes against them. I have always said it was their greatest fault.

Rushing through the struggling ranks afoot, I finally reached the gates of the city, and made for the palace. I was still dazed by the suddenness of the misfortune that had overtaken me. At the palace I expected to find Antenor and prevail on him to carry the sad news to Dares, my father. They had long been friends.

Luck was against me. I had just passed Doreon Square and was turning through the old marble gate when I found myself suddenly confronted by my father in person. How his face lit

up as he caught sight of me! He ran forward, forgetting his
staff in his consuming eagerness.

"Idaeus! My son! And Phegeus? Where is Phegeus?"

My face must have told the story, for as he caught sight of
the expression in my eyes he released me from his embrace
and took a faltering step backward.

"Phegeus? Tell me, what of my son Phegeus?"

I answered bruskly:

"He is dead."

At that dreadful word I thought for a moment that my father
would fall to the ground. I sprang forward to support him, but
before I could reach his side he had straightened himself stiffly
to the full height of his tottering old body. Again he spoke, in
a firm tone:

"It is the will of Jove." Then, as though struck by a sudden
thought, he added swiftly: "But what of his body? You bring
it to me? Idaeus, you did not desert him?"

But by that time a crowd had gathered, and not caring to
air our family woes in the street, I took my old father by the
arm and led him to his house, but a short distance away.

There, seated in the great marble court which had been his
chief pride, where Phegeus and I had been wont to play together in the sunshine of our youth, I related everything to
him in detail. Grief at the loss of his son and anger at my
failure to recover the body were almost forgotten in the glo-
riousness of his death. I remember that he repeated over and
over the words:

"He died in battle, and by the hand of a Greek king!"

In this thought he appeared to find consolation, but still it
was easy to see that the calamity had added ten years to the
burden of his shoulders. For an hour we talked together, while
I did my best to comfort him, but the depth of his feeling was
shown in the strange request he made of me at the end. It was,
in short, that I should lay down my armor and leave the field
for good.

"But, father," I expostulated in amazement, "do you then
advise me to play the part of a coward?"

His reply was half wistful:

"You know well, Idaeus, that no son of Dares can be a coward. I am but a merchant, though holding the office of a priest, and my bones are old and cracked, but still I carried arms during the first three years of the siege. Was it not my lance that slew Amyclas? But now I have lost one son, and I would not lose another—the only one left to me. King Priam, with his fifty, can afford to be prodigal. Besides, have I not often heard you scoff at this war and its object? You should be glad to leave it."

"That I know, father. 'Tis a silly business from beginning to end. To die so that fool Paris may keep his woman calls up my choler. Still, I would do nothing unseemly; and how can I now lay down my arms, when Troy is in direst need of all?"

My father actually smiled. "So stupid a question from the subtle Idacus! My son, there are other things besides the bearing of arms to be done in Troy. Only tomorrow there is a caravan of silks to be conducted to Phthia."

"But that is beneath me."

"Then, the garrison at the Scæan Gates?"

"Nay. I will either fight or not; I will have no half measures."

At this second refusal my father paused and appeared for some time to be lost in thought. Then suddenly he inquired:

"What would you say to the post of kesten in the palace?"

I looked up quickly. "The palace of Priam?"

"Assuredly."

"But it is not obtainable," I objected. "It is held by Ialyssus."

"But if I could get it for you?"

"I would take it gladly."

"Do you promise before Jove?"

"Such a promise would not strengthen my will."

"I know, I know," and my father's face darkened. "I tell you, my son, it is ill to renounce the gods. But there, we will not argue the matter. Then you promise? Oh, Idaeus, to keep you—forever! I could not bear to lose you—the last! The post shall be yours. I shall see Antenor—here—my staff, my cloak of hide, my *zoster*—I shall see Antenor. In an hour I shall return.''

He departed. Finding myself alone I sought a marble bench at one end of the court and sat down to reflect. My thoughts would scarcely allow themselves to be shaped, overcome as I was by the so recent memory of the body of my dead brother stretched out on the ground before me.

It was only then, in fact, that the seriousness of the conflict that had been carried on for nine years between Greeks and the men of the Troad was apparent to me; and still I had difficulty to keep myself from regarding the thing as a huge joke. But Phegeus was dead—Phegeus, the brother of my heart—gone forever! In that was solemnity enough. Thoughts and memories of him raced through my mind for upward of an hour; then, with a deep sigh for his fate, I turned to the present perplexities and those of the future.

I had little hope of my father's success in his petition at the palace. The post of kesten had been held for three years by Ialyssus, who was generally supposed to be one of King Priam's favorite sons. It was most unlikely, it seemed to me, that he would be deprived of this honor at the request of a mere merchant of Troy, even so important and wealthy a merchant as my father.

Besides, my father had already been favored with the appointment of Priest of Mulciber.

What, then, to do? Return to the conflict, the morning pilgrimages to the temple, the absurd sacrifices to the gods, the hopeless and never-ending struggle—and all for nothing? All, forsooth, because Menelaus could not conquer his desire for a woman who had been weak enough to run off with a young rake like Paris! Olympus! Who would want a wife like that? One would expect a man of sense to consider himself well rid of her.

I had seen Helen—we called her "Helen of Troy" to miff the Greeks—many times in the temple, on the street, in the corridors of the palace, on the Scæan Towers; and I must say that I had never been able to understand what either Paris or Menelaus saw in her. But every man to his taste.

Jove! Did not I remember a little Thessalian girl, fair as Briseis—.

"My son! Idaeus! You are kesten!"

It was my father's voice. He came stumbling into the court from the outer portal, leaning on his staff and breathing heavily.

I jumped to my feet in surprise.

"Father! What do you mean?"

"You are kesten in the palace of King Priam. I have seen Antenor. You know his influence. The post is yours."

I stared at him, scarcely believing. "But what of Ialyssus?"

"Ialyssus takes the field, glad of the relief. Everything is settled."

"And when—when do I go?"

"On the morrow. With the chariot of Phœbus Apollo. There is but little time, my son, and much to be done. There must be splendid mantles, of golden cloth and rich weaving, and many other things. Come, Idaeus, come."

CHAPTER II

HELEN

EARLY IN THE MORNING OF THE FOURTH DAY FOLLOWING I gave my father a last tearful embrace, leaped into the lofty, gilded chariot, and gave the driver the word: "Forward!"

I was leaving my father's home permanently, to take up my residence in the palace of Priam in the capacity of royal kesten.

I looked backward as long as the house was in sight, while tender memories filled my thoughts. To think that Phegeus, the companion of my youth, was no more, only made it the more difficult to leave; for my old father was thus left alone. But after all, I knew that he would not have it otherwise, for, like a good Trojan, he placed the honor of his family before his personal happiness.

The appointment of royal kesten was an honor any family would be proud of. It made me a member of the royal household. The duties were precisely the same as those of the kesten in any ordinary household. All the royal parchments would be in my care—civil, religious, and military. The order of feasts and sacrifices—that is, those pertaining to the family of King

Priam—were to be communicated by me to the priests. All military orders would pass through me, save those originating on the field.

I had been within the palace many times before, but somehow it had never presented the appearance to me that it did on that morning. My eye saw new magnificences. The immense pile of white marble, dazzling in the sunlight, towering into the sky, struck me almost with terror.

As we passed the guard, with their glittering shields and upright lances, at the outer gate, they saluted respectfully. The next moment we found ourselves at the beginning of the grand corridor—a long, lofty passage of yellow *giallo antico* marble, flanked on either side by immense pillars of jasper.

Down this we passed to the foot of the main staircase, also of yellow marble, and up to the corridor above, which led us to the room of state, where the ceremony of induction was to take place.

I confess that I was just a little frightened. The elegance of the assembly gathered in my honor, the majesty of King Priam and Hecuba, his queen, seated on the throne, the very magnificence of the room itself, all contributed to my embarrassment. Great pillars of red *nero antico* ran the entire length of the room in four massive rows. Around the walls was the famous circle of carved gold; the walls themselves, of whitest marble, shone with an astounding brightness. Across the end of the room where the throne was placed were hung sweeping folds of silken tapestry embroidered in gold, culminating in the point of the great canopy above the heads of Priam and Hecuba.

A quick glance around showed me the faces of all those most prominent in Troy. It was easy to guess from their expression that they took little pleasure in this household ceremony. Old Priam, in his dotage, had grown inordinately fond of display, and, though they bent to his wishes and whims, they found little pleasure in it.

I noticed that Rhesus, King of the Thracians, wore an open frown of displeasure, and Hector was pacing impatiently up and down between two giant pillars. Paris and Helenus were grinning together behind their hands, no doubt at some joke at my expense.

At one side were Polyxena, daughter of Priam, and Andromache, wife of Hector; to their left, near Queen Hecuba, stood her daughter Cassandra, wearing, as usual, a solemn phiz; and a little to the rear stood the woman who had caused the death of so many Greeks and Trojans, and who was fated to become the instrument of Troy's destruction: Argive Helen.

She stood under a stretched length of tapestry depicting the labors of Hercules, her face partially concealed by its shadow, and she stood alone. Troy, feeling that it owed its misfortunes to her baneful presence, shunned her.

Her large, shapely form was suggested by the pliant folds of her white himation; her golden hair was gathered in a magnificent coil, heavy and lustrous; her eyes were hard with aloofness, and at the same time tender with sympathy. Crowned as she was with beauty and surrounded with magnificence and luxury, something in her attitude brought home to me the fact that she was in truth an unhappy exile, and I felt pity for her.

Absurd, perhaps, for the humble kesten to feel pity for glorious Helen, but the emotion came unbidden.

The ceremony itself amounted to nothing: it would appear that Priam had gathered every one together merely for the pleasure of looking at them. He mumbled a few words and Antenor beckoned; I approached and made my obeisance before the throne. He made mysterious passages in the air with his hands, chanting the while, and ended by placing in my hands a rod of twigs and a roll of parchment—symbols of my new authority.

Then, after a word of notification to the assemblage, he gave the signal to disperse.

I descended again to the floor and began to make my way through the throng. Two or three of my friends met me with hands upraised in congratulation—for already I had friends at court.

Suddenly, as I was pushing my way toward the door by the side of Cisseis, I heard my name spoken by some one in the rear, loud enough to be heard above the buzz of conversation now going on all over the room. I knew the voice at once: it was that of Æneas, reputed son of Anchises and Venus. As for that story—well, Anchises must have been a better-looking man in his youth than in his age. He certainly wasn't very pretty to look at when I saw him. And—to continue the digression—I heard only the other day that Æneas has even the favor of Queen Dido of Carthage. She must have rather poor taste.

"Fine man for the job, that Idaeus!" Æneas was saying, with scorn in his voice. "Only yesterday he left his brother's body lying on the field, and his horses and chariot into the bargain. And now they make him kesten!"

Turning like a flash, I found myself looking directly into the face of the speaker.

"Æneas," I said, "you would do well to manage your own affairs and let others do the same. When you acquire the wisdom of Antenor you will possibly possess his influence. It is to him I owe my appointment."

"Akh!" Æneas snorted in return, "you do well to speak of old Antenor. Wisdom! That is very funny. If it weren't for the fact that he happened to marry Hecuba's sister, where would he be with his influence? Besides, I repeat that you abandoned your brother's body and lost your chariot and horses."

I opened my mouth to retort, but was dragged away by Cisseis. After us came the sound of Æneas's mocking laughter, and my face grew hot. Not that I intended to pursue the quarrel; where would be the good of it? His reputation and influence in council would have been too much for me.

Cisseis and I had made our way to the door and were leaving the chamber when a curious incident took place, unnoticed by all save myself. Indeed, it was so trivial that it can scarcely be called an incident, but it made an impression on me by its unexpectedness.

As my feet struck the threshold I had a sudden feeling that someone was eying me intently from behind, and turned sharply. My eyes met the gaze of Helen! She was standing on a raised step before the throne, and thus was easily seen over the heads of the crowd. There could be no doubt of it: she was gazing straight at me, and there was significance in the gaze.

As I turned she shifted her glance, and I saw a rosy blush mount to her brow.

What did it mean? I tried to answer the question as I descended the main staircase with Cisseis, who apparently had not noticed the occurrence. Was it possible that I had gained the attention of Helen?

After all, I reflected, I was not a bad-looking fellow. Stranger things have happened. I was aware that Helen was an inveterate coquette—perhaps she had been taken with a fancy to amuse herself with me.

I smiled and came to myself with a start, realizing that Cisseis had repeated a question three times and was looking at me in amazement.

To return to Æneas. I have forgotten now whether it was the following day or the one after that, but it makes no difference. The point is that his insult to me was speedily avenged, though not by me.

It was in the afternoon. I was strolling along the broad white walk leading to the entrance to the Scæan Towers when the gates nearby suddenly swung open and a throng of soldiers burst through, shouting, "Æneas! Make way for Æneas!" In an instant a crowd had gathered round them so that they had difficulty to force a passage.

Grasping the arm of one of them, I pulled him to one side and demanded to know the cause of the excitement. He was covered with dust and blood, and was so hoarse he could scarcely speak. Finally I made out these words above the din:

"It is Æneas. He is wounded. They are carrying him!"

"Wounded! How?"

"A stone hurled by the mighty Diomed. Æneas and Pandarus attacked him together in a chariot with the famous horses of Tros. The arrow of Pandarus could not pierce the armor of Diomed, made strong by Pallas. Pandarus escaped by flight. Æneas, badly wounded, was rescued. Diomed captured his horses and chariot."

A grin overspread my face as I dismissed the fellow with a piece of gold. Æneas wounded by Diomed, and his horses taken! I turned in time to see the son of Anchises enter the gate, carried on a stretcher. I could not refrain from shouting at him mockingly:

"Great Æneas, why do you not return with your horses and chariot? Surely you would not leave them on the field!"

He sent me an angry glance, but said nothing; and, crossing to a clepsydra near the gate, and seeing that the point was quite low, I returned to the palace to attend the daily meeting of the council.

I was thus the first to tell them of Æneas's injury, and I noticed that the news was not exactly displeasing, though it gave uneasiness. Æneas, by his overbearing manner and superior talents, had awakened their envy, and none grieved at his discomfiture.

After the meeting of council, at which plans of war were discussed to the exclusion of all else, I went to my lodgings in the palace. They were situated in the east wing, beyond those of King Priam. Further on were the lodgings of Polites and Agavus, sons of the king. My rooms, finished in red marble and decorated with Pylian tapestries, had a great door at one end leading to the sanctuary of the kesten, containing the archives and parchments under my care.

Thither I betook myself for the purpose of becoming familiar with the articles arranged in mathematical order on the long rows of ivory shelves. I had already spent the better part of two days at this task, and there was little left to do. There remained one corner which I had not inspected, containing, I soon discovered, some records which had never been made public—a lucky circumstance for the good fame of Theseus. Even now I cannot persuade myself to divulge the nature of their contents.

With an armload of these documents I retired to a curtained alcove at one end of the room and seated myself on a marble bench before a table of ebony. I was soon buried deep in their perusal, for, being new to me, they were extremely interesting.

Some letters of Theseus to friends across the bay were particularly rich.

I had finished this pleasant task and was preparing to return the documents to their shelves when I fancied that I heard soft footsteps in the room beyond the curtain of the alcove. I rose to my feet with a frown; the sanctuary of the kesten was sacred, and no one, not even a member of the royal household, was supposed to set foot there without permission.

I sprang to the curtains, but another hand was there before mine—a soft, tapering hand of purest white. The curtains parted, and in the opening appeared the form and face of white-armed Helen.

I bowed, stammering:

"You—I am surprised—"

"No doubt," she interrupted with a mischievous smile. "I am in the habit of surprising people—it is my chief amusement. Come; admit that it is not unpleasant."

I continued to frown. "But it is wrong—this is a serious trespass. Do you not know that none must enter here?"

Her smile broke into a rippling laugh as she advanced within the alcove and seated herself beside me on the marble bench. Her girdle of *serica* fell across my knee; she allowed it to remain there, and I felt it burn into my flesh through the folds of my himation. A subtle Grecian perfume came from its hiding-place somewhere in her soft garments.

But these wily tricks were by no means new to me; I smiled within myself and waited for her to speak. I had not long to wait.

"Idaeus," she said, and she put into the name all the sweetness of which she was capable, "Idaeus, I beg of you, do not disappoint me. Must you begin by telling me that I cannot enter where I already am? How absurd!"

"But, madam—this room is sacred—"

"Silly! Rules are made to break. Will you not forget them for my sake? Is it nothing that Helen comes to ask a favor of you?"

"Helen has a husband," I observed dryly.

She shrugged her white shoulders.

"Akh! A dolt—you know it well. But I did not come to talk of him. This is something that can be granted by no one but you. You must promise me beforehand."

"There is King Priam," I suggested, a little uneasy.

"He cannot help me. Come, promise."

I steeled myself. "It is impossible, madam. I am sorry. But—tell me what it is."

"A true Trojan!" she exclaimed scornfully. "Have you no spirit? Can you not say yes, and risk all to gain much? But there—I will tell you. It is really a very simple matter."

"Anything possible I will do."

"That is well. It is this. Three days hence is the time for my annual sacrifice on the shrine of Venus, my protectress and the friend of Leda, my divine mother. As you know, these things are arranged by the Priest of Thamyris. As luck would have it, Oileus has been appointed to that post, and Oileus is my enemy. He will somehow manage that the sacrifice shall be a failure, and the protection of the daughter of Jove will be lost to me. And if—what, Idaeus! You are laughing at me!"

"Not at you," I hastened to say, "but at your superstition. However, that is beyond the question. The point is that I do not understand how I can be of service to you in your difficulty."

"Superstition? You mean—"

"I mean that I regard your Venus and your divine birth as a pretty myth and nothing more. Do not be offended because I am a skeptic, like all men of sense. I repeat, how can I help you? I have no authority over the Priest of Thamyris. King Priam is the only man can aid you."

"I have seen the king. He says that Oileus would not dare trifle with the sacrifices."

"Which is absurd."

"Certainly. Therefore I come to you."

"But what can I do?"

Helen looked at me, edging herself a little nearer. "You can transfer the sacrifice to the Priest of Mulciber," she said softly.

This request, as anyone would know, was thoroughly characteristic of Helen. She would not hesitate to ask the life of any man, and would think him well repaid with a smile. That this transfer of authority from Thamyris to Mulciber was calculated to incur the wrath of Jove did not bother her for a moment, since it was on my head that the wrath would fall. Which was a fair sample of Greek cunning.

I could not repress a smile of admiration at her cleverness. Knowing my irreligion, and my loud profession of it, she was well aware that I could give no good reason for a refusal of her request. And since my own father, Dares, was the Priest of Mulciber, she would at the same time assure herself of a propitious sacrifice—for it was well known that the priests arranged things to suit themselves.

Still, I had no intention of being taken in lightly.

"It surely must be," I protested with some feeling, "that you do not appreciate the serious consequences of your request."

"Consequences!" she cried incredulously. "Does Idaeus talk to me of consequences?"

"Idaeus himself." This ironically.

"But then—are you made of stone?"

"By no means."

"Have you not eyes to see?"

I looked at her. Her meaning was plain. An inviting, provoking smile was on her lips; her own eyes were filled with promise. I made a sudden determination; but I resolved at the same time that she should know me for no fool. I am always ready to toy with a pretty woman, and Helen was undeniably that, but I wish them to understand that I know coquetry when I see it. It was amusing to see her start of surprise as I asked abruptly:

"Do you mean to give me permission to call you Helen?"

Her reply was ready enough. "That is for the future, sir. You must not press matters. I will confess this much: you interest me; and have I not condescended to ask you for a favor? You see, I am perfectly sincere. But you must not expect too much—now."

I smiled. "As you wish, madam. As for your request, I grant it. I shall prepare the documents with tomorrow's sun; your sacrifice shall be performed by the Priest of Mulciber. For the rest, I shall be content to wait."

Helen made a quick movement, grasping my hand with both her own. "Idaeus! You are a man indeed! This shall be remembered. Count on me. He who pleases Helen has no regrets."

"No? What of Menelaus?"

It was foolish, of course; the words were out before I realized what I was saying. I fully expected her to blaze with anger, and involuntarily drew back a step as though to avoid a physical blow. But somehow the observation struck her as amusing; a smile appeared on her lips and her eyes twinkled.

"Ah," she said, "but Menelaus did not please me. He was merely my husband."

She gave my hand a quick pressure, turned swiftly, and before I had time to utter a word was gone. I slowly gathered up the parchments to return them to the shelves, thinking meanwhile that my post of kesten bade fair to be more productive of entertainment than I had anticipated.

CHAPTER III

The Lodgings of Paris.

THAT NIGHT, WHEN MY FRIEND CISSEIS CAME TO SEE ME in my rooms at the palace to talk over the events of the day, I told him of my meeting with Helen. At first, as I could plainly see, he doubted me; but I at length convinced him of the truth of my recital. His surprise knew no bounds.

"Then you have attracted Helen herself! Lucky Idaeus! Most favored son of Troy!"

"Most favored bowstrings," I retorted. "To hear you talk, Cisseis, one would think that Helen is the only woman in the world. Is it so great an honor to be noticed by her?"

In which I was utterly insincere. The days of youth are past now, and I am able to smile at their folly, which was none the less inexcusable. I can hardly expect my conceit and hypocrisy to be forgiven, but it may at least be understood.

I *did* feel that it was a great honor to be noticed by Helen. What young man would not? She had been the prize and pride of the Greek world, and had come to be the recognized type of feminine beauty. She had been Queen of Sparta, and might be so again. Pretend as I might before my friend Cisseis, my giddy brain was, in fact, transported into ecstasy by the thought that I had attracted her attention.

And my case—this much may be said in extenuation—was certainly not without precedent. She drew men toward her as a magnet draws iron. I had already forgotten Briseis. Helen had promised me nothing, but I hoped for much, and I set about doing my best for her in the matter of the sacrifice to Venus.

The priest of Mulciber, who was Dares, my father, made no difficulty in the matter, and I silenced Oileus by a promise of the second feast of Apollo. I had expected some opposition from King Priam; but at the audience which I obtained with the next sun, he merely said that he was content to leave all such matters to the discretion of his kesten. The sacrificial beasts were that same evening conveyed to the temple of Mulciber, and all preparations were made for the ceremony.

I decided to carry my report to Helen in person, thinking it a good opportunity to advance myself in her graces. Accordingly, early in the second morning I made my way down the pavement of the court to the lodgings of Paris and presented myself at the wicket on the farther side.

Owing to the authority of my official position, I was admitted without question and allowed to proceed alone down the inner corridor to the flight of steps leading to the chambers above. But at the top of these I found myself suddenly halted by the sound of a soft feminine voice:

"You may not go farther."

I stopped, and not unwillingly. Before me, not ten paces away, stood a girl of the purest Graean type, all of graceful curving lines, and with the seductive olive skin. As I stood regarding her in silence, wondering who she was and how it happened that I had never seen her before, she spoke again, repeating the same words:

"You may not go farther."

"And why?" I demanded.

"It is forbidden," was her reply.

"Do you not know that I am kesten of King Priam?"

She merely repeated:

"It is forbidden to go farther."

"But I must see Argive Helen, wife of Paris."

"You may not. Helen is at this moment with Paris and his brother Hector. They are not to be disturbed."

"Where are they?"

"Within." She pointed to where a heavy embroidered tapestry covered a door on the right.

Suddenly and unaccountably, I was possessed of an eager desire to hear what was being said beyond that door. Mostly, I suppose, it was curiosity; but underneath was a vague idea that it would not be a bad thing to know how Paris stood with his wife. Rumor had begun to whisper that neither was very well pleased with the other; it behooved me, for the sake of my own plans, to find out. I glanced speculatively at the girl in my path.

"You say that Paris and Hector are with Helen?"

"It is so."

"And they are not to be disturbed?"

She nodded.

I tacked. "Tell me—you are from Graea, are you not?"

She showed her white teeth in a smile of pleasure. "How did you guess that?"

"I would be blind not to see it. Such beauty as yours comes only from the valley of the straight river and the golden hills." I advanced a step toward her. "Are you in the service of Helen? What is your name?"

"Yes. My name is Gortyna. I am a serving woman of Helen." Her face darkened a little—on a fair face it would have been a blush—as she added: "A slave-girl. Four years have I been in Troy. You knew Graea?"

"Yes; well. You have a pretty name, Gortyna, and a pretty face. Shapely you are, and good to see." I advanced to her side, chucked her under the chin, and passed my arm around her waist.

"Nay, nay!" she exclaimed and drew back; but I pressed forward, encircling her with my other arm, and held her close. "What do you mean?" she cried.

"You know well, Gortyna."

"But I cannot believe—"

"Have you lost your mirror? Come—do not hold me off!" I drew her close against me.

"Venus! Venus, thy aid!" she cried, but still was careful not to raise her voice.

"An untimely prayer," I laughed.

"What do you want?"

"You are mine."

"Idaeus! What—"

"You are mine."

Suddenly her form relaxed, and she leaned back in my arms, looking up at me with glad, wide-open eyes.

"Ah! Then you would take me away?"

"Of a surety. No more shall you be the slave-girl of Helen."

"When?"

"Soon. In five days."

"So long—ah!"

"It must be. You may count upon me. And listen, Gortyna, this is important; you must let me in there." I pointed to the door covered with the embroidered tapestry. "Never mind why, but I must hear what Hector says. You would not understand; it is a matter of state."

She shrank back, exclaiming:

"It is impossible—I would not dare!"

In the end I persuaded her, though with considerable difficulty. Indeed, the poor girl is hardly to be censured for her treachery—beautiful as she was, to have been for four years the slave of Helen. I had no intention of fulfilling my promise to take her, but she could not know that; and when, somewhat later, she discovered it, she proved herself to be a girl of spirit and a true daughter of Graea.

But the main thing is that I was allowed to enter unannounced. With a last word of encouragement to Gortyna, who was thoroughly frightened at the proceeding, I slipped quietly through the curtained door.

Once inside, I had all I could do to repress an involuntary cry of amazement. Paris had indeed spared no pains or expense in the preparation of a nest for his Grecian bird. Much had been said of the luxury and magnificence of Helen's apartments, but all description fell short of the fact.

Everywhere was marble of the purest yellow and white. Benches of ivory, inlaid with red *nero antico,* were placed here and there about the room, while the walls were hung with tapestries of the richest and heaviest *serica.* In the center was a miniature court, with a fountain of sparkling water; on its sides were four reliefs of Parian marble, glistening through the spray.

All this I saw in a glance; for no sooner had I entered the room than my attention was caught by the sound of voices in an adjoining chamber.

I crossed silently to the hall leading in that direction and secreted myself behind the curtains of an alcove near the inner door. From where I stood the voices were plainly audible— or rather, the voice, for it was Hector that spoke.

"Wretched man," came in the tones of Priam's favorite son, "of timeless and dishonest spite! We fight for you; for you our slaughtered friends besiege Troy with their carcasses; the cries of wives and babes are heard within, and all for you. O man without spirit! Without—I dare say it—without honor! Come forth to battle, lest Troy be burned about your ears!"

The voice of Hector ceased. Paris began to speak, but in so low a tone that I was unable to distinguish the words. It was easy enough to guess what he was saying; Paris was always good at the gentle art of making excuses. He was burdened with sorrow at the misfortune he had brought on fair Troy and the unhappiness of Priam; he had consulted the oracle of Apollo, and been advised not to seek the field; he had a toothache—truly, the man was capable of any meanness to avoid any physical exertion.

But it was soon apparent that he had overreached himself; he was suddenly interrupted by the voice of Helen, raised in protest:

"Paris, you lie! Oh, the gods that have foreseen my plagues! Brother Hector, I honor you—but as for him, Paris; the coward! Why could they not have seen that he they put in yoke with me had been a man of spirit, or had noblier dared to shield my honor with his deed? He is senseless, nor conceives what any manhood is, nor now, nor ever after will; there hangs a plague above him. Leave me, Paris; begone from my sight; but do you, good brother Hector, rest you here and sit with me."

There was a short silence; then came Hector's voice, seconding Helen in her arraignment of his brother. He ended by saying that he had no time to rest; he must seek Andromache and then return to the field.

At this I shrank back into a corner of the alcove, and soon I heard his heavy footsteps pass not more than an arm's length away.

As soon as their sound had died out I peeped forth from the alcove again; and was nearly discovered, for as I did so the curtains leading to the inner room were violently thrown aside and Paris stalked forth, wearing a gloomy frown and incased in shining armor. Luckily he did not see me, and I again shrank back into my corner, and remained there until sufficient time had passed for him to have left the house. Then, coming boldly forth from my hiding-place, I stood at the end of the hall and called in a loud voice.

"Argive Helen! It is Idaeus would enter!"

A sudden cry of surprise came from the room within, and the curtains parted in the middle, disclosing the form of Helen. She was dressed in a flowing mantle of white, caught together at the waist with a girdle; her arms were bare, and her white feet shone between the straps of her sandals, while her golden hair fell over her shoulders almost to the ground. For a moment she stood there regarding me in amazed silence, then spoke sharply: "What would you? How did you enter?"

I took a step forward, smiling. "Is this my welcome? For two days have I labored at your request; your wishes are fulfilled; and your greeting is, 'What would you?'"

"But how did you enter?" she demanded, and her brow contracted in a frown. "Where are my women, that my house should be as open as the public temple? Speak!"

"Venus has made me invisible to all but you," I laughed.

" 'Tis an ill-timed jest, Idaeus," she retorted. "When the vengeance of the gods overtakes you, you will lose your vaunted humor. But what do you say? My wishes are fulfilled?"

"Yes. Your sacrifice will be performed by the priest of Mulciber. The sacrificial beasts are at this moment in his temple."

"Ah!" A smile overspread her face. "Then—so much for Oileus! Was there much difficulty? What had King Priam to say?"

"Nothing. He left everything to me. To be honest, the thing was absurdly easy. Still, as you say, I have perhaps awakened the wrath of Jove."

"It is well," said Helen, and she beckoned to me to enter her apartment. I did so.

If I had thought the outer room magnificent, what shall I say of this, her private chamber? Every article in sight spoke of wanton and lavish luxury. It was furnished in the early Spartan style—everything in long, sweeping lines of blending colors. White was predominant, except in the benches and chests, which were studded with the purple gems of Crete.

Great soft cushions, placed everywhere, would scarcely allow one's foot to touch the floor. The toilet vessels were all of lustrous gold; tall Nisyra vases stood in the embrasures of each window, half covered by the clinging folds of rare tapestries, on which were inwoven the figures of graceful swans and beautiful women.

Scenes of battle and love were carved in relief on the marble walls, and above and below these decorations ran a wide ribbon of glistening gold on all four sides of the room.

In the center of the apartment a miniature shrine, on a raised pedestal, was flanked by four benches of white marble inlaid with blocks of ebony and purple stones. Scattered about on the benches in careless profusion were piles of cushions, covered with priceless tapestries of gorgeous coloring and unique design.

Leading the way to one of these benches, Helen sat beside me on the cushions. Her face wore an expression of uneasiness, which I understood very well. She was wondering whether or not I had heard the conversation between herself and the two sons of Priam.

I resolved to put her mind at rest.

"It is an old observation," I began, "that a man in love will stoop to anything. I have never felt the full force of its truth till this morning."

Helen looked at me inquiringly. "What do you mean?"

"This. I have just been listening to something not intended for my ears."

"Ah! Then you heard—"

"Everything."

"But Idaeus—you amaze me! It is dishonorable—"

"I have said that I am in love. That is my excuse."

I was surprised at the sudden laugh that burst from her lips. "In love!" she exclaimed. "No, Idaeus, you are not in love; you are too selfish even to know the meaning of it. Or if you *are* in love, it is with your father's gold."

"You laugh at me," said I sulkily.

"I do," she agreed, and laughed again.

"Then," I retorted, "Helen insults Helen. I have always thought myself incapable of love until I saw you. I laughed at Paris for his painful efforts to gain you; I laughed at Menelaus for his heroic struggles to restore you to Sparta. Then I saw you, and I laughed no more. This puny war is not worthy of your beauty; it is a farce. They fight in the morning, and then lay off for a week. Paris the effeminate, Menelaus the timorous, are not for you. Nor yet warriors, such as Hector and Achilles, nor a counselor, as Æneas."

"Aï! Are all gone for me?" Helen sighed mockingly, with a twinkle in her eye. "I am not to have the effeminate nor the timorous, the warrior nor the counselor? I am, then, to have no man?"

"There remains Idaeus," said I, striking my breast.

"Indeed! But you have been a warrior."

"I am so no more."

"What then do you call yourself?"

"A philosopher."

"A philosopher? What does that mean?"

"It means a man who laughs at all men, including himself, because he understands them."

"And women, too, I suppose?"

"Yes. All except one. With me, that one is you."

"How amusing! Really, Idaeus, I like to hear you talk. But you must not call me Helen—not yet."

"Then I may hope?" I demanded eagerly, grasping her hand.

She drew the hand away, but withal gently and with a smile. "You are bold," she said—not in a tone of displeasure. "You would seem to forget that I am Argive Helen, wife of Paris. Come; I would talk with you of the sacrifice to Venus."

There was nothing else for it; I acquiesced. I told her the number of the sacrificial beasts and described the golden vessels for the wine. That the sacrifice would be propitious was assured; how pleased she was!

I took advantage of the occasion to pass a few remarks concerning the foolish superstition of religion, showing how plainly its myths originated in the glorification of old heroes who had been nothing but mortals, and quite common mortals.

"You will not convince me," said Helen, shaking her head with firm determination; then her lips moved silently; she was murmuring a prayer. She continued aloud: "What do you say to the golden apple awarded to Venus? Think you that Paris could have lured me from Sparta without the promised help of the goddess?"

"Akh!" I exclaimed contemptuously. "That was all arranged, and you know it. My friend Cisseis has asked Paris about that apple business at least twenty times, and do you think he can get any satisfaction? Hardly. Paris evades as long as he can, and then changes the subject.

" 'Did you actually see Venus?' Cisseis will ask. 'No,' Paris answers. 'I didn't exactly see her.' 'Well, did you see Juno and Pallas?' 'No.' 'What *did* you see?' 'I saw the apple.' And that's as much as he will say; he saw the apple. Silly rot! And to think that men like Æneas pretend to believe it!"

"It is ill to renounce the gods," said Helen, resorting to the stock phrase of the priests.

But I had not come to argue religion with her, and I tried once more to extract an avowal. Cautious—like all Greeks, both men and women—she would admit nothing and promise less. That I had performed a service worthy of gratitude in her behalf she could not deny; but she would go no further, except to say that I could count on my reward when the time should come.

"But, Helen, how can I wait? How can you ask me to wait when you see me all impatience? By the gods, have I not said I love you?"

"That oath comes halting from your lips, Idaeus, and betokens falsehood."

"I swear by my girdle, by the memory of Phegeus, by the gold of my father!"

"Ha! That is like you. However—let us wait. You say you heard what I have said to Paris—you know, then, what I think of him. He is a coward, a woman-man. I find you amusing, and I was deadly dull; is not that enough? Do you sing?"

"A little."

"The songs of Greece?"

"I know them."

She pulled a rope, and when a serving woman—it was Gortyna—appeared a minute later she sent for a lyre. Then, as Helen lay back lazily on the soft mass of cushions, I began the slow chant of the "Hymn of Astyache."

Gortyna stood nearby regarding me with steadfast, questioning eyes.

CHAPTER IV

THE GRECIAN CAMP.

A T THIS TIME LITTLE ANXIETY WAS BEING FELT IN TROY as to the outcome of the siege. Achilles, angry with Agamemnon for his forced appropriation of Briseis, had been for many days retired to his tent, and the Greeks had been almost powerless without his assistance. Hector had many times swept the field, driving all before him.

Nothing much had really happened; a few common soldiers had been killed and one or two chieftains; about the same number as would probably have died with fevers and pneumonia if there had been no war.

But, notwithstanding the triviality of the whole affair, the members of the Trojan council were accustomed to gather together every afternoon, talk at great length, shake their heads with grave solemnity, and consume all the wine and cakes they could lay their hands on. It was one of my duties as kesten to attend these meetings and keep a record of the proceedings; a dreary enough task, rendered tolerable only by the excellence of the wine.

On the afternoon of the day following my visit to Helen I

arrived at the council chamber a few minutes earlier than usual. Rhesus, King of the Thracians, and Antenor were already there, talking together in low tones. Soon Hector and Hicetaon appeared, to be followed shortly after by Æneas and Clytius, with Paris.

In another ten minutes the lofty council chamber was filled, and a messenger was despatched to summon King Priam.

At the very beginning of the proceedings I felt that something important was in the air. The routine business was disposed of with unprecedented swiftness, and almost before I had time to prepare a new sheet of parchment the king had arisen to inquire if there were any new proposals to be submitted to the council.

With the word Æneas was on his feet. I do not remember the details of his speech, but its substance was to the effect that the Trojan soldiers and heroes—meaning by the latter term, I suppose, Hector and himself—had become thoroughly tired of expending their energy and blood to the end that Paris might keep his stolen wife. He reminded the council of the wound he himself had received but a few days before. He asserted that the affair was childish and absurd from beginning to end, and ended by proposing that an offer be made to the Greeks to return Helen and all her wealth to Menelaus, her rightful husband.

As Æneas sat down, Paris jumped to his feet and began to bellow. What? Give in to the impudent Greeks after these nine years of glorious combat? Deprive him of his jewel, his treasure, his life? As for Helen's wealth, let them take it and welcome; but he could never consent to give up Helen herself!

Antenor arose to support Æneas. Two or three voices were upraised in Paris's defense. The son of Anchises had indeed stirred up a hornet's nest; they had it hot and heavy for an hour, and seemed no nearer to a decision than at the beginning, when King Priam suddenly stilled the tumult by declaring that he would put the question to a vote.

He did so. The result was fourteen to eleven in favor of Æneas's proposal!

The faces of everyone in the room went white at the announcement. Paris rose to his feet and stalked angrily from the palace, followed by two or three of his friends. Æneas, wearing a smile of satisfaction on his wily countenance, rose to ask King Priam to appoint an ambassador to carry the offer to the Grecian camp. He expected, no doubt, to receive the appointment himself; but he was no more surprised than I myself was when I heard these words from the mouth of the king:

"Idaeus, son of Dares, I charge you to carry our message to the Greeks."

On that somebody moved to adjourn, and the members gathered in little groups about the hall, discussing this most momentous decision of the council. Hostilities were to be suspended for the day; royal couriers were sent forth to proclaim the truce. After receiving from Antenor and Hector orders to the effect that I should make my visit to the Grecian camp that same evening, I hastily left the council chamber and made my way down the broad marble walk to the lodgings of Paris. Eager voices accosted me on every side—it appeared that the news had already leaked out into the street—but I paid no attention to them, save when Cisseis halted me by grasping my arm, and him I told to await me at my rooms in the palace in half an hour.

Much to my relief, I found Helen alone in her chamber, save for her waiting-women. Them she dismissed at the announcement of my arrival, and I found myself seated beside her on the selfsame benches where we had talked the day before. I asked her abruptly:

"Have you seen Paris?"

She looked at me in surprise. "No. Why do you ask that?"

I told her in as few words as possible of what had just occurred at the meeting of council. As I spoke I fancied that I detected a gleam of gladness in her eyes; but either I was mistaken, or she dissembled when she turned to me with a sorrowful face and said sadly:

"Idaeus, what you tell me is matter of grief. I must, then, leave Troy? Not that I have found overmuch happiness within its walls, but—but—"

"Say it, Helen."

"To leave when I have just found you!"

In her voice was a note of the utmost sincerity; how was I to guess that she was toying with me? As she turned her eyes to the floor I saw a shining tear on the edge of each heavy lid. In an instant I was on my knees before her, clinging to the folds of her mantle, and she, bending over till her golden hair fell as a veil over my head, was murmuring in my ear:

"Idaeus—Idaeus—Idaeus—"

I was intoxicated, and I talked wildly. I swore that I could not give her up; that the Greeks should not have her. At that moment, indeed, I really loved her; and how beautiful she appeared, with her white breast heaving with sighs, her great gray-blue eyes wet with tears and looking into mine with an expression of the sincerest devotion.

The woman was a born actress. What her motive was I do not know to this day; but it must have been that, believing herself about to leave Troy forever, she wished to enshrine her image in another heart before she departed. Or, being above all things a woman of love, she may have found enjoyment in the mere mimicry of the passion.

"You shall not go, Helen! I love you! You shall not leave Troy—I will not permit it!"

She sighed. "Aï! What can you do, sweet Idaeus?"

"I know not, but I shall do something. After all, who knows that the Greeks will assent to this proposal? It would not be strange if they should refuse, wishing as they must to avenge the blood of their fallen comrades. And—yes—that is it—I have it! Helen, have you forgotten that *I* am to carry the offer to the Grecian camp?"

She looked up quickly, while her expression of grief gave way to one of curiosity. "Well, what of that?"

I smiled; already a plan was forming in my mind. "It will be strange if I cannot find a way to make them refuse," I replied. "Anything will serve; any impossible condition; if nothing else, I shall arouse the anger of Agamemnon; you know his temper."

"You will do nothing of the sort." Helen spoke calmly, but

uneasiness dwelt in her eyes. "Would you betray the trust of
your king? For shame, Idaeus! The message must be carried
as it has been given you; let the Greeks decide."

I saw then, or fancied I saw, that Helen's real wish was to
return to Sparta; and I regretted having spoken so rashly. I
decided more firmly than ever that she should not go. I was,
in fact, blinded by the brightness of her presence; my only
thought was that she should be mine, and I forgot everything
else in that desire.

So, dissembling my real purpose, I pretended to be moved
by her censure of disloyalty, and protested that I had only
suggested it to try her love for me. I ended by saying:

" 'Tis a poor affection, Helen, that will admit of no weakness. Verily, I believe you are glad to leave us—to leave me,
and my love for you—you, the daughter of love!"

"Idaeus, you do me wrong."

"You do not love me."

"I have never said I did."

"You permitted me to hope."

Helen turned her eyes away. "Hope is denied to no man,
sweet Idaeus," she said falteringly. "Would you force my
confession? Would you make me an unfaithful wife? Must I
beg your mercy?" Her voice broke, and stopped.

"What?" I cried eagerly. "Your confession?" I tried to
look into her eyes, but she kept her face turned away, and I
placed my hands on her cheeks and drew her slowly toward
me. I could feel her trembling under my touch, and my blood
was fired.

"Helen! Your confession!"

"Must you have it?"

"I beg of you—I implore you!"

She turned, facing me, and laid her hands on my shoulders;
then, with her mouth close against my ear so that I could feel
her hot breath on my skin, she whispered tenderly:

"I confess—I confess—I love you."

At that I tried to clasp her in my arms, but she sprang hastily
to her feet and drew away, saying that Paris might return at
any moment and must not find me there.

"Go, Idaeus; carry your message to the Greeks. If it be that they assent to the proposal of Priam, there is naught to do but obey the will of the gods. But in that case, do you return to me this evening that we may say farewell and give each other our blessing; you may come safely, for Paris is going to the home of Hector."

I could get her to promise nothing more, nor would she allow me to stay longer. She would not even permit me to touch her hand; and, considerably piqued—she knew her business, all right—I left the house and returned to my own lodgings.

I found Cisseis there waiting for me. He was full of news. Simoïsius and Democoön had that day been killed by the Greeks; Pirus Imbrasides and many others had been captured and led in triumph to the Grecian camp. On our side, Thoas Aetolius and Antiphus, a son of Priam, had raged over the field, killing twoscore or more; it appeared that there had really been some fighting.

"It is too bad," Cisseis protested, "that just when we have really started something they should end everything by offering to return Helen to Menelaus. It's just like a Trojan; fight for a thing till it is within your grasp, and then throw it away."

I smiled. "Helen is still in Troy, my dear Cisseis," I observed sententiously.

"Ha! What does that mean—that knowing air? Idaeus, you have something up the sleeve of your tunic!"

"Perhaps. Have you forgotten that I am to be ambassador to the Greeks?"

"Well?"

"Well—leave it to me."

Cisseis opened his mouth, no doubt to demand an explanation of my design, but at that moment a messenger appeared to say that my presence was commanded by King Priam. With a word of apology to my friend, I hastily perfumed my hair and hands and clasped my girdle, and followed the messenger.

I found the king in full court in the room of state where the ceremony of my induction into the office of kesten had taken place. All Troy was present, even to Andromache, who seldom allowed herself to be seen in public. Cassandra and Polyxena, daughters of Priam, sat on his right hand. I heard someone whisper that Queen Hecuba was indisposed; and someone else whispered in reply: "No wonder; did you see the number of oysters she ate last night?" Which accounted for the smile on my lips as I pushed my way through the throng to the foot of the throne.

It transpired that Priam had sent for me to give my instructions as ambassador to the Greeks. He loved so to hear the sound of his own voice that he never entrusted this sort of commission to his advisers.

The proper thing to do would have been to call me into his closet and tell me in two words what to say, but he must needs make an oration on the subject.

"Idaeus," he said, after he had talked half an hour about nothing—"Idaeus, son of Dares, you are charged with our message to Agamemnon and the kings of Greece. Thus: that we of Troy renounce all claim to Argive Helen and the wealth of the ship which carried her hither; we undertake to deliver her into the hands of Menelaus, her rightful husband; we shall return the ship, laden as it arrived, to the Argive fleet. This on the promise of King Agamemnon to withdraw his troops from before the walls of Troy, to lead them to their ships, and leave our city in peace. This with the authority of King Priam, and in all measure as befits his dignity."

He ceased; a great shout of approbation arose from the assembled multitude, leaving little doubt as to the popularity of the proposal. King Priam smiled on them benignly from his throne.

Old Antenor approached to whisper in my ear that a royal chariot was awaiting me without, and that couriers had already been despatched to announce the embassy. It was time to depart.

Most of those in the place followed me to the terrace, and stood waving their mantles as I mounted the white-and-gold chariot and gave the signal to the driver. The horses sprang forward. Through the broad streets of the city we passed swiftly, urged on by a cheering multitude, and soon had reached the Scaean Gates. Then across the plain without, when we found ourselves traversing the field which had that day been the scene of bloodshed.

Suddenly, observing a whitish, indistinct line some distance ahead and to the right, I called to the charioteer, pointing. He nodded:

"The tents of the Greeks."

He turned the horses' heads sharply to the right, and in another ten minutes we had arrived at our destination—that is, the outer edge of the camp.

We found them ready for us. The soldiers, drawn up at attention before their tents, saluted as we passed, and we had not proceeded far before we found an escort waiting to conduct us to the tent of Agamemnon.

It was the first time I had entered the camp of the Greeks and I was observing everything about me with intense curiosity. The tents themselves were dirty and poorly placed; no three of them were in a straight line. The armor of the common soldiers was thrown about in untidy heaps; the soldiers themselves were unkempt and scraggy-looking. An unpleasant odor of garlic filled the air.

Suddenly there was a great blast of trumpets, and the escort came to an abrupt halt. We had arrived at the tent of Agamemnon.

Dismounting from the chariot, I found myself confronted by a tall, anemic chap with pale-blue eyes and wavy hair, whom I recognized at once as Menelaus. He saluted me courteously and, motioning to me to follow, disappeared within the tent. A moment later I found myself in the presence of all the kings of Greece.

The tent of Agamemnon presented a very different appearance from that of the common soldiers. Not, perhaps, on the score of cleanliness; the less said about that the better. But its furnishings were nothing short of luxurious; and the bright trappings of war, covering the walls on all sides, gave it an added touch of splendor. One side, I remember, was completely hidden by a collection of immense cuirasses and gorgets, that could only have been worn by a race of giants or ancient fabled heroes.

Agamemnon was evidently as fond of display as King Priam himself.

The king of kings was seated on a raised dais in the center of the tent—not at all a bad-looking fellow. At his right stood Ajax Telamon—a huge frame was his, with arms the size of the shoulders of an ox. On Agamemnon's left was a medium-sized man with little, cunning eyes and a bushy red beard; him I recognized as Ulysses, King of Ithaca.

Beyond these the others stood in careless groups: Menelaus, Diomed (he who had killed my brother Phegeus and wounded Æneas), old Nestor, Menestheus, Ajax the Less, Agapenor, Philoctetes, and many others.

I advanced and stood before the dais while the royal herald announced my name. As he finished every one in the tent saluted; I returned the courtesy, then stood silent, waiting for Agamemnon to speak.

Finally he did so in a deep, guttural voice:

"Idaeus, son of Dares, you bring a message from Priam, King of Troy?"

"I do."

"What is his pleasure?"

I cleared my throat and spoke in a loud voice that all might hear. During my speech I kept watching Ulysses out of the corner of my eye, but I might as well have been looking at a sphinx for all I got out of it. I said:

"Hear the words of Priam, most mighty King of Troy by the grace of Jove:

"We of Troy do renounce all claim to Argive Helen and the wealth of the ship which carried her hither; we undertake to deliver her into the hands of Menelaus, King of Sparta, her rightful husband; we shall return the ship, laden as it arrived, to the Argive fleet."

There was a start of surprise throughout the tent; Menelaus bent forward eagerly, his pale face lit up with a smile of joy; Ulysses alone stood like a man of stone. I continued:

"This on the promise of King Agamemnon to withdraw his

troops from before the walls of Troy, to lead them to their ships, and leave our city in peace.''

I paused. The voice of Agamemnon sounded:

"These are King Priam's words?"

For a single moment I hesitated, scanning the faces of those around me, trying to decide from their expression whether the proposal would be accepted or refused. It was plain that most were pleased; but what of Ulysses? I knew that his voice would be the deciding one, and his face told me nothing; it was as blank as the face of an old rusty shield. I had decided that Helen should not be returned to Sparta, and was determined to play cards of my own if necessary. Now was the time.

Again I spoke in a louder voice than before:

"Not all, King Agamemnon. Further, this:

"That the kings of Greece shall agree to permit the oracle of Apollo at Delphi to be transferred to the city of Troy, in grateful recognition of his protection of the city. This with the authority of King Priam, and in all measure as befits his dignity.''

It was amusing to observe the change of expression on their faces as they listened to this last demand. Threatening gestures, ejaculations of anger, sullen mutterings filled the tent. Deprive them of their Delphi oracle! I knew very well that they would never consent to it.

Frowning heavily, King Agamemnon spoke in a voice deeper than before:

"It is not needful, insulting Trojan, to consult with my counselors on your proposal. You may see their will and wishes in their faces. This is my answer to the King of Troy: We of Greece will repay his insult with blows and the fury of war! You may go in peace.''

Ulysses remained silent, immovable; the others showed plainly their approval of the king's words. Nothing more remained to be said. With a stiff salute I turned, left the tent, and mounted the chariot. My driver urged the horses forward; a little more, and we were again traversing the bloody field, on our way back to the gates of Troy.

CHAPTER V

Outwitted by Helen.

To say that King Priam was surprised when I acquainted him with the outcome of my mission to the Grecian camp would be to put it mildly. Of course, he was unaware of my demand regarding the Delphic oracle, and thus was unable to account for their refusal.

That same night he called a special meeting of council, at which I was present. It was decided that the combat should be resumed on the following day with renewed vigor, and each captain was assigned to duty at some particular part of the field. Hector continued in general command of the forces.

After the meeting of council I betook myself to the lodgings of Paris and asked to see Helen, but was informed that she had shut herself in her chamber and would see no one. Gortyna, with whom I managed to get a word aside, informed me that her mistress had denied herself even to Paris. With this I was perforce content; and, evading Gortyna's questions concerning my promise to her of three days before, I returned to my rooms in the palace and sought my couch.

The following morning I awoke late; the sun was streaming

in at the windows with the brilliance of a summer's noon. Dressing hurriedly and snatching a hasty breakfast of fruit and cakes, I made ready to make another attempt to obtain an audience with Helen.

During the night I had dreamed of a purple crow pursued by blackbirds, which was manifestly a good omen. Not that I am the slightest bit superstitious, but it cannot be denied that these things do sometimes amount to something.

I had left the palace and was proceeding down the broad marble walk toward the lodgings of Paris when I suddenly heard my name called from behind. Turning, I saw a royal courier running toward me. He brought a summons from King Priam to attend him at once in his private chambers.

Unwelcome interruption! There was nothing to do but obey; I retraced my steps to the palace.

There I received news more unpleasant still; I was to go to the field in search of Hector with special orders for the day. It would take at least two hours to go and return, possibly more; I gave up my visit to Helen with a sigh. Sending a messenger to the stables to order a chariot and horses, I returned to my rooms to put on my armor.

Fifteen minutes later I was on my way to the field. News that the combat was on with redoubled fury had evidently spread all over the town; the streets were filled with old men, women, and children talking in excited tones and gesticulating wildly.

A pang of genuine remorse shot through my breast as I realized that but for my treachery of the day before these people would at that moment have been reposing safely in the arms of their sons, husbands, and fathers. But still there was no regret. I was determined that Helen should be mine. It was all on account of Helen—Helen the witch, who would have been worthy the protection of the laughter-loving goddess, if there had been any.

Passing through the gates, we found ourselves on the plain before the city. Far off rose the dust of the conflict—a thick, whirling cloud that obscured the gaze completely and had the appearance of a coming summer's storm. My driver halted the chariot to ask me at what part of the field Hector might be found, but I knew no more than he, and we drove straight at the center of the whirling cloud.

That morning, I remember, I had laughed at the bravado of the Trojan leaders—at their loud assertions that they would on that day carry the fight to the very lines of the Grecian camp. I was soon to discover that they had not talked lightly.

The din of conflict reached our ears when we were still far removed from its scene. The clang of brass on brass and steel on steel, the throaty shouts of the warriors, the singing of arrows through the air, the thundering of the wheels of the war chariots, all combined in a horrid, deafening clamor.

Soon the tremendous roar denied all thought of speech; my driver merely went straight forward, nor turned his head.

Almost before I knew it, we were at the edge of the fight. About us lay scores of wounded and dead, and my heart leaped within me as I saw, by the color of their garb or the style of their armor, that they were mostly Greek. They were being driven toward their tents, leaving their fallen comrades behind.

Suddenly an arrow whizzed past my ear; I knelt behind the bulwark of the chariot. Still the driver spurred the horses forward—a nervy devil he was, and I admired him for it. He sat exposed, protected only by the inferior armor of the common soldier.

How shall I describe what followed? All was chaos and hopeless confusion; the fight was so thick that it was impossible to tell friend from foe. Off to the right, behind a hill, I caught sight of Pandarus, with his archers, sending deadly shafts over the heads of the Trojans directly into the hostile ranks. Toward the front the chariots swept like wagons of fire, carrying destruction in their path; around, on every side, the foot soldiers surged forward in irresistible fury, while the Greeks fell back at the very points of their lances.

I saw Æneas, some distance to the front, pushing steadily forward at the head of his troops. With his right hand he wielded a ponderous sword; in his left was a thin Ætolian dart. These he whirled about his head, stopping now and then for a thrust at some Greek who unluckily stood in his path.

Nearer still were Troilus and Antilochus. They rode side by side in one of Priam's royal chariots, dealing death as they passed. Their foot soldiers, by some miraculous effort, kept pace with them, and transfixed on their steel points those whom their leaders missed.

Everywhere the Trojans were driving forward victoriously, while the Greeks, with desperation in their faces and death at their heels, flew toward their camp in rout.

Suddenly I caught sight of Hector riding the famous white steed. As I looked he raised his lance, and then I saw just in front of him the mighty form of Ajax Telamon, in the act of hurling a great stone. The stone flew through the air, missing Hector by inches, and falling on the head of a soldier in the rear. Hector's lance left his hand, singing as it went, and pierced the curvet of Ajax.

The Greek staggered and fell to his knees, shouting to his comrades. They rushed forward, and had just succeeded in lifting Ajax into the chariot of Meleager when Hector was upon them.

With the first stroke of his lance four Greeks fell; he dashed forward in irresistible fury, striking down all in his path; none was able to keep pace with him. The shaft of his lance broke squarely off near his hand; he grasped a javelin from the hand of a Greek who was rushing at him and thrust its point into his assailant's neck.

The Greeks, terror-stricken, turned and fled ignominiously, pursued by Hector, who had thrown off his helmet and rode with his face exposed to the enemy's darts. He was covered with blood and dust; his shining armor had lost all its brightness. Still he rode on.

Others tried to stay him—Menelaus, Diomed, Agamemnon himself—but he drove them all before him like sheep. At his heels thundered the foot soldiers, cutting down the laggards. The retreat became a rout; yells of dismay and despair filled the air; it appeared that the Greeks would be forced to take to their ships.

"Forward!" I shouted to my driver, for it seemed that he was pulling on the reins.

His mouth opened to reply, but the answer never came. Instead, he threw up his arms with a spasmodic gesture and tumbled to the ground. The horses, deprived of a guiding hand, stopped short like the well-trained beasts they were.

I sprang from the chariot and ran to where the driver lay on the ground. He was dead. A stream of blood issuing from a wound on his neck told the story; a Grecian dart had passed through and out on the other side.

My first thought was to drive the chariot myself after the flying armies; then a second thought struck me—that I should be the first to carry the glorious news to Troy. With the point of my lance I cut off the harness of one of the horses, leaped to his back, seized the reins, and turned his head toward Troy.

The poor beast, fatigued as he was, answered nobly to my summons. He flew over the field like a second Pegasus, treading numberless dead bodies underfoot. Once he slipped in a pool of blood, and I thought I was gone; but he quickly righted himself and sped onward.

Soon we had passed the field and entered the plain without the city; the walls were in plain view. The sight increased my eagerness; I sank my heels in the horse's flanks; he sprang forward. In an incredibly short time we passed through the gates, enveloped in a cloud of dust.

Eager voices assailed me at the entrance; I did not stop for them; but, crying, "Victory for Troy!" at the top of my lungs, I hastened on toward the palace. Women and children tried to stop me, demanding further news; I drove through them, nor halted till I reached the lofty portals of marble and stone.

I found King Priam closeted in his chamber with his daughter Cassandra and old Antenor. A guard halted me, but I pushed him aside and pressed forward till I saw the king.

I brought joy to the palace that day. Nothing is more pleasant than to be the bearer of good news. Priam wept with happiness, crying aloud the greatness of his son Hector; Hecuba and Polyxena embraced each other tearfully; Cassandra sat in a corner with a knowing smile. Finally, when Priam had thanked me for the thousandth time and sent off a dozen messengers for further tidings, I sought my own rooms and took a much-needed bath.

I trust that I will be pardoned if I indulge myself in a short digression. It is apropos of the bath. Imagine my dismay if you can, when, on going to my chest of perfumes after leaving the front, I discovered that my oil of Ciletus had entirely disappeared—both jars! Truly, thieving slaves are the bane of man's existence! I had to use an inferior extract from Pylos, and nothing is more distasteful to a man than to call on a lady smelling of some common and cheap perfume.

The lady in this case, as you will probably have guessed, was Argive Helen. She could not but be pleased with the news I brought from the field; all in all, it was a most opportune time to advance my cause.

I know that Helen has been accused by many of entertaining a secret sympathy for the Greeks; but, though it is certain that she would at this time have willingly returned to Sparta in order to end the combat, I cannot believe that she would not have grieved to see the Trojans defeated in battle.

Alas, for the vanity of man! I am now able to laugh at myself, but 'twas not so then. With how light a heart did I present myself at the ivory wicket of the lodgings of Paris! I was going forth to conquer, and to conquer Helen, most desired of all women!

She received me graciously enough in her private chamber, where she sat alone. More, she rather seemed to have expected me; this I could not understand until she volunteered the information that Polyxena and Cassandra had left her but a few minutes before, having called to tell her of the joyful news I had brought from the field.

"Then I am too late," I observed, a little crestfallen. "I had hoped to be the first to bring you the tidings."

"It is of no consequence," said Helen carelessly, "since it is already known all over the city. They are expecting the return of Hector and the others at any moment. Ah, there is a man! I have just been having an argument with Polyxena. I claim for Hector greatness above all other men; she will hear of none but Achilles. Rather curious, it seems to me, for a daughter of Priam.''

''A matter of prejudice,'' was my indifferent comment.

There was a short silence, then Helen spoke abruptly:

''Idaeus, I am going to ask you a question, and I want the truth.''

I looked at her in some surprise, and, I confess it, a little uneasiness. ''Have you reason to fear that I would tell you otherwise?''

''None—perhaps. I know not. But I shall know. Look in my eyes. So! Now tell me: Did you carry the message honestly to the Grecian kings?''

I suppose I colored a little, though I did my best to avoid it. My voice was even enough as I answered:

''I did. The message was carried honestly. Why should you doubt?''

''It is not that I doubt,'' said Helen, keeping steady eyes upon me. ''It is merely that I would know. Have I not this morning seen wives tearing their breasts and old men wringing their hands in sorrow? There is already a heavy burden on my weak shoulders, Idaeus; I would not have more.''

I bent over her and repeated:

''Your weak shoulders? Nay, Helen, the word is 'beautiful.' Must I wait longer for your smile?''

''Do not change the subject,'' said she dryly. ''You have not answered my question.''

''Have I not?'' I exclaimed, a little impatient.

''Nay. Not to satisfy me. Do you think I act beyond my warrant in insisting on double assurance? Very well; then I shall see King Priam and advise him to send a second ambassador to the Greeks.''

I sprang to my feet in dismay, caught entirely off my guard. ''Helen!'' I cried in a tone of alarm. ''You would not!''

Then, warned by the expression in her eyes that I had fallen clumsily into the trap she had set for me, I stopped abruptly, biting my lip in vexation. She sat perfectly still, looking into my eyes, while her own filled with a dangerous light. When she spoke her voice, though calm, was tense and significant.

"Idaeus," she said, "you have betrayed Troy."

If I had realized how seriously she regarded the matter I would still have attempted to conceal the truth; as it was, I abandoned the effort. Her eyes might have warned me, filled as they were with the flaming light of anger, almost stern; but it seems that I was blind. With a careless shrug of the shoulders I said airily:

"If it be so,'twas for you."

"Then it is true!" she cried. I nodded my head.

She sprang to her feet and stood facing me; I shrank back involuntarily at the blaze of horror and contempt that came into her face. She advanced toward me swiftly, raising her clenched fist as though to strike; then she stopped short, while her hand dropped to her side and a short, bitter laugh came from her lips.

"Venus!" she cried, raising her eyes to heaven. "Holy protectress! Why dost thou lend the light of thy beauty and mercy to so miserable a creature as I? Thy sacrifice was propitious for me; why, then, dost thou load my shoulders with guilt and my name with infamy? Was it not enough to make me an ungrateful sister and a faithless wife? Tear out mine eyes, flay my body, visit me with the tortures of the shades below!"

And, falling to her knees, she beat her breasts and began a mournful chant. Grasping her wrists, I tried to raise her to her feet; but she shrank from my touch, exclaiming

"Leave me! Leave me, traitor to Troy!"

Then, quite suddenly, her manner changed. She rose to her feet, and stood regarding me for a time fixedly in silence; I stood, returning her gaze, likewise silent. Finally, with a deep heaving sigh, she returned to her seat on the marble bench and spoke in a tone of firm composure:

"Listen, Idaeus! It is not for me to blame you. If you have betrayed Troy for me, as you say, I should rather blame myself. Tell me—had I, in fact, given you reason to hope?"

"Had you not?" I exclaimed, somewhat amazed and not a little piqued. "Was I not promised a reward for your propitious sacrifice? Were not my ears filled with tender words in this very room? I lied to the Greeks, and am not ashamed of it; it was to gain you. I love you; could I become the instrument of your departure from Troy?''

"I know not," said Helen wistfully after a short pause. "Alas! Idaeus, the curse of Venus is upon me. I cannot see a man but he must be mine. Of this be assured: I despise you, and have ever held you in contempt. Still I sought your devotion. 'Tis the curse of Venus!''

"At least, you are frank," I observed, trying to smile.

"Yes, now that it is too late and my breast is filled with remorse. The misery of Troy tears at my heart. But for my weakness and your treachery I might at this moment be in the Grecian camp; today's bloody battle would have been averted; Trojans and Greeks would be united in a feast of joy. There is but one way; Idaeus. We must try to repair the wrong we have done.''

"How is that possible? What can we do?" I demanded, though I knew full well what she meant.

"You must go again to the kings of Greece. Renew your offer, and honestly. Say that I would willingly return to the arms of Menelaus; that I pine for him. Weak fool that he is, his breast will be fired at that.''

Now, I was anything but desirous of returning to the Grecian camp. In the first place, such a mission would be fraught with danger; the truce was ended, and the chances were ten to one that I would be either killed or captured as a spy, and all for nothing. For after that day's conflict, when so many Grecian heroes had been laid low, and after their humiliating defeat at the hands of Hector and his troops, the Greeks would be in anything but an amiable frame of mind.

But greatest danger of all, if the news of my visit should get abroad it would mean the exposure of my treachery. The loss of name, of honor, of life itself—the disgrace would break my father's heart and earn for our family the contempt of future Troy.

I told Helen with the firmness of sincerity—for I really believed what I said, and future events proved me in the right—that such an attempt as she proposed would be worse than useless; that the Greeks would not now be satisfied with anything short of the destruction of Troy. I ended by declaring flatly that I would not go.

She answered determinedly:

"You shall go, Idaeus, and I will expect you to be successful. Aï! All day long I have heard the wailing of women and their curses. Do you think me heartless? I would descend even to the shades below to relieve myself of this burden of guilt. You shall go to the Greeks!"

"I will not," I repeated stubbornly.

"Nay? We shall see." Her tone was hard. "If honor will not drive you, then it shall be fear." She stopped for a moment, then continued in a voice of exaggerated distinctness: "This very night you shall carry your offer to the Greeks, or I will go to King Priam and tell him your treachery."

I sprang toward her, exclaiming:

"Helen! You would not!"

"But I would. Have I not said I despise you and hold you in contempt? If you are killed, what matter? And I warn you, do not try to deceive me. I have word from the Grecian camp—no matter how—and I shall know. You must carry the message, and honestly."

She meant what she said; there could be no doubt of that. She would indeed betray me to King Priam, after corrupting me with her black wiles and sorceries of Venus. It was a time for action, and quick action.

I did not hesitate. Almost before the last words were out of her mouth I had thrust my hand within the folds of my mantle and drawn forth a thin Ætolian dart. Another moment and it would have been buried in her white breast; nor Greek nor Trojan would evermore have fallen victim to the wiles of Argive Helen.

But evidently she had foreseen just this situation. As I stretched forth my hand to grasp her, she sprang lightly to one side, clapping her hands together and calling out. Immediately the curtains across the door were parted and a dozen huge blacks rushed into the room, seizing my shoulders and hurling me to the floor. Then, standing over me, they looked at Helen, as much as to say: "Shall we finish him?"

She stepped forward, instructing them not to harm me.

"So," she exclaimed, "you would take the life of Helen! If I spare your own, 'tis only for the sake of Troy. You have heard my bidding; do it. No later than tonight; if not, I shall go to King Priam."

With a motion of her hand she bade the slaves stand back. They did so; I rose to my feet. Still they stood between me and Helen, and with a muttered curse I turned to go, stopping only for a backward glance at the woman who I thought was sending me to destruction. She stood half hidden by the curtains of the window, wearing a mocking smile on her lips.

I had passed through the door and started down the corridor without when I heard my name whispered by someone in the rear. Turning swiftly, I found myself face-to-face with Gortyna, the serving woman.

"Idaeus," she whispered, creeping up to me and laying her hand on my arm—"Idaeus, four times has the chariot of Apollo raced through the heavens, and still your promise to Gortyna is unredeemed. You said five days; is it then the next?"

I was in no mood to humor the little Graean peasant, and I pushed her roughly from me, saying:

"Not the next, nor any. Begone!"

As I left the house I heard Gortyna's voice raised behind me in a wail of despair.

CHAPTER VI

In the Hands of the Enemy.

It was toward the second hour of evening that I left the lodgings of Paris, to find myself again in the street. Darkness was falling; lights were already shining from the high, arched windows of Hector's lodgings adjoining the palace. I stopped for a moment in the expectation of accosting one of the servants to obtain news of Hector, but no one was to be seen.

I went on down the broad marble pavement, in a state of mind not easy to describe. Its basis was utter detestation of myself and my actions.

I know not what it was that had brought me to my senses. Perhaps the words of Helen. Like all Trojans, I had taken it for granted that she was fundamentally immoral, a mere creature of the senses; and now I found that even she recoiled in disgust at the revelation of my baseness.

But what was worse, I had been provoked by her righteous contempt into making a cowardly attack on her person!

I shuddered, thinking, "It is no fault of mine that I am not at this moment a foul murderer."

I stood aghast at my wretched folly, wondering how I had ever allowed myself to be led into such a depth of iniquity. I had never loved Helen, though now, for the first time, I respected her. For nothing more than a mere caprice I had betrayed Troy, and been faithless to an honorable trust. Thersin, my Thessalian slave, was a better man than I. I felt debased, degraded, smothered with shame and remorse, and I felt that it would be impossible to return to the palace and meet the gaze of old Antenor, or the searching eye of King Priam.

My only thought was to repair the damage I had caused. I can honestly say that I was moved not in the slightest degree by Helen's threats. They were in fact empty, for I could not believe that she really possessed a secret avenue of intelligence from the Grecian camp. They had nothing to do with the resolve which I now formed, of making my way to the camp that very night in an effort to renew the negotiations.

This resolve in itself was an earnest of the sincerity of my remorse, for such an excursion would be fraught with imminent danger, and I had ever been timorous in adventure.

One thought partially consoled me: the doubt that the Greeks would not have accepted the proposition to return Helen under any circumstances. Ulysses and Agamemnon, in particular, desired, not the person of Helen, but the downfall of Troy, and I did not believe that we could so easily have purchased peace.

It was to relieve my own mind from the tortures of self-accusation that I decided to carry the true message of Priam to their tents.

I went first to the halls of the palace, to learn what news was in the air. I found the place crowded. Everyone was there, from old Antenor down to little Helicaon, Laodice's husband. They were all drinking wine and laughing and talking at the top of their voices; a thousand lamps, placed in the niches of the marble walls, flooded the scene with brilliant light. Priam and Hecuba, seated on the ivory throne, looked on with smiles of benignant pleasure.

The costumes and headdresses of the women flashed with designs of gold and precious stones, and their white shoulders and arms gleamed and shone even against the whiteness of their garments. The men, faces flushed with wine and the news of victory, pressed those arms with a joyous air of gallantry. Troy was gay.

Accosting friends and acquaintances here and there, I made my way across the room to where Cisseis stood talking with Polyxena.

He was amazed at my ignorance of the final outcome of the day's battle, and wanted to know where I had been for the past few hours; but, seeing my embarrassment, he did not press the matter, and ended by giving me the information I sought. It appeared that the Trojans, though victorious, had not succeeded in utterly routing the Greeks, who had made a desperate stand at the very line of their camp. But for the approach of darkness they would almost certainly have been driven to their ships; as it was, Hector had been forced to lead his troops back to Troy to prepare for the following day.

The whole town was jubilant and withal gay; but twoscore Trojans had been killed, while hundreds of Greeks had fallen and many more taken captive.

"The tale would be a different one," said Polyxena suddenly, interrupting Cisseis, "If mighty Achilles had been there."

"Mighty my aunt!" exclaimed Cisseis scornfully. "Daughter of Priam though you are, Polyxena, I dare tell you your folly. Achilles would have flown before the wrath of Hector."

"All right; wait and see," retorted Polyxena, tossing her head. "The day Achilles leaves his tent—if ever he does—will see every Trojan entrenching himself within the walls, if he is lucky enough to get that far."

"Has he not been met before?" Cisseis demanded hotly. "What love have you for Achilles?"

But Polyxena, instead of answering, turned abruptly and crossed the room to meet Helen, who had just entered on the arm of Paris. I was staring across at them, feeling my face grow red at sight of Helen, when I suddenly heard my name pronounced at my side.

Turning, I found myself confronted by Antenor, who desired to know why I had not attended the meeting of council that day. I answered:

"You know well that I was sent to the field."

Then, not caring to submit to further questioning, I caught the arm of Cisseis and asked him to come with me to my rooms.

My purpose in taking him there was to tell him the story of my treachery and the mess I had got myself into with Helen, and ask his advice. But somehow I could not bring myself to the point. Cisseis, I knew, would be shocked and horrified; I might even lose his friendship; it was that thought that restrained me.

We talked for an hour on various subjects, when finally I spoke of my intended visit to the Grecian camp that night and asked Cisseis if he cared to accompany me.

"To the Grecian camp!" he cried in a tone of astonishment. "Why, this is madness! What do you seek there?"

"Glory!" I replied, assuming a tone of lightness.

"Glory! Well, 'twill be that, perhaps to the point of death. Do you not know that after today the Greeks will kill every man of Troy they can lay their hands on? Idaeus, I know you well; it is some woman lures you there. Beware!"

I took up the cue gratefully. "Yea, Cisseis; 'tis a woman. You should see her! And you shall. Will you come with me?"

But that he would not do, exclaiming against the foolhardiness of the venture and begging me to renounce all thought of it. Would that I could, was my thought. Then, after pleading with him in vain to accompany me, I bade him return to the halls that I might be left alone to make my preparations, and asked him to stop at the stables on his way and see that one of the white Thessalian steeds was bridled for me and left at the gateway of the palace.

Finding myself alone, I took my armor from the wall and began to dress. You may be sure I spared no pains, for I had no mind to fall before some stray Grecian javelin. I put on everything, even to the curvet, except only my helmet and shield. Over all I threw a long mantle, so that the glint of my armor was entirely hidden by its folds. I hoped thus to escape question; one does not usually dress in full armor in the middle of the night.

Discovering that one of the hinges in the gorget squeaked, I even went to the trouble of taking it off again and oiling it.

With a cap of panther's skin pulled over my head, for the night was cool, I was ready.

Thanks to Cisseis, I found a horse waiting for me at the postern. As I stepped hurriedly down the walk to the block I fancied I heard footsteps, but I could see no one. I was sure at the time that it was Helen, come to assure herself of my departure, but it may have been my fancy.

Another moment, and I was speeding through the darkness of the night on the back of one of the best of Priam's stable.

As I have said, the night was cool, but I was amply protected by my armor and mantle. Once outside of the city, however, I threw the latter aside that it might not stream behind me in the wind like the trappings of Astyoche.

At the gate I was halted by the voice of the guard; I saw their lances shimmering in the dim light of the moon.

"Who goes there?"

"Idaeus, kesten of the king."

"On what mission?"

"By the king's order."

And I was allowed to pass without further question, though not without a close scrutiny of my face as I rode beneath the torches on the portals.

The silence of night, descending over the field, had taken place of the din and roar of conflict. Whichever way I looked, nothing was to be seen save the ghostly forms of the floating river vapor, and I heard only the pounding of my horse's hoofs. For a while I handled the reins with caution, fearing a stumble; but the ground appeared to be free of obstruction; the Greeks had evidently removed their dead under cover of the night.

Finally I gave the horse his head, and we flew over the plain with the speed of the flood of Scamander.

We continued thus for so long a time that I began to fear I had lost my way, made nervous, I suppose, by the danger of

my venture and the dread silence of the night. At length my
fears in that direction were allayed when I caught sight of the
lights of the Grecian camp, few and dim, but not to be mistaken.

Another few minutes and I had approached so close that I
could see the uncertain white line of the tents directly ahead;
and, at a short distance beyond, the waters of the Scamander.

I brought my horse to a dead stop, still undecided as to the
best plan of entry. One thing was certain: I had no desire to
enter the tent of Agamemnon. It was not with him I would
treat. I had that day seen him flee ignominiously before the
mighty onrush of Hector, and I knew with how little ceremony
he was apt to receive any Trojan.

Having sat for some minutes in a state of indecision, and
having determined to trust myself to the vagaries of blind
chance—I was very near praying to Apollo at one time—I
started my horse forward toward the line of tents. I had nearly
reached them when I was halted by the ringing voice of a
sentry:

"Who goes there?"

Disguising my Trojan accent as well as possible, I answered
in a loud tone:

"One who would speak with Nestor."

"What would you with him of Athens? Approach."

I obeyed the summons, and found myself almost immediately surrounded by a circle of a score of Greeks, who did not
conceal their astonishment at my appearance, garbed as I was
in full armor and mounted on a steed of war.

I heard low mutterings, "He is of Troy. Unhorse him. Drag
him before the king. Let him feel a lance." But putting on an
air of bravado I spoke boldly:

"Lead me to the tent of Nestor. You scurvy villains, would
you affright a friend of Athens?"

Whether I really succeeded in overawing them I know not,
but they did not offer to harm me. The most likely conclusion
is that they believed me to be a secret spy of the Greeks from
within the walls of Troy; perhaps they were more or less accustomed to such nocturnal expeditions. At any rate, one of

their number who appeared to be the leader turned and led the way down the line of the camp, while the others, following at my back, contented themselves with muttered threats and insults to Troy.

The procession continued, I should say, for a length of sixty tents, when the guide suddenly halted before one set considerably forward of the others and of an unusual size. Muttering some words to the others which I did not catch—but which evidently were to the effect that I should be watched, for they gathered close around me, jostling my horse and eying me ferociously—he disappeared within.

In a few minutes he returned, saying that Nestor would receive me. I thought I observed a malignant gleam in his eye, but, thinking it due to his personal hostility, I dismounted, threw him the reins of my bridle and entered the tent.

The tent was divided into two compartments, both unusually large. The one at the right was open to view from the entrance, and it was in this I found myself; the other was completely hidden from the gaze of the curious by an immense embroidered tapestry of coarse and heavy weave.

On the walls were hung a few scattered pieces of armor, long unused; probably old trash which Nestor had worn some half century before. In a corner was a table laden with scrolls of parchment—presumably the treasured wisdom of the "wise old Greek," as they called him. Some rude mats were scattered about on the earthen floor, and a few benches were ranged in the center of the room.

On two of these last were seated an old man with flowing white beard and hair, and a big, haughty-looking fellow with yellow, leathery skin, dressed in a lion's hide.

The first could be none other than Nestor himself; the second was Ajax Telamon.

Both men arose to their feet as I entered and gave me a courteous salute; this appeared to augur well for my safety. I advanced a distance from the door, returning the salute, and stood waiting for them to speak.

Nestor broke the silence:

"You come from Troy?"

"I do."

"From King Priam?"

"Nay. That is, not officially."

"Do you seek the protection of a truce?"

"No more than that of Nestor's honor."

"It is well. What is your mission?"

"A delicate one," I replied, scarcely knowing how to begin, "and one that requires many words."

"Then rest yourself." Nestor motioned me to a bench. After we had all seated ourselves I began again, speaking slowly, for I had difficulty to find the words:

"You know well, O Nestor and Ajax, that with yesterday's sun I came to the Grecian kings with an offer from King Priam."

"An offer of insult," broke in Ajax with a frown.

"That may be. 'Tis for the gods to decide. But whatever insult it held was my own and not of the men of Troy. You refer, of course, to the stipulation concerning the Delphic oracle."

Ajax sprang impetuously to his feet, opening his mouth to speak, but at a gesture from Nestor he reseated himself, glaring at me savagely. I continued imperturbably:

"That stipulation was inserted in the conditions of peace by my own stupidity; I misunderstood the directions of the council and rendered them wrongfully. It was not the intention of the Trojans to request the transfer of the Delphic oracle."

"And you have traveled to our camp to tell us this?" came from Ajax. It was a verbal explosion rather than a question.

"I have," I replied firmly. "Do not think to intimidate me by the force of your bull's voice, Ajax. It is to Nestor I speak. I come to withdraw the demand concerning the oracle of Apollo, to apologize for the insult offered, and to renew the proposal to return Helen and her wealth to the Grecian camp."

"Base dog of a Trojan!" bellowed Ajax, but Nestor restrained him and turned to me with a mild question:

"You have finished, Idaeus?"

I nodded my head in the affirmative; then, suddenly remem-

bering what Helen had said of her former husband, I spoke
again:

"But for one thing, Nestor. I would speak to Menelaus,
King of Sparta. I carry a message to him from Argive Helen."

"What is the message?"

"I crave your pardon; 'tis for his ears alone."

"But he is sleeping in the tent of Agamemnon."

"Then, by your leave, he must be sent for."

"The message is important?"

"He will think it so," I replied with a smile.

"No doubt," said Nestor dryly. Evidently he was as well
acquainted with Menelaus's weakness as was Helen. "You are
passing bold, Idaeus, to come to our camp thus alone; I admire
you for it. I will send for King Menelaus."

Walking to a table at the end of the tent, he wrote something
on a scrap of parchment; then clapped his hands for a messenger. Soon after a rough-looking fellow entered and stood
at attention while Nestor instructed him to carry the parchment
to the tent of Agamemnon and place it in his hands. I broke
in with a protest, saying that my message was for Menelaus,
not Agamemnon; but the old Greek silenced me with a look
and sent the messenger off with an admonition to use the utmost speed.

After he had gone we three sat on our benches in silence.
Nestor gazed at the armor on the wall in a fit of abstraction,
drumming on the arm of the bench with his fingers; Ajax
glared at me as though his fingers were itching to be about
my throat, as no doubt they were—I believe it was only the
presence of the other that restrained him.

What a man he was! His leg was like the trunk of a giant
tree; his arms were almost as big. And yet only that day he
had been forced to give way before the attack of Hector. No
wonder he was sulky!

For my part I was anything but easy in mind. The last thing
I desired was to let Agamemnon know of my errand; I feared
his temper, which must be in a pretty state, indeed, after the
events of the day. I still believe that if I had been able to
negotiate with Nestor and Menelaus alone I would have been

successful; as it was, my fears proved to be only too well grounded.

We had waited for half an hour or more when the messenger returned. He brought a scrawl on parchment for Nestor, who read it through at a glance and then turned to me with what I fancied was an air of compassion. But there was nothing of it in his tone as he said:

"Do you wait here, Idaeus; I will return shortly. Ajax, come with me."

They rose from their benches and walked to an opening in the tapestry which divided the tent, but halted as they heard my voice:

"Nestor—I beg of you—my long ride has made me dry—I would wet my throat."

"Of a certainty; I should have thought of it before; I will send you wine," he answered, and a moment later had disappeared behind the tapestry, followed by Ajax.

Finding myself alone, my first thought was to rush from the tent, leap on my horse, and make a dash for safety. I had no doubt but that the message was from Agamemnon, and that it meant no good to me; very probably Nestor and Ajax had gone to meet the king himself in the other compartment of the tent. I stepped silently to the door by which I had entered, and, lifting the flap a small space, looked without.

My worst fears were confirmed. My horse was not to be seen. A group of soldiers stood a few paces from the entrance with their eyes on the door. I was a prisoner!

I turned and started for the tapestry through which Nestor and Ajax had disappeared, thinking to find them unguarded, and at least to get my revenge on them. A typical Greek trick, this, I thought—to lull a man into security, to lay his caution with honeyed words, and then betray him!

I had crossed to the middle of the tent and was drawing myself together for a spring onto the backs of my prey, when I was suddenly startled by seeing the curtains part slowly in the middle. At sight of the person who entered I uttered an involuntary cry of amazement and stopped dead in my tracks.

It was a woman, bearing a tray on which were placed a cup

and a vessel of wine. But I did not notice the tray at first. My gaze rested on her face and remained there—a face of the most wondrous beauty and sweetness in all the world.

I am not an over-brave man, but at sight of this woman's face all thought of my danger and wish to escape from it flew from my mind. My first thought was that she was some Grecian princess, perhaps a daughter of Nestor; but why, then, was she sent to serve Idaeus the Trojan?

The woman—or girl, for she was scarcely more—seemed unconscious of my gaze of astonishment and admiration as she crossed to a table near the center of the tent and placed thereon the tray. Then she turned to me with a smile that reminded me of the flowery bank of the Simoïs on a sunny spring morning.

"It is wine of Lemnos, and cheese of the milk of a goat. Shall I pour for you?"

I did not answer; I could not. Instead, I moved toward her with slow, fascinated steps, without removing my eyes from her face. Everything else was forgotten; I was shocked into dumbness by her incomparable beauty.

"She is a goddess," was my thought; "at last I believe in goddesses; I have seen one!"

Finally I succeeded in forcing words from my throat—husky, trembling words:

"Who are you? Tell me; who are you?"

It is no wonder if she was frightened by my manner; I must have resembled a priest in transport. She shrank back toward the wall of the tent, groping behind her for the opening.

Fearing that I was about to lose sight of her forever, I forced myself to calmness.

"Do not fear," I said pleadingly, "I would not harm you for all of Troy and Mount Olympus. It is your beauty that stuns me. I implore you, tell me your name."

A little reassured, she allowed her hand to fall at her side and stood regarding me gravely as she answered:

"My name is Hecamed. Hecamed, daughter of Arsinous, King of Tenedos."

I knew that the Greeks, led by Achilles, had taken Tenedos

some time before, and without thinking, I exclaimed:

"You are then a slave-girl!"

Instantly I regretted my words. Her face colored and her eyes blazed. "It is not the part of a man to remind me of it," she said proudly.

I stepped quickly to her side, pleading for forgiveness. "I meant nothing, Hecamed; at least, I meant not to twit you with your misfortune. It was my joy at finding you a mortal, for I thought you a goddess. Will you pour my wine?"

Her face softened, but she said nothing as she walked to the table and raised the heavy vessel to fill the cup. I followed her and stood on the other side, admiring the perfect curves of her neck and shoulder and the firm whiteness of her arm. When the cup was nearly full she set down the vessel and looked up at me inquiringly:

"Do you wish the cheese?"

I never take cheese in my wine, but I answered:

"Yea, if you will put it in with your fingers."

She could not restrain a smile at the eagerness of my tone, and, taking a pinch of the yellow powder between her forefinger and thumb, she sprinkled it lightly over the surface of the wine. Then she turned to go.

"Hecamed!" I exclaimed, and then stopped, not knowing what to say. She stood regarding me gravely. At length I continued:

"Hecamed, have you forgiven me?"

"I have forgiven you," she replied in a sweet liquid voice.

"Then I am happy. It is much to have seen you, Hecamed. You are as beautiful as your name. More I will not say, for I would not offend you. Are you of Nestor's tent?"

She replied simply:

"Yes. I was given to him by Achilles after the taking of Tenedos. I have to thank Pallas that it was old Nestor and not a younger man."

"You are right, Hecamed. I am sorry for you, and thankful for your forgiveness. If it were not for my own peril—"

Her face had suddenly filled with an air of indecision, which had as suddenly given way to one of resolve. Abruptly she stepped to my side, seized my arm, and said in a low tone:

"Your peril is great. Beware of the Greeks. Farewell!"

And then, as if attacked by a sudden fear, she turned and ran from the room before I had time to ask her for an explanation of her words or thank her for the warning.

I stood by the table with the cup of wine in my hand, gazing stupidly at the swaying curtains through which she had disappeared. Even then I had difficulty to persuade myself that her appearance had not been a celestial vision; I had not thought such beauty was in the world.

I was quickly and rudely awakened from my dream. I had just raised the cup to my lips when I was startled by a sound from the door of the tent. Turning, I saw a dozen Greeks rush into the room from the blackness without. After one quick glance around they made straight for me.

Leaping to the other side of the table, I caught up the heavy wine vessel and hurled it full in the faces of the foremost. It stopped them for a moment, but only for a moment; another rush, and they were upon me.

I overturned the table for a barricade and held them off for a while with my bare fists, but their numbers proved too much for me. Maddened by my resistance, they struck savagely; I sank to the floor; they continued to kick and beat me. It seemed to me that this lasted for hours; my breath was gone; I covered my face with my arms and waited for the end.

Then my senses left me, and all was blackness.

CHAPTER VII

Hecaméd of Tenedos.

WHEN I REGAINED CONSCIOUSNESS I FOUND MYSELF enveloped in the darkness of night. No ray of light, however dim, was visible; after the return of my senses I lay for a long time in a sort of stupor, thinking myself the victim of some bad dream.

Suddenly came the rush of memory. With the first conscious thought arrived the realization that I was lying on hard ground, on my back; I started to rise to my feet, and discovered that my wrists and ankles were tightly bound! Muttering a curse, I rolled over on my side and began to pull at the thongs, but the effort was fruitless; the job was well done. My hands were tied behind my back, so I could not reach the cords with my teeth.

I strained my eyes on every side, but could see nothing. It was as though I were at the bottom of some deep pit. In fact, that thought entered my mind and made me fear that I had been left to starve to death, though it must be admitted that such barbarous cruelty was hardly to be expected of the subtle Greeks. I raised my voice, calling I know not what, and was immediately reassured by hearing the gruff tones of a man off to the right and not at any great distance:

"Be quiet, you dog of a Trojan!"

Disregarding the injunction, I burst out with a volley of questions. But I got no answer save a repetition of the order to be quiet, with an added warning that if I did not obey it would go ill with me.

The tone was a significant enough; I exercised discretion and became silent. At least, I was not alone. No doubt I was imprisoned in one of the three tents I had noticed directly opposite that of Nestor; the voice came from the soldier set to guard me. Why my life had been spared it was impossible to conjecture, unless I surmised correctly that I was being held for an examination by Agamemnon on the following day. It was well known that he had tried to extort information from Thacylus for three full days before he had ordered him sacrificed.

This, then, I reflected, was the outcome of my nocturnal expedition to the Grecian camp; this was the end to which I had been sent by my own weakness. That weakness still persisted, for I found myself trying to blame Helen for my predicament. But I could not do so in justice. Granting that she had entrapped me by her sorceries, the deed of treachery was still mine own; the cancer had grown in my own heart; even as I lay on the hard ground, bound hand and foot, I had the courage to admit it.

I gave myself up for lost, and entered on a meditation of death with what calmness I could muster. I knew full well that the Greeks would never permit me to return to Troy with both life and honor, and I had so endangered the latter that I determined to hold on to what I had left of it.

The four hours till dawn—I had entered the tent of Nestor a little before the middle hour of night—passed on leaden feet. I lay on my back, my belly, either side, trying to find ease, but without success. I thought the darkness would never end. Few sounds were audible. Occasionally I heard a faint tramping of feet outside, no doubt those of a passing sentry; and once, when the time came for the relief of my guard, there was some talking quite near me in the tent.

But with the first ray of light which crept through a small slit in the flap of the tent, there was activity and noise enough. I could hear soldiers running up and down the lane outside, calling to one another in a dozen different dialects. Someone brought my guard, as he sat on a bench at one side of the tent, a bowl of some steaming brew, a slice of turned meat, and a handful of salt-cakes. Watching him attack his rations with evident gusto, I was reminded of my own hunger; but when, a few minutes later, a similar portion was brought to me, I found that it was not as good as it looked.

As for the meat, it must have been cut from the thigh of some old Pylian dog; the brew was strong of garlic, and was filled with what appeared to be bits of leather. The salt-cakes were at least possible; I ate all of them.

The meal finished, my hands were rebound behind my back. I turned my attention to the guard. I had tried, while the tent was still in darkness, to get some information from him, but he had been even more surly than the other. His looks confirmed his tone and words. Bushy, disheveled hair covered the greater part of his face and neck: his mantle, which covered his huge form like a weather sheet on a sack of grain, was dirty and torn. In his belt were stuck a number of wooden darts; on the ground at the side of the bench lay a thick wooden lance, brass-tipped.

Of course all thought of resistance on my part was absurd, bound as I was and helpless.

A corner of the flap of the tent had been raised by the attendant who brought our food, and through it streamed the broad light of day. By turning on my side I could see a spot of sunlight on the ground outside. Through the opening came also the shouts of the soldiers, ever increasing in volume and number; evidently some unusual activity was in the camp.

For a long time I lay listening to their cries and the orders of the officers, wondering meanwhile what would be my fate and when it would be decided. My meditations were ended by the entrance of a soldier in full armor, which, by its brightness and completeness, marked him for an officer, probably of high rank. As he entered the guard sprang to his feet and stood at attention.

The officer, without noticing him, approached me and said:

"Idaeus, you are held at the wishes of King Agamemnon, who would speak with you. At this moment he arms for battle; when he returns from the field you may expect further."

With that he turned and left as suddenly and unceremoniously as he had entered.

My surmise had been correct; Agamemnon was hoping to gain information from me regarding the weakness of the Trojan walls. You may be sure I had determined that if he did get any information from me it would be false and to his own disadvantage, and my resolution was strengthened, rather than weakened, by the news that I was to remain, bound like a common soldier, on the hard ground of the tent throughout the wearisome day.

I worked myself into a pretty state of anger at the thought; then, realizing my impotence, resigned myself to the inevitable with what cheerfulness I could command.

Gradually the shouts of the soldiers grew fainter and less numerous; the sharp, gruff commands of the officers sounded at intervals. I heard Nestor making a speech to his troops without the tent; if he had possessed as much endurance as a fighter as he did as a talker he would certainly have been a mighty hero. Still, it afforded diversion; I listened to his flowing sentences and flourishing periods with considerable amusement.

At length the sound of his voice ceased and was replaced by the tramping feet of the soldiers as they marched away; to that succeeded silence.

The silence lasted so long, unbroken, that I decided that all the soldiers had departed for the field and left the camp deserted. This thought brought with it the idea of escape; I examined the strength of my thongs and looked across at the guard speculatively. Evidently he guessed what was passing in my mind, for he grinned at me malevolently and raised his lance from the ground, resting it against his knee. I saw that he would be only too glad of an excuse to bury it in my breast;

no doubt my first movement, if I made any, would be my last.

At this realization of my helplessness, despair began to creep into my heart for the first time. The action of the soldier in lifting his lance somehow conveyed vividly to my mind the certainty that all was over and my end was near. I began, in short, to weaken; fear seized me; it was only by an extreme effort of the will that I kept myself from breaking out into pleas of mercy from the impassive guard.

Much good it would have done me! I like to remember now that I was able to summon sufficient fortitude to keep silence and return his leering gaze with eyes quite as steady as his own.

Time crawled. It seemed to me that many hours had passed since the departure of the soldiers, that it must be nearly time for their return, when I was startled by a sudden rush of light in the tent and looked up to see that the flap had been lifted to one side and thrown over the pole. The fact was, as I soon discovered, that it was not yet the middle of the day. The guard had remained seated on the bench at one side of the tent, almost without moving.

When the flap was lifted he, too, saw the rush of light, and jumped to his feet with an exclamation of surprise. A moment later I imitated his cry as the form of a woman appeared in the opening, carrying in her hands a great bowl of some blue metal.

It was Hecamed, the slave-girl of Nestor!

She stood for a moment in the entrance, then, flashing me a quick glance of warning, she stepped within and started across to where the guard stood leaning on his lance.

"See," she said, holding out the metal bowl, "I have brought you a vessel of the wine of Lemnos."

The soldier was regarding her with open suspicion. "A great favor, I suppose, from the daughter of Arsinous," he said sneeringly.

"What!" she exclaimed with an appearance of surprise. "Do you doubt my intention?"

"I know naught of it," said the soldier. "I doubt your kindness, and with reason. Why should a girl of Tenedos quench the thirst of a man of Athens? Give your wine to your father; it cannot harm him."

At this brutal illusion to her dead father Hecamed's eye flashed and her lip trembled with anger.

"I care not for your thirst," she retorted resentfully, but without surrendering her dignity. "Do you think I find pleasure in waiting on you and your kind? Old Nestor, in his tent yonder, bade me carry you a vessel of wine; I have done so; I will tell him that you do not care to drink."

And, still holding the metal bowl in her hands, she turned to go.

"Stay!" cried the soldier. "Say you that Nestor sent the wine?"

"I have said so," replied Hecamed. She continued sarcastically: "Shall I tell him that you would prefer to receive it from his own hands?"

Still the soldier hesitated; then, as Hecamed turned again to go, he crossed in rapid strides to her side and seized her by the arm, saying roughly:

"Give me the wine. I know not what has made Nestor generous, he who is ever stingy; but your words are honest. Give it me."

Whereupon Hecamed freed herself from his grasp with a jerk, spilling a little of the wine on the ground, and handed him the bowl.

In my own mind there was no doubt but that the wine was poisoned. Perhaps I may be thought to have flattered myself in thinking that Hecamed had come to my rescue, but I knew that, being a woman, she must have been moved by the honest admiration and fervor that had shone from my eyes the night before.

Besides, I had not forgotten the significant glance she had sent me as she entered the tent.

In that I was mistaken. The wine was entirely harmless in itself. But it played its part. The soldier sent a glance toward me to make sure of my harmlessness, then lifted the rim of the bowl to his lips, muttering something to the effect that she might as well have brought a cup to drink from while she was about it.

Standing thus, with his line of vision cut off by the bowl in front of his face, his eyes could not see what mine saw plainly.

It happened so quickly that I scarcely realized the beginning before the end. Hecamed's hand crept stealthily, yet with quick movement, to the folds of her gown; again it came forth, holding a shining dagger; a quick lunge forward, and the bowl went tumbling to the ground, followed by the soldier, with the dagger buried in his side.

But Hecamed had neither the strength nor knowledge of a warrior. It was soon evident that the dagger had failed to reach a vital spot. The soldier sprang to his feet with the blood streaming from the wound and started after Hecamed, who had retreated to the other side of the tent, covering her face with her hands. I dared not shout a warning.

In another instant he had reached her side and encircled her white throat with his dirty fingers.

CHAPTER VIII

FOR LOVE AND GLORY.

A T THAT I AWOKE TO ACTION. BOUND AS I WAS, BUT
one kind of movement was possible; adopting it, I wrig-
gled sidewise, and began rolling over and over on the
ground toward the two across the tent. Suddenly feeling some
obstruction beneath me, I looked down to see the lance of the
guard; in another instant I had twisted myself around and was
sawing away on its point with the thongs that bound my wrists.

Working desperately, and tearing my flesh in a dozen
places, I at last succeeded in severing them.

A glance across the tent showed me that in another second
I would be too late. The soldier, forgetting all about me in his
fury, had borne Hecamed to the floor, and was kneeling across
her body, gripping her throat in his powerful hands, the while
muttering and growling like a wild animal.

I lost no time. Jumping and crawling along on my knees,
feet, hands—my ankles were still bound—I reached them
somehow, and, lunging forward with all my strength, drove
the lance into the soldier's back, just at the base of the spine.

He twisted around like a writhing serpent, gave a yell of

agony, and fell motionless across the body of the girl.

In another moment I had cut the thongs about my ankles, pulled the soldier to one side, and knelt over the form of Hecamed. She was breathing heavily, in short gasps; her eyes were closed; there were marks on her throat. I looked around in desperation for means to revive her; as I did so a low moan came from her lips.

I began rubbing her throat, on which the marks of the soldier's fingers appeared like splotches of mud on a statue of Parian marble. Her breathing seemed easier, and finally she opened her eyes, while her hand sought her forehead with a groping, helpless gesture.

"Hecamed!" I cried in a low tone, tense with anxiety. "Hecamed, speak to me!"

At length words came, thick and hoarse, while her face contracted with the pain of forcing speech from her bruised throat. "Idaeus," she murmured, "you are safe?"

"Do not think of me. What of yourself? Are you in much pain?"

"I? Nay. I shall be all right—soon." She smiled up at me sweetly. Tears came to my eyes to see it.

I helped her to her feet, and soon she was able to speak with little difficuly. Catching sight of the body of the soldier, she exclaimed with sudden fierceness:

"Him! Is he dead?" And, having assured herself of that fact, she turned again, urging me to instant flight.

I smiled. "That is impossible, Hecamed. In this armor I would be stopped within ten paces of the tent; besides, my face is known. I dare not; it is as safe here."

At that her face filled with despair, and she wrung her hands, crying: "Then is all that I have done of no use to you? But you shall escape; I have sworn it! There must be a way— if I could think—Nestor is in his tent—"

She paused for a moment appearing to reflect; then, calling to me over her shoulder to await her return, she fled from the tent.

I had no idea what her purpose was, and contented myself with examining the body of the soldier. There was nothing there in the way of clothing that would help me; the soiled and torn mantle was all he wore. I extracted the dagger with which Hecamed had pierced his side and concealed it within my armor; the lance, which had passed clear through his body and out at the other side, it was impossible to withdraw.

I was tugging away at it when I heard Hecamed's voice from the doorway:

"Come, Idaeus; hurry! This is for you."

How she ever managed to carry it is beyond me, but there she stood, holding in her arms a complete suit of armor! It was heavy and of passing thickness, as I soon discovered.

I crossed to relieve her of the burden. "How did you get—" I began; but she interrupted me:

"Hurry! Do not ask for explanations. It is the armor of Meneston, son of Nestor; I took it from Nestor's tent while his back was turned. Quick; put it on; cover your face with the helmet, and you are safe!"

The excellence of the plan was clear to me at once, and I needed no urging. As I took the armor from her, Hecamed abruptly turned her back, and I saw a blush, rosy-red, cover her neck and shoulders; even in that moment of danger I found time to smile in approbation of her modesty. With desperate haste I divested myself of my own armor and put on that of Meneston. The greaves were small for my legs, but I managed somehow to get the silver buckles together; this I fastened to the cuirass on my breast, then the gorget and scabbard, and last of all the shield.

Casque in hand. I approached Hecamed and accosted her:

"I am ready. I will not try to thank you—"

"Nay, do not—do not stay. Go—go!" And she placed her hands on my shoulders as though to push me from the tent.

"But Hecamed—I must know why—"

"I implore you, go! Have I saved you, only to see you lost by your own tardiness? Go!"

"If I could only take you with me—"

"You cannot; it is impossible! Go, Idaeus—and remember Hecamed, if you will. May the gods be kind to you." With

that she turned and flew from the tent, seeing, no doubt, that
it was the only way to hasten my departure.

I followed her, having first pulled the helmet firmly over
my head and fastened it to the cuirass. Once outside in the
sunlight, I felt courage rise strong within me. Going to the rear
of Nestor's tent and finding several horses tethered there,
ready-accoutered, I leaped astride the one that appeared to be
the fleetest and set his nose toward the field and Troy.

That was a wild ride and a dangerous one. At any moment
I might have been halted by any one of the Greek chieftains,
who, knowing that Meneston was that day absent from the
field, would seek to know who wore his armor.

But luck was with me. The conflict proved to consist of
nothing more than skirmishes between small detachments of
troops, and I made my way between the lines without hin-
drance. Once on the Trojan side of the field, I cast off my
helmet and rode bareheaded. Several recognized me, but I
stayed not to answer their questions. Spurring my horse forward across the plain before the city, I entered the gates as
the booming of gongs on the Scæan Towers summoned the
priests to the second feast.

At the portals of the palace I turned the horse over to a
member of the guard and mounted the great marble steps three
at a time. Down the main corridor and up the stairway I went
unmolested; at the top of the latter I heard my name called,
and, turning, saw Cisseis coming out of the rooms of Polites
at the rear.

"Aha! Idaeus!" he cried gaily. "I have been anxious for
you. Have you returned safe. Did you see the lady?"

"I did," was my reply; "but I am in no mood for jest.
Come with me, Cisseis; there is much that I would tell you."

Approaching, he linked his arm in mine, and we went to
my rooms together.

I had expected, with sufficient reason, as I thought, to encounter some difficulties in the explanation of my visit to the
hostile camp and my return to the palace in the armor of a
Greek warrior. In which I would seem to have overestimated

my importance, for no one took any notice whatever of my absence with the single exception of King Priam, and he contented himself with an indifferent question as to the reason for my failure to attend him at the usual hour for our morning conference. He did not even wait to hear my answer.

After this short talk with the king in his private chambers, I returned to my own room to rest till the council should meet in the afternoon. One thought filled my mind to the exclusion of all others: the thought of Hecamed. Nor was there any vagueness in it; I had already communicated to Cisseis the outlines of a project to be executed that same night, and had wrung from him the promise of his assistance.

He had gone off to obtain the help of two or three others—mutual friends whom we felt we could rely upon.

The council meeting that afternoon was a dull and tame affair. Every one was suffering from the reaction of the great events of the day before. No one was present save a handful of the older councilors, Antenor, Panthous, Lampus, Clytius, stout Hicetaon, Thymoetes, Ucalegon, and half a dozen others. The warriors were either resting or gone to the field.

There was much talking, but nothing was said; I left the chamber with a feeling that if the Trojans were victorious it would be in spite of these old gabblers and wine-bibbers, rather than on account of them.

One task which had been postponed till now could be put off no longer; Helen must be made acquainted with the failure of my mission to the Greeks. With this purpose in mind, I made my way to the lodgings of Paris immediately after the council meeting.

Among other reasons for my dislike of this visit was the fear of a meeting with Gortyna. This was the fifth day since I had first seen her; the day set for the fulfilment of my promise. I knew what the Graean girls were like: fiery little devils with quick tongues and unexampled boldness; and I have said that Gortyna was a typical Graean.

However, there was nothing else for it; I knocked for admission at the wicket with a determined hand.

Luckily I found Æthra and Clymene alone in the upper hall.

Gortyna was not to be seen. In answer to my request for an audience with Helen, Clymene informed me that her mistress could not be seen.

"And why?" I demanded.

"It is her order. Paris is with her in her rooms."

"It matters not. I must see her. Go to her and tell her so."

Still Clymene hesitated. I exclaimed:

"Do you know that I am an officer of the household of King Priam? Obey! Tell your mistress that the kesten Idaeus would speak with her concerning the sacrifices."

At that she turned and went to deliver the message; not, however, without shrugging her shoulders and turning up her nose. The impudence of some waiting-women is amazing; and what can you do about it? One can pull their ears, of course; but it has no effect on them.

Soon Clymene reappeared to say that Helen would see me at once. I followed her down the long corridor and along a passage to the right. At the door to the outer room she left me, after calling my name aloud.

Entering, I heard the voice of Helen from the inner room:

"Idaeus, you may attend me here."

I half expected to find Paris with her, and entered with an air of official reserve. But she was alone; her husband had evidently been sent away at the announcement of my arrival. She was reclining on a heap of cushions on a long *nero antico* bench, her hands clasped idly above her head and her golden hair falling loosely over her shoulders.

"Well," she said impatiently, as I approached and stood before her, "what news?"

"None, or bad, whichever you will," I replied. "I went to the Grecian camp—"

She interrupted me:

"Did you see Menelaus?"

"No. I went to the tent of Nestor and conferred with him. Ajax was present. They pretended to send for Menelaus at my request, but, instead, a troop of soldiers entered and overpowered me. At no time—I know it now—would the Greeks have accepted of your return as the price of peace to Troy.

My errand was useless."

For a moment Helen was silent, then asked abruptly:

"You say they overpowered you?"

"Yes, and imprisoned me in a dirty tent like a common captive. I have suffered much for my treachery; as much as you could desire."

"Imprisoned! How, then, did you escape?"

"What does that matter to you?" I retorted. "I am nothing to you; it is enough to know that I am in Troy. In a word, I killed my guards with their own lances, secured the armor of Meneston from Nestor's tent, and rode through the field."

From Helen's lips came an exclamation of wonder, and she rose, leaning on her elbows, and regarded me with an expression very like admiration. It will not be difficult to understand why I preferred not to mention the name of Hecamed.

"Killed your guards?" cried Helen. "And they the soldiers of Athens! Am I to believe this tale, Idaeus? Are you indeed such a man?"

"It is a matter of indifference to me what you believe," I replied calmly.

"Ho!" Helen raised herself still further and sat upright. "What is this in my ears? Do you flout me? Indifferent? And but a short time ago you professed to love me!"

"It is so. Many a man is ashamed today of yesterday's folly. It is so with me."

At that the old, dangerous light appeared in her eyes; the light that had lured men to her, to find death and disgrace. I had escaped both narrowly; she must have thought me poor of wit, indeed, to imagine that I could be beguiled a second time. But the light was there, unmistakably; I smiled to myself as I recognized it.

"Do you think your love for Helen was but folly?" she asked, looking at me through her lashes.

"I force myself to regard it so," I replied, finding no little amusement in the game. Still, I must be careful not to offend her seriously, for it was yet in her power to expose my treachery to King Priam. I continued: "I know not if I loved you, Helen; rather, say I was fascinated by you. Or"—I pretended to hesitate and consider—''shall I tell the truth? It will not offend you. Well, then—I sought diversion. You know how dull and tiresome our city has been since the beginning of the siege—no theaters, no races, no dances, no anything. I was horribly bored, and the idea of a flirtation with you promised entertainment. Love? No, I did not love you.''

I stopped, hardly knowing what to expect; a flash of anger, perhaps an outburst of scornful contempt.

For two full breaths I waited, then the storm came; but it was a storm of laughter. Helen rocked to and fro in ever-increasing mirth; it was no forced gaiety.

I stood regarding her in silence and not a little surprise, finally demanding:

''Pray tell me, what is so funny?''

''Really,'' she cried as soon as she could get her breath, ''this is too amusing!'' Her eyes still danced. ''Idaeus, you have said to Helen what no man ever said before; but truly, I deserve it. I acknowledge myself in the wrong; I played you for a fool, and I find you somewhat of a man. I did, in fact, despise you; it is no longer so, and I beg your pardon. I would be your friend.''

This was a new Helen, and one I had never known to exist. Now I understood why it was that sensible men like Hector and Rhesus were on friendly terms with her without falling victims to her wiles. It was with fools she amused herself—fools like Menelaus and Paris—and I had come very near falling into their class. There was more to her than I had thought.

''Come,'' she was saying, thinking, no doubt, that my silence proceeded from hesitation—''come, will you not be my friend, good Idaeus? There shall be no question of love between us. I respect you quite as much as I formerly despised you.''

''I would willingly be your friend, Helen; let us both forget the past.''

''That is well. Shall we seal the pact?'' She clapped her hands and, when Clymene appeared in answer to the summons, sent for wine and cheese. ''Let it be wine of Pramnius,

unmixed and neat," she said; "it is for an important ceremony."

And when the wine appeared, a little later, we filled the
golden cup and drank from it in turn, pledging our friendship.
Helen's mirth had given way to gravity; after the cup and
vessel had been removed she turned to me with a serious smile
and said:

"You should consider yourself honored, Idaeus; I have but
three friends in the world; you are the fourth. If you knew
their names you would not be ashamed of the company."

"And they are?"

"That I may not tell you. But come; you have said you are
horribly bored. Good Heavens, so am I! Amuse me. You have
called yourself a philosopher. Teach me philosophy."

I sat down beside her on the cushions, and we chatted agree-
ably for an hour. Indeed she was no fool; when it came to
philosophy, she should have been the teacher. The doctrines
of Thersicles rolled off her tongue like the glint of the sunshine
from her hair. But in the matter of religion, she was a confirmed bigot. She reiterated her belief in the divinity of her
own birth from Leda of Zeus, declared herself to be under the
special protection of Venus, and scoffed at my natural theories.

I found the conversation so pleasant and diverting that I was
like to forget my engagement to meet Cisseis at my rooms at
the falling of the last clepsydra. Recollecting it suddenly, I
sprang to my feet, saying to Helen that I had an appointment
at the palace. She herself was surprised at the discovery that
it was nearly night.

"It has been a pleasant day," she declared, standing before
me. "But then it is always sweet to find a friend. I will not
detain you. Farewell. May the gods breathe the smoke of your
sacrifices."

With that I left in haste, striding rapidly through the ante-
room and down the corridor, for my business with Cisseis was
of supreme importance.

But it was decreed that our meeting should be still further
postponed. I had nearly reached the end of the corridor when
I heard my name called from behind in a woman's voice.

Turning, I saw Gortyna emerge from an open door at one side of the hall.

Impatient as I was to get to my rooms, I had no time to waste on serving-women. So, paying no attention to her repeated voicing of my name, I continued on my way and started down the stairs.

Immediately Gortyna's voice was upraised in a series of frightful screams. You might have thought the girl was being murdered. There is no other word for it; she positively screamed.

"Idaeus! Wait for me! Idaeus!"

I halted. There was nothing else for it. She came running to the top of the stairs and stood looking down at me with an appearance of the greatest excitement.

"I am ready to go with you," she announced pleasantly.

"To go with me? Where?"

"To your home—to your rooms. Do you not remember your promise?"

"I remember no promise," I lied.

"What," she exclaimed, "you remember no promise? Well, *I* do. You promised to take me from the service of Helen—in five days. The day has come. I am ready."

Seeing plainly that no evasion would serve, I decided to end the thing once and for all. I looked at her in the eye and said distinctly:

"If I do not remember my promise, Gortyna, it is because I wish to forget. Do you understand that? Must I make myself plainer? I do not intend to take you."

At hearing these words the girl's face was a study. Disappointment, chagrin, humiliation, all raced across it in rapid succession; then quite suddenly all were displaced by a swift wave of fury. I had expected an outburst of reproach and recrimination—that was all; yet I should have known better for I have said that Gortyna was a typical Graean. She lived up to her type.

For a second she stood gazing down at me from the top of the stairway, while her face grew white with rage; then she acted with startling suddenness, bounding like a panther down the steps toward me.

Before I had time to move aside or raise a hand she was upon me, screaming at the top of her voice. Fastening her fingers in my hair, she swung herself out like one crossing a stream on a hanging vine.

Down we went together to the bottom of the stairs, tumbling and rolling and bouncing on the hard marble and on each other.

Nor was she satisfied with that, nor did she loosen her hold. I was as helpless as though I were in the grasp of a raging whirlwind—as, indeed, I was! She bit, kicked, tore, and scratched, all the time yelling and screaming with all the strength of her lungs. But for the most part she confined herself to the operation of pulling hair.

To this day I cannot understand how it was that she left one in my head.

Finally, urged to desperation by the absurdity of the situation as well as the very real pain she was causing me, I managed to get hold of her wrists and rise to my feet. Still she held on, while her screams were unabated. With one violent shove I released myself, sending her sprawling to the ground; then, hearing footsteps coming rapidly down the dark corridor, and not caring to have any witnesses of my plight, I turned and fled through the hall, past the wicket, and into the street.

Night had nearly fallen, but still there was sufficient light to recognize a face, and I threw my mantle over my head as I ran down the white pavement to the entrance of the palace. I succeeded in passing the guard at the inner portal without being halted, and made my way as quickly as possible to my rooms, where I found Cisseis waiting for me.

As I entered, throwing my mantle aside, he sprang to his feet to gaze at me in amazement.

"Great Mars!" he cried. "What is it, man? Have you been in a tussle with wild boars? Or did you go alone for your lady and find a hard welcome?"

I crossed to a mirror, and saw that his astonishment was not without reason. I was indeed a pretty sight. My hair stood up

like the bristles of a pig of Thessaly; no doubt most of the
ointment was on the fingers of the fair Gortyna. My face and
neck were covered with scratches and bruises; blood was trick-
ling from the skin in a hundred places.

Philosophically speaking, I suppose I should have been grat-
ified; here was ocular and indisputable proof of the correctness
of my estimate of the girls of Graea.

I turned to Cisseis.

"Hear me, my friend. You see me in a sorry plight. No man
nor woman—not yourself nor my father, nor King Priam himself—could make me tell how I got there. Swallow your curiosity." And with that I sought my bath and my chest of
ointments and perfumes.

A little later I emerged, a different man. Cisseis had been
shouting questions at me through the door, punctuated with
shouts of laughter, but I paid no attention to him. Now I came
forward, inquiring eagerly:

"Have you been busy, Cisseis? Is everything in readiness?"

"This long while past," was his prompt reply. "You are
late. Evenus with twenty men—"

"Wait," I interrupted, "I am hungry, and will eat as you
talk. Will you join me?"

He replied that he had already dined. Summoning Thersin,
my man-slave, I ordered a platter of roast fowl, some stewed
herbs, and a bottle of Lemnos wine, directing that it be fetched
from the royal kitchens. Soon he returned with the food on a
large golden tray, and I refreshed myself while Cisseis reported his success.

"First of all, I saw Evenus," he began. "He will join us at
the western gate with twenty men of Thrace. Rhesus, their
king, was but lately killed by the Greeks, and they will do
anything for vengeance. Echinaus would not come; he gave
no reason, but I imagine he expects to disport himself at a
certain house not far from that of your father. Alus and Orchomen, sons of Priam, both agreed willingly—indeed, with
enthusiasm; they both love a lark, and each will bring with
him ten tried men of Troy. They also will join us at the western gate."

"That is well. And what of the guard?"

"I have made all arrangements. I have the word of exit and entry from Hector himself. Evenus hath been granted leave of absence; King Priam will not expect you at the palace. Everything is done."

"That is well," I repeated; and then, after a moment's silence, continued: "Cisseis, you are a true friend. This project is fraught with danger; once more I warn you."

He smiled.

"Danger? Why Idaeus, it is the only thing that makes life worth living. But if I am a true friend, you are a secretive one. Who is this Hecamed that you should desire her so strongly?"

"I have told you—she is a slave-girl in the tent of Nestor."

"But who is she?"

"That I will tell you later."

"And do you think, truly now, that we can possibly reach the tent of Nestor, procure this girl, and return with her to Troy?"

"I have told you, Cisseis, that there is great danger. But it is possible—yes."

"And you are honest— you cannot be happy without her?"

"I cannot be happy without her."

There ensued a silence. Cisseis gazed reflectively through the window at the great torches ranged along the walks and terraces without, while I finished the fowl and wine. Soon the platter was clean. I rose, saying to Cisseis:

"The time is approaching. Do you go home and get your horse. I will obtain one from the king's stables and meet you at the door of your house."

"My horse is ready at the gate of the palace," returned Cisseis. "And see—the clepsydra—the time is not yet near. You are impatient. Let us sit and talk."

He was right about the time and my impatience, and there was nothing to do but sit and wait. Cisseis entertained me with tales of the city and news of our old friends, for since my appointment as kesten I had seen little of them. I had not formerly moved much in court circles, though at the schools

I had become acquainted with not a few of the younger nobility and several of the sons of Priam.

At length we arose and made ready to depart, covering ourselves from head to foot in long, black mantles, with nothing for protection but thin, pliable curets underneath. Beneath the folds of the mantles we carried swords, daggers, and an assortment of darts.

Thus accoutered, we left the palace. I procured a horse from the royal stables, while Cisseis found his own steed at the entrance. A moment later we had mounted, and were making our way through the streets of the city.

During the siege, Troy was perfectly safe at any hour of the night. Guards with flaming torches were posted at every street corner; the town was as light as day. This was not exactly agreeable to Cisseis and me on that particular night, for we did not care to be recognized by any of our friends and be forced to answer their foolish questions. But by drawing our mantles closely about our heads, bending down over our horses' necks, and making detours through the lesser streets, we managed to escape recognition.

My eagerness brought us to the rendezvous ahead of time. Passing through the Scaean Gates and following Cisseis to the spot he had designated as the place of meeting, we found no one there. Immediately I was seized with the fear that our friends had failed us, and began to break out into reproaches, but was silenced by Cisseis, who upbraided me for so little trust.

He was right, of course, and we had not long to wait. We had just dismounted to stretch our limbs when we heard the voice of Evenus within the gates. In a moment the bars were opened and he appeared, followed by his troop of twenty men. Even in the dim light from the torches at the gates I could see that they were sturdy fellows and well mounted.

They had reached us, and we had barely finished the exchange of greetings when the bars were again opened, and Alus and Orchomen, sons of Priam, appeared, followed each by ten men.

There were forty-five of us in all. My heart rose high within me as I gazed at the band of resolute warriors, draped each in his mantle of night and armed, as I knew, to the teeth. The horses were pawing restlessly on the ground and champing on the bits; the men were saluting one another jestingly and in the best of humor, but with an underlying note of exaltation and firm purpose. Alus, Cisseis, and Orchomen were talking together aside in low tones.

Evenus approached me.

"Idaeus, this is your affair; we shall expect you to lead. We are ready," he said.

I turned to the soldiers and said:

"Men, our purpose is known to all of you. This is an expedition of adventure and revenge. If glory comes, so be it; if death, it is the will of the gods. I thank you now, and pray that it will be possible to reward you later. Silence is the word, and forward!"

A moment later we were on our way across the plain. I led, with Cisseis at my side; Evenus, Alus, and Orchomen followed, each at the head of his men. There was no occasion for caution yet; we rode swiftly, and the thundering of the horses' hoofs rang and raced across the deserted plain.

Very different this from my lone expedition of the night before, and with a far different purpose. Then I had been downcast, mistrustful, and not a little afraid; now, with these friends at my back, and with a great desire in my heart, I was resolute, daring, and anything but fearful. I felt willing to meet the mighty Ajax Telamon alone and ask no odds.

The blanket of night lay close over the vast plain, for there was no moon; we were guided only by the stars. Still it was not hard to keep the way, for the path of the Trojans going and returning from the field lay like a dim white ribbon before us.

On through the darkness we sped, so swiftly that it seemed but a few short minutes had passed when we entered upon the field itself.

There I called a halt, and turned to command the men to cease all talking, and proceed as silently as possible.

"We have mufflers for the feet of our horses. Idaeus; shall we use them?" said Evenus.

This was a precaution I had hardly thought it necessary to employ, but on advice from Orchomen I assented. Each man dismounted and wound pieces of thick cloth about the hoofs of his horse, securing them with strips of hide. This operation required so much time that before it was ended I was consumed with impatience.

" 'Tis cold," commented Cisseis, drawing his black mantle closely about his shoulders as we started forward again.

"Yes," I replied in a low tone, and added: "Silence."

We proceeded across the field with our horses at a walk. Now the time for action was near, I kept my eyes strained intently ahead. I looked so long in vain that I began to fear we had wandered out of our way, but that seemed scarcely possible. Little tremors of excitement began to run up and down my body; I had all I could do to keep myself from urging my horse into a run.

Finally my gaze ahead was rewarded by the sight of a dim, flickering light off to the left, and a moment later a hazy, uncertain blur appeared at a distance, stretching away to the other side.

It was the line of tents of the Grecian camp.

CHAPTER IX

IN THE TENT OF NESTOR.

WITH THE KNOWLEDGE GAINED BY MY VENTURE OF the night before as a guide, I had led the way, as I could best judge, to that part of the camp where was pitched the tent of Nestor. But before we could proceed farther it was necessary to settle this point definitely; and, leaving Evenus in charge of the men, I dismounted and prepared to reconnoiter on foot.

Cautiously and silently I approached the line of tents. It was now near the middle of the night, and the camp was in total darkness. Nearing my goal, I dropped to my hands and knees and crept forward, stopping every now and then to listen. No sound came of whatever kind.

Soon the form of one of the tents loomed up directly before me in the dim starlight. Creeping to its edge, I placed my ear over the slit near the ground. So quiet was it that I could hear the beating of my own heart; but above that rose another sound—the sound of a number of men breathing regularly in sleep.

I remained thus, straining every sense, for several minutes;

then, deciding that nothing was to be learned there, I crept on to the next tent.

The result there was the same as at the first, but at the third I had better luck. Two men were conversing inside together in low tones; I could hear their voices distinctly, and I felt a thrill run through me as I perceived that they spoke in the Athenian dialect. I was on the right track.

Backing away cautiously, I crept farther along the line; and, knowing that I must soon reach the tent of the old chieftain, which would certainly be well guarded, I grasped the dagger in my right hand with a firmer hold, and proceeded even more warily than before.

It was well that I did so. I had not gone far before I found myself in the center of a large open space caused by a break in the line, and directly before me was an isolated tent, much larger than any of the others. This I surmised to be the quarters of Nestor.

My surmise was confirmed when, just beyond it in the rear, I caught sight of three smaller tents in a group. It was in one of these that I had been imprisoned the night before.

Fancying that I saw a ray of light issuing through a tiny slit in the tent of Nestor, I approached for a closer inspection. Suddenly I stopped short and dropped flat against the ground. I had heard footsteps on the other side; and as I looked a man came from the rear into the open space and started directly toward me, swinging in his hand as he walked a lance twice as long as himself.

I was not yet discovered, but I saw that I soon would be, and decided to act while I yet held the advantage. Gathering myself together, I waited till he had approached within ten paces, then bounded to my feet with a mighty spring, and leaped toward him.

Taken completely by surprise, he had not even time to utter a cry. My dagger found its home in his breast at the first lunge, while the fingers of my left hand closed around his throat. He sank to the ground with me on top of him, while the lance flew from his hand a dozen feet away.

Kneeling over him, I heard the death-rattle in his throat; at that I left him with his gods.

I took no time then for an investigation of the ray of light, knowing as I did that the dead sentry might be discovered at any moment by one of his comrades. Instead, I turned to retrace my steps to the spot where I had left my companions.

I found them consumed with anxiety and impatience at my long absence, but this changed quickly to elation and another sort of impatience when I told them of my success. There began immediately an argument between Evenus and Orchomen as to whether we should keep to our mounts or advance on foot.

I interposed: "We shall stick to the horses. It would be folly to lose sight of them."

"Could we not leave them guarded?" Evenus retorted.

"Evenus," I replied, "you have said I am leader. It is decided. Mount!"

Then, having given explicit directions of the location of Nestor's tent, I placed myself at the head, and gave the word to advance.

The horses leaped forward as with one set of muscles. The mufflers had been removed by the men while they waited for me, and they had thrown off their mantles—no need for caution, the time had come for action.

Almost with the first bound we reached the first tent in the line, and, swinging to the left, urged our animals forward down the lane. The din of their hoofs on the hard ground was tremendous. As we passed the third or fourth tent I caught sight of the dim form of a man, no doubt a sentry, rushing into the lane just ahead.

When he saw us coming he raised his voice in a mighty shout of warning.

Instantly the camp was in an uproar. The flaps of tents were raised, and soldiers came leaping out half naked, crying in alarm. One sprang for my bridle; I brought my sword down on the top of his head, and he fell beneath my horse's hoofs, cursing and bellowing.

The next moment, seeing the tent of Nestor directly ahead,

I pulled my horse up sharply to call to my comrades, then charged straight for the door. As I reached it I swung my sword, ripping the cloth from left to right, leaving an opening for our entrance.

With the first glance inside I understood that ray of light I had seen on my scouting trip. A group of men had been sitting around a table in the center of the room, no doubt at council; at the noise of the riot without they had left their seats and sprung to the entrance, reaching it just as we arrived. I suppose most of the Greek chieftains were there; I recognized Ajax, Ulysses, and Diomed.

With a yell to my companions I urged my horse forward, striking desperately at the group with my sword. I heard Evenus and the two sons of Priam shouting behind me; Cisseis's voice sounded at my side.

"There is Diomed! For Phegeus!" And he rushed at the Greek in resistless fury.

A dozen of the Greeks had run to where the armor of Nestor hung on the walls, and were snatching down javelins and swords in desperate haste. I saw Ulysses spring at the bridle of Orchomen and receive a stunning blow on the shoulder for his pains. Ajax Telàmon leaped forward, grasping my leg in his mighty hands and pulling with all his strength. I felt myself falling to the ground, but just in time Alus rushed forward and urged his horse full at the breast of Ajax, who was forced to release his hold to avoid being trampled underfoot.

I was spurring my horse forward headlong, for my main business was in the other compartment of the tent. Through the struggling, pushing mass I fought my way, and at length reached the curtain at the farther end. Here I was alone; the Greeks had all they could do with my followers at the entrance.

Throwing myself to the ground and leading my horse after me, I passed within.

I could see nothing; it was dark as the shades below. I raised up my voice that I might be heard above the roar of the conflict, shouting at the top of my lungs:

"Hecamed! Hecamed!"

There came an answering cry in the shrill voice of a woman from somewhere in the darkness, but I could not distinguish the words. I called desperately, advancing:

"Hecamed! It is Idaeus!"

Again the answering cry came, and it was a cry of joy. In another moment I felt a hand on my arm and heard a voice in my ear:

"Idaeus! Is it you, indeed? What would you? What is this—"

"I have come for you," I replied; and, waiting for no more words, I picked her up in my arms, threw her onto the back of my horse, and sprang up after her. She kept shouting questions at me, but I had no time to answer. Turning the horse around, we reentered the first compartment of the tent.

The Greeks, having secured the weapons of Nestor, were fighting desperately. Ulysses stood directly in the entrance, wielding a sword so huge that an ordinary man could scarcely have lifted it; as I looked two Trojans fell before him. Dead and wounded were lying all over the tent.

In a corner Cisseis and Diomed were fighting foot to foot; just as I called to my friend to join me, I saw him lunge forward viciously, and Diomed fell with blood pouring from a dozen wounds. A score of my followers were in the center, engaged with Ajax alone, who had caught up a heavy, double-edged ax and was whirling it like a tongue of flame around him on every side.

Orchomen and Evenus sat their horses side by side at the entrance, using an overturned table as a barricade, over which they used their swords on all who tried to enter.

All this I saw at a glance; and, knowing that Greek reenforcements in overwhelming numbers would arrive at any moment, I spurred my horse to the entrance, holding Hecamed high in my arms and calling to the others to follow. Cisseis, after the fall of Diomed, had mounted his horse and rushed to join the attack on Ajax. I saw that he heard me, and, knowing that he would follow, I urged my horse out into the lane, with Orchomen and Evenus on either side.

Instantly Cisseis and the others joined us, cutting their way through tooth and nail. We had not been in the tent altogether more than four or five minutes.

The Trojans formed a solid three-cornered wedge, with me in the middle; this for the protection of Hecamed. It was impossible to return the way we had come, for the lane was filled with Greeks, attacking us from all sides. We turned sharply to the left, heading for the open field.

Somehow we fought our way through. Cisseis and Evenus led, side by side. It seems to me now a miracle that any of us ever escaped with our lives, for by that time the entire camp was up in arms and around us. Several Trojans fell and many Greeks.

Finally we found a clear road ahead, and urged our horses forward at full speed, pursued by the few Greeks who had found time to mount.

Three only overtook us, and we left them dead on the field. The others, disheartened by this, fell back, and we headed our horses for the plain before the gates of Troy.

I heard Hecamed's voice from my shoulder:

"Idaeus, why have you done this? So great danger! Are you wounded?"

I silenced her with a pressure of my arm, and rode on.

"Did you know that Alus was killed?" asked Cisseis at my side.

"Nay; I did not know," I replied soberly; and Orchomen, who had overheard us, said in a tone almost of joy:

"It was a glorious death, and by the hand of Ajax!"

The men started to talk and sing as we entered the plain, but I silenced them, reminding them of the comrades we had left dead behind.

"Akh!" one retorted, "they are better off than we are. It is a glorious death."

Which may be accepted as the philosophy of Troy.

We rode hard and fast, and it was not long before the lights of the Scaean Towers could be seen shining in the distance. At that we spurred our horses on to even greater effort, and in another five minutes found ourselves before the walls of the city.

As we entered the gates we counted ourselves. Of the forty-five who had ridden forth a short two hours before, but twenty-nine returned, and hardly one of the twenty-nine possessed a whole skin. In the light of the torches at the gates we were a sorry-looking crew, covered with blood and dust, and our clothing hanging from us in rags.

We parted at the Square of Doreon and went our several ways, after arranging a meeting for early in the day. Cisseis rode with me to the palace entrance. There we dismounted. He took charge of the horses, while Hecamed and I proceeded afoot through the grounds to the private walk and down that to the lodgings of Paris.

"Where are we going?" asked Hecamed, drawing close to me with a shiver. I had pointed out the palace as we passed and told her my rooms were within. "Where are we going?" she repeated. "I am frightened; I would not leave you."

"But, my dear girl, I cannot keep you with me! Our laws are as those of Tenedos; I must first see King Priam. Have no fear; I will not be far away, and I have a good friend who will take care of you."

With that I knocked loudly on the wicket of Paris's lodgings.

I had the very deuce of a time to arouse anyone, and my heart beat loudly in the fear that the summons would be answered by Gortyna. But it was a man-slave of Paris who finally appeared, after my oft-repeated noisy knockings.

"Who is it?" he cried sleepily through the wicket.

"Idaeus, kesten of King Priam," I answered in a bold voice. "I would speak with Argive Helen, your mistress."

"Speak with my mistress! What would you?"

"I have said, speak with Helen, and at once."

"But it is long past the middle hour of night! Argive Helen is in her chamber."

"I care not. Go to her."

He ended by doing so, though not until I had threatened him with every punishment on the code of Troy. After he had disappeared there was a long wait before he returned to say that Helen would receive me.

"Who is this?" he cried, catching sight of Hecamed as we entered. "I had no orders to admit anyone but Idaeus."

"Be off, fool," was my reply, thrusting him aside in exasperation.

At the landing above we found Clymene, who conducted us to Helen's chamber. I entered with considerable trepidation, for in truth the procedure was somewhat bold, while Hecamed clung to me timorously. But I had no reason to fear; after a start of surprise at my bloody appearance Helen received me with a gracious smile, and with a sidelong glance of amusement and wonder, at sight of Hecamed.

"Helen," said I, advancing and leading Hecamed by the hand, "you have said you are my friend."

"It is so, Idaeus," she replied, inclining her head.

"It is soon, perhaps," I continued, "to ask a favor of your friendship. I would not do so if any other course were possible. To be brief—this is Hecamed, daughter of Arsinous of Tenedos. I have come to ask you to care for her."

"That Hecamed who was taken by Achilles?" asked Helen, looking at the girl with interest.

"Yes."

"And given to Nestor?"

"Yes."

"How, then, is she in Troy?"

"The story is a long one," I replied, "and it is late; I would not detain you. Another time will suffice for that. Will you care for her?"

Then—I know not exactly how it happened—Helen smiled at Hecamed, and Hecamed smiled back, and in another instant they were in each other's arms, laughing and weeping together.

That satisfied me. "Both exiles from their native land, and both unhappy," I said to myself, and turned to go.

I was stopped by the voice of Helen:

"Have no worry, Idaeus; Hecamed shall be well cared for. I see you are going; it is best. Good night."

With a word of thanks and a last glance backward I left them together.

CHAPTER X

JR

FROM JEST TO EARNEST.

I T WAS LATE WHEN I AWOKE THE FOLLOWING DAY, AND
when I did arouse myself to the point of tumbling from
my couch I was so stiff and sore and lame that I was barely
able to stand. I staggered somehow to my bath; after which,
finding myself considerably refreshed, I made a hearty breakfast.

I had thought that my first act of the day would be to make
a call on Hecamed, but was forced to postpone it when I discovered that I just had time to fulfil my engagement to meet
Orchomen and Evenus at the home of Cisseis. Since it was
but a short distance away I did not stop to order a chariot, but
went on foot.

It was a day of bright sunshine and soft breezes. One walking through the streets of Troy, flanked by the lofty buildings
of granite and marble, would never have guessed the town to
be suffering in the tenth year of a great siege.

The truth was, it never had amounted to much. There had
been fighting, of course—a skirmish here and there, especially
when Ajax saw fit to come forth. He always made things more

or less lively. And it probably would have been a far different story but for the anger of Achilles and his retirement to his tent. As it was, it had been tame enough, with only the battle of three days before, which I have described, to relieve the monotony.

Groups of children were laughing and playing on the streets, watched over by mothers and maids. At one spot I passed a line of young lads marching to the tune of a battered old drum, carrying sticks at their sides for swords and a look of grim resolve on their faces. They were training, no doubt, for future sieges, when the generation of their sires would be dead and gone. As I ascended the steps to the door of Cisseis's home I was lost in a half-amused contemplation of the mutability of existence.

Aï! Those poor young lads! I remember them now with sorrow. Their time never came.

I found my three comrades waiting for me. Having met, we realized that there was really no occasion for our meeting, save for the purpose of talking over the events of the night before. The news of Alus's death had been communicated at the palace by Orchomen. He had been reprimanded by Priam for his failure to bring back his brother's body, but that was all.

To me it was not surprising that the loss of Alus caused so little commotion; it had always seemed to me that a man with fifty sons must have some difficulty even to keep track of their names.

Evenus reported that the news of our exploit had spread all over Troy, being greatly exaggerated in the journey as a matter of course. One rumor had it that we had killed all the Grecian princes except Achilles, and had brought him a prisoner to Troy; which at least served the purpose of giving us a hearty laugh.

What with these stories and the excellent food and wine provided by Cisseis for our refreshment, I came nearly forgetting my purpose to visit Hecamed. But when Orchomen turned to me to ask "how the lady was," I leaped to my feet on the word and made ready to depart, giving Orchomen and

Evenus presents of gold for their men who had so valiantly served me.

It was past midday when I arrived at the lodgings of Paris. I entered not over boldly, for I half expected reproaches from Helen and Hecamed at my tardiness. Imagine my surprise, then, when, on being ushered into their presence in Helen's chamber, I observed on the face of each an expression of distinct annoyance!

But I understood at once when I perceived that they were surrounded on all sides by mantles, veils, sandals, and other articles of feminine apparel which shall be nameless. When a woman is considering the subject of clothes she wants the interference of no man, whoever he may be. I will wager that when Eurydice came up from the shades below for her annual visit with Orpheus he got no kiss till she had fastened some twig or flower in her hair and examined herself at length in some nearby brook.

In this particular case the conference had produced immediate results. You will remember the impression Hecamed made on me when I first caught sight of her in Nestor's tent. Then she had been dressed in the coarse garments of a slave-girl, while I now beheld her in a choice costume from the most expensive and fashionable wardrobe in the world.

She was too lovely for words. Her face glowed with color under my admiring gaze; her hands sought the folds of her gown; in her eyes was the light of pleasure and joy, to replace the dull and stony expression of grief at the humiliation of her captivity.

I advanced boldly; she, seeing my purpose, caught up her girdle and fled to the arms of Helen for protection.

"You need not run," said I, amused. "I am no monster, Hecamed."

"No?" Her eyes flashed merrily.

"Nevertheless, I do not trust you. You looked just now as though you were ready to eat me."

"And so I was," I declared. "Are you not the daintiest morsel in all the world?"

"For shame, Idaeus!" cried Helen, laughing. "Have you forgotten me so soon?"

"I will never forget you," I replied gallantly, with a sweeping bow. Then I continued, suddenly grave: "To say truth. Helen, I will never forget what you have done for me. If there may be gratitude between friends—which some philosophers deny—my heart is full of it for you. What other place I could have found for Hecamed I do not know."

"You should indeed be grateful," Helen returned, still with a twinkle in her eye, "for you have broken my heart. Has not all the world called me the most beautiful of women? Is it any wonder that I have been persuaded to so regard myself? And you have brought me Hecamed to prove that the world lies."

I looked from one to the other with the critical expression of a judge at the Olympic games.

"Aï," I said at last, fetching a deep sigh, "I fear, Helen, that you have lost the palm. But to be serious, what a lucky dog am I! To have one of you for a friend and the other for a—a—" I hesitated, stammering with embarrassment.

Helen clapped her hands in glee at my entanglement. "Well, go on, Idaeus," she said wickedly. "For a what?"

"I am unhappily in ignorance on that point," I replied, recovering myself. "But I will not be so for long, if you will leave us together for ten minutes."

On that Helen arose. "Call me if he threatens you," she laughed, stooping to kiss Hecamed's cheek. "Ah, child, if I only had the color of your youth! You see—" she pulled at her own cheek—"I am an old woman now. What, Idaeus? Are you all impatience? Very well; I am going."

Hecamed and I, left alone, stood regarding each other in silence. For my part, I knew what I wanted, but I knew not how to ask for it. There seemed to be no words anywhere. I wanted to laugh at my own stupidity, standing there open-mouthed like an awkward schoolboy. Hecamed sat on the edge of the bench where Helen had left her, regarding the toes of her sandals with downcast eyes.

At length I found my tongue.

"Hecamed," I stammered desperately, taking a step forward, "I would speak with you."

She raised her eyes and let them fall again, but spoke not a word. I forced a laugh.

"Do you know," I exclaimed, "we are just like two silly children!"

Still no reply. Great Olympus! Was she going to give me no assistance whatever? What did the girl expect? Did she think me an orator? Taking my courage between my teeth, I advanced another step, longer than before, and spoke hurriedly:

"Hecamed, do you remember what I said to you in Nestor's tent?"

"I do remember, Idaeus," she replied composedly. "But I no longer give any weight to your words, for I have learned that you had said exactly the same things to Helen only the day before."

Thunders of Jove! Here was a pretty mess of Helen's mixing. She had spoken, no doubt, in a spirit of pure mischief; still, if she had told Hecamed everything—

"I know not what you mean," said I to the daughter of Arsinous. "Helen is my friend."

"Of course. Because she will be nothing else. 'Tis not the end of your desire."

"I swear to you, Hecamed—"

"Do not. Do not perjure yourself. Helen has told me all. You are indeed a lover of adventure, Idaeus, to brave the dangers of the hostile camp for me when you had given your heart to another woman. What more can I say except to thank you?"

"I swear to you, Hecamed, that I love you!"

"What of Helen?"

"You are the most desirable woman in the world."

"What of Helen?"

"I went to the Grecian camp solely for you. I am not a hero; I am scarcely a brave man, in the ordinary meaning of that word; but I put on the cloak of both for your sake. To look at your fires my brain and sets my temples throbbing. I am Idaeus, son of Dares, the Priest of Mulciber, and I would have you for my wife.''

"What of Helen?''

This question, thrice-repeated, exasperated me. "You are playing with me!'' I cried angrily. "You know well the truth of my words!''

"I know nothing of the sort,'' was her calm reply.

I grew angrier still. "I repeat, you are playing with me!'' I almost shouted. "That is folly, for you are in my power. I took you from the tent of Nestor by force. I brought you to Troy before me on my horse. You are mine. Your resistance is useless.''

"I know it well,'' she replied, still calm, though her eyes flashed. "I grant your power.''

"Then why do you resist?''

"I do not resist. Hear me, Idaeus. I am, as you say, yours. You can force me to be your slave-girl. So be it. But as for your wife—nay! I must have the heart of my husband, and yours belongs to Helen. I will be your slave, but I will hate you.''

"Lies! Lies!'' I cried furiously. "Helen has not my heart. It is yours, Hecamed. I would not have you for a slave. I love you!''

"Will you answer a question?'' she demanded. "I expect the truth. Did you, but three days before this, in this very room, offer your heart to Helen and beg for her favor?''

I was silent.

"Answer me!'' she demanded.

"That was before I met you,'' I replied at last.

"But you did so tell her?''

"I did.''

"And yet you have the temerity, but three days after, to ask me to be your wife! Shameless man!''

There still lurked in my mind a suspicion that she was but toying with me; but even so, what could I say? I felt that I was being made ridiculous—a very disagreeable feeling—and had opened my mouth to offer her a choice of alternatives, when I was interrupted by the voice of Helen from the doorway:

"Well, good Idaeus, can you now complete your sentence?"

Then, advancing across the room and observing my face red with anger, she continued mischievously:

"What! A quarrel—so soon!"

"If there is a quarrel, 'tis of your own making," I retorted hotly. "Is *this* the friendship of Helen? Was it for this we sealed our pact with the wine of Lemnos? That you should betray me!"

"Betray you? How? Where? When?" Helen's face wore an expression of utter innocence and surprise.

"He means," put in Hecamed in explanation, "that you told me of his love for you."

"Of a certainty," said Helen, "I did that, but I was not sworn to confidence. I see no wrong in it. I was proud of your love, and I could not conceal my pride."

"Akh!" I exploded, "so you make merry with me!"

"By no means." Helen maintained her air of injured innocence. "But I cannot deny that you have made love to me."

"And but three days ago!" This from Hecamed.

"And but three days ago," Helen agreed.

"And but now—this very moment—he made love to me—passionately!" cried Hecamed.

"What!" exclaimed Helen, raising her hands to express incredulous surprise and horror, and sending a glance of reproach at me. "Faithless man!"

At that I had sense enough to perceive the jest and enter into its spirit. "Alas," I sighed, "is it any fault of mine that no woman can look upon me without desire?"

This brought them up short and silenced their tongues.

I continued: "It is but too true, Hecamed, that Helen loves me. What could I do? I was forced to simulate a return of her guilty passion. It is true also that I love you—"

I was beginning to enjoy myself, having, as I thought, turned the tables on them rather cleverly. Again I felt sure of Hecamed, having considered all the time that she had committed herself by assisting me to escape from the camp of the Greeks. So I continued in a tone of mingled assurance and sorrow:

"Yea, Hecamed, I love you and would have you for my wife. And you refuse! So be it. The daughter of Arsinous shall not be the slave of Idaeus. I renounce all claim to you; you have broken my heart. Cruel you are—cruel beyond—"

I hesitated, seeking a sounding finish for my sentence. But the sentence was never finished. As I stood facing the two women, with my back to the door, there suddenly came from behind a sharp, eager cry in another voice, while an expression of astonishment appeared on the faces of Helen and Hecamed.

I turned. In the doorway, with her hands outstretched toward me and a glint of satisfaction in her eyes, stood the serving woman Gortyna!

It was Helen who spoke first. "Gortyna," she said sharply, "what do you mean by entering thus unannounced?"

Undaunted, the little Graean advanced to the center of the room with firm steps.

"It is him I seek," said she, pointing a finger at me.

"What?" cried Helen, and this time her surprise was genuine. "What would you with Idaeus? Is there a message for him?"

"Yes—a message from me," replied Gortyna in a tone of desperate resolution. "I would ask him for the fulfilment of his promise, and before you."

Even at so slight a hint, Helen's quick brain began to divine the truth; I saw it in her eye.

"Know, O queen," continued Gortyna, "that Idaeus is a faithless man. He gave me his word to take me from your house; his eyes were filled with desire for me; his hand trembled on my arm. The day came. He denied me."

A little smothered cry came from Hecamed. Helen asked quietly:

"When was this, Gortyna?"

"But six, seven days before this. He promised to take me on the fifth day, and I believed him. Do you remember that evening when my screams in the corridor brought the household running, even to yourself and Paris? It was then he denied his promise. I held onto his hair, but he escaped me. Now I would know—"

Helen interrupted, her eyes twinkling:

"Did he make love to you?"

"Yes. Passionate love. He desired to have me in his house. He said I should no longer be a slave-girl."

Helen looked at me. "Really, Idaeus, you are setting a strong pace. A voracious lover, indeed! Is there truth in the story of Gortyna?"

I was looking at Hecamed. Her face had gone white, and she was staring straight at me with her lips curled scornfully.

"Answer!" she said, in a voice that trembled despite her effort at control. "Is there truth in this story?"

I knew not what to say. I ended by declaring weakly that if there were truth it could easily be explained.

"Explained!" cried Hecamed contemptuously; and Helen put in:

"Come, Idaeus, tell us the truth; explanations can come later. Have you set yourself up for a rival of the love-god? Tell us!"

Gortyna, becoming impatient, advanced a step toward me. "And your promise—what of that?" I saw her hand steal within the folds of her gown.

"Why do you not improve your time by making love?" inquired Hecamed ironically. "There are three of us here; we can await our turn."

"Is it your intention to outshine Priam and his fifty sons?"

"Would you furnish the temples of Troy with priests of your own making?"

"Your promise! *Your promise!*"

Thus badgered on every side, speechless and helpless before the bite of their tongues, I saw only one possible course. Adopting it on the impulse, I turned without a word, sprang through the door, and ran down the corridors and stairs to the street! Nor did I slacken my pace till I had reached my own rooms in the palace.

CHAPTER XI

I TAKE A SLAVE.

THE MAN WHOSE MIND IS DOMINATED BY A SINGLE thought and purpose is, of course, tortured with anxiety till that purpose is either gained or lost; but he is at least rid of a thousand other perplexities that might otherwise arise to haunt and harass him. Which observation serves to describe the state of my mind as I paced up and down the length of my rooms with a wrinkled brow and clenched fists.

I no longer reproached myself for my betrayal of King Priam's trust. Although Gortyna was but a peasant slave-girl, the fact remained that I had treated her rather shabbily; but that thought did not disturb me. I had been placed in a foolish and false position by the taunts and gibes of women, but, though ordinarily no one is more keenly sensitive to ridicule than I, my breast held neither shame nor anger.

All other emotion and sensation were driven back by the overwhelming tide of love that surged within me.

It had needed only this—her scorn, and the fear that she was lost to me—to force upon me the realization that I desired Hecamed as I had never desired anything in all my life. I trembled at the memory of the contempt of her parting glance. I ran from one side of the room to the other; I shook my fist in the air; I swore aloud. Then I sank down on a bench and buried my face in my hands with a groan.

I remained thus two hours.

Finally I arrived at a decision—or, rather, a decision was forced upon me. It was repugnant, and I hated myself for it; but no other course was open to me. I jumped to my feet, and saw by the glass without the window that the time had arrived for the council meeting. Dressing and perfuming myself hurriedly, I arrived at the chamber a few minutes late.

As on the day before, only the older councilors were present. Excitement was in the air; rumor had it that Achilles, being offered rich presents by Agamemnon and restitution of Briseis, had, at the earnest pleadings of the Greek chieftains, agreed to return to the field on the morrow. A dozen messengers had been despatched to obtain confirmation or denial of this report, but none were successful.

The Trojan councilors were plainly worried over the prospect; they who had an entire army at their disposal! They talked and wrangled till evening—getting nowhere, as usual—and I at length found myself free to return to my rooms.

At the door of the chamber I hesitated, considering within myself whether it would be advisable to address King Priam on my own account. Finally, deciding it best to carry with me some corroboration of my story, I left the palace and made my way through the grounds to the low-roofed marble dwellings at the edge of Pilamon Square.

At the outer portals I secured the services of a member of the guard, who conducted me through a maze of winding corridors to the apartments of Orchomen. Though night had not yet fallen, it was all but dark within, and lamps were set in the niches of the walls. Their rays shone and glittered on the polished surface of the yellow stone, displaying in all their magnificence the luxurious furnishings of the immense palace maintained by Priam for the convenience of his natural sons.

''All this is what makes Troy poor,'' I thought, stopping at Orchomen's door.

No such idea would seem to have entered the brain of Or-chomen. I found him reclining on a tapestried divan heaped with cushions, watching with languid eye the graceful move-ments of a Phthian dance-girl. As I entered he waved me to a seat without removing his gaze from the limbs of the dancer.

"Fie on thee and thy Lydian graces!" I exclaimed, when the entertainment was finished and the Phthian had taken her-self off with a bow to the floor. "Is this the part of a warrior?"

"It is the diversion of one," replied Orchomen, stretching himself and yawning. "How are you, Idaeus? Wait! I will send for wine."

"You will do nothing of the sort; I am come to drag you forth from your paradise." And I explained my mission, end-ing with the request that he accompany me at once to King Priam.

He agreed to go, though not without grumbling. "And so your Grecian beauty needs the spur?" he commented laugh-ingly as we left the rooms on our way to the palace.

Luckily we found King Priam in the best of humor. Word had just reached the palace that the rumor that Achilles was to return to the field was without foundation; Hector had again driven the Greeks from the field single-handed. He listened to my story with attention and not a little surprise, and when I had finished turned to Orchomen to ask if the adventure of which I spoke was that in which Alus had met his death.

"It is, sire," replied Orchomen, "and I can answer for the truth of Idaeus's story, having been present myself. He took Hecamed of Tenedos from the tent of Nestor by force and carried her with him to Troy without parley or agreement. You know the law; she is his."

"Without doubt." The king nodded his head. Then, turning to me:

"You say she is now at the lodgings of Paris?"

I nodded my head.

"And that she refuses to attend you?"

"No; she does not refuse. But I would have the necessary authority to bring her to my rooms; if there is resistance I wish

to be able to meet it. It is possible that I will met with opposition on the part of Helen.''

"Have you already a slave-girl?"

"None."

"Very well. Send hither the captain of the guard and the
roll of my household; the latter is in your care as kesten. You
shall have your Hecamed, good Idaeus."

He waved his hand to signify that the interview was ended,
and I departed, while Orchomen remained, no doubt to take
advantage of the king's pleasant humor by asking a favor on
his own account. He was always in need of money, was Orchomen; and no wonder, since he entertained with the lavish
display of a wealthy merchant.

Joy and misgiving were strangely mingled in my breast. On
the one hand, I was certain of having Hecamed for my own
in my own lodgings; on the other, I feared that she had spoken
truly when she said that as my slave-girl she would hate me.

But it was too late now to draw back, and an hour after the
fall of darkness saw me marching down the broad marble walk
to the lodgings of Paris with a roll of parchment under my
arm and a captain of the guard with twenty men at my back.

As a matter of fact, I expected no resistance either from
Helen or Hecamed; the guard served merely to support my
own courage and to take charge of Gortyna if she attempted
to make trouble.

Æthra answered the summons at the wicket. The captain of
the guard spoke to her in the measured tones of authority:

"We come on behalf of Idaeus, kesten of King Priam, son
of Dares, the priest of Mulciber, to demand that Hecamed of
Tenedos be delivered into his hands. By authority of the
king."

Peering over the shoulder of the captain, I could see Æthra
make a little face at him before she disappeared to carry the
summons to her mistress.

A long wait followed, during which the captain took occasion to question me concerning the exploit of the night before.
He got little satisfaction, for my mind was so preoccupied with
the perplexities of the present that I scarcely heard his ques-

tions. For one thing, I was by no means sure that Gortyna was finished with me—indeed, I was convinced of the contrary—and for another, I knew not what would be the outcome of this seizure of Hecamed.

At length there was the sound of footsteps approaching the wicket from within. They halted, and a voice came—the voice of Hecamed:

"Who is there?"

"A captain of the guard."

"What would you with Hecamed of Tenedos?"

"It is the order of the king to carry her to the rooms of Idaeus."

"Is he with you?" Hecamed's voice was calm and firm; her questions were following one another like those of an attorney in court.

"Who—King Priam?" asked the guard foolishly.

"No. Idaeus."

I answered for myself. "I am here."

"Akh! Idaeus, do you sanction this brutal proceeding?"

"Yes, and more. I instituted it," I replied, thinking that if the thing were done at all it should be with boldness.

"Very well; I will come," said Hecamed quietly. An instant later the wicket was opened and she stepped out before us. From within came the voice of Helen—I could not see her in the darkness:

"Idaeus, I had not thought this of you; 'tis an outrage!"

"I am only taking what is mine," I asserted, with a resoluteness all assumed; and without more ado I grasped the arm of Hecamed and led her off, followed by the guard.

The walk back to the palace seemed all too short, for I was dreading the time that should find me alone with Hecamed in my rooms. To treat her as men are accustomed to treat slave-girls was out of the question; that was not at all what I wanted. My own action depended entirely upon hers, and that was a conundrum too deep for me.

What would she do? Would she rebel at once, preferring to take her chances in the public market rather than remain with me?

I sighed and gave it up just as we reached the outer portals
of the palace, where the captain of the guard took his leave,
saluting respectfully.

Hecamed and I ascended the great stairway side by side.
She had not spoken a word since we left the lodgings of Paris.
When we reached the door of my rooms I stood aside for her
to enter; then I followed her within and went to the ebony
stand at the further end of the room to light the lamps.

I turned to find her standing rigid in the center of the room
with her arms held straight at her sides and her eyes set straight
ahead, like a soldier at attention.

"This is your home," I said, in as natural a tone as I could
command. "What do you think of it? Come; look around."

She remained motionless. "You are mistaken; it is my
prison," she replied.

I advanced and took her by the hand; she passively allowed
herself to be led to a marble bench in the embrasure of a
window overlooking the palace grounds. Then, seating myself
beside her, I spoke earnestly:

"Hecamed, I beseech you to abandon your attitude of hostility. This is no prison for you; rather you are confined in my
heart. I will not repeat that I love you; you know it well. But
I will say that I love you with honor and good intent; can I
prove it better than by begging you to be my wife?"

Hecamed sat looking straight ahead, nor did she turn as she
answered me in a quiet voice, impersonal and hard:

"I am your slave; how then can I be your wife?"

"That is mere quibbling."

"It is not." She looked at me for the first time. "Hear me,
Idaeus. You have humiliated and disgraced me in the eyes of
Troy. For that I hate you, and will forever hate you. You have
dragged me from the house of Helen to be your slave; so be
it. But as for being your wife—I would sooner marry your
Ethiop servant, or a dog in the streets. Akh! I despise you!"

"You had best choose your words," I cried, while my face
went white. "If you are my slave, remember that my power
extends to the scourge!"

"It is not necessary to remind me of it," she replied evenly, but I saw a slight shiver run over her body. "Such a threat is like you—coward!"

At that word I sprang to my feet in fury; then, restraining myself with a great effort, I stood in front of the bench, looking down at her. My voice was hoarse with agitation.

"That was but an empty threat, Hecamed. 'Twas my anger spoke it, not I. Your white shoulders were not made for the Trojan scourge, nor could I calmly see your punishment. You are over bold in your speech, but words break no bones. Know this: I have never intended, and do not now intend, any harm or insult to you. Rather shall I protect you; if against your will, so be it. I have done nothing to make you hate and despise me; your words come from your own hard and unforgiving heart."

I stopped. She was silent. How lovely did she appear in the soft lamplight, with her veil thrown back over her shoulders, while her skin glowed and her eyes flashed with the spirit of resentment that filled her breast! Words of entreaty arose to my lips, but I held them back, vowing that when she came to me it should be of her own will.

So I left her, saying that the duties of my office had been neglected for several days and needed my attention. She did not even lift her eyes as I spoke, but as I reached the door I was suddenly halted by the sound of her voice:

"You have not told me what I am to do."

"What you are to do?" I really did not understand.

"Yes. Am I not your slave? You will be cheated of your bargain if I remain idle. What is my duty?"

I smiled in spite of myself as I replied:

"Your duty is to amuse yourself and preserve your beauty. I did not carry you to Troy for your strength, but for your large eyes and white arms and shapely form. There are handmaidens enough and to spare; I would not have you prepare my couch and cook my meals, but share them with me."

With that last speech I was very well pleased; I was acquainted with her fear, and was not sorry to have fed it. This was my thought as I entered the large compartment in the rear of the palace, on the same floor as my rooms, where the royal archives were kept.

It was in this compartment, it will be remembered, that I had received a visit from Helen the day after my induction into the office of kesten.

I had not been there five minutes before I found myself powerfully impelled to return to the side of Hecamed. The desire was ludicrous enough, and I was considerably amused at my own expense. What chance of welcome was there to attract me? I tried to work, and actually carried an armload of parchments to the table of ivory and opened the rolls, but I could not get my mind upon it.

At length I abandoned the effort and gave myself up to the consideration of my own affairs.

I had indeed made a sorry mess of things with Hecamed. What to do? Make her in fact my enforced slave? But in that event I was sure to lose all chance of ever winning her affection—though I knew full well that that was exactly what she expected me to do. Well, I would surprise her. The idea had always been repugnant to me anyway; I had never been able to understand how a man could get any real enjoyment from an intimacy forced and unwelcome.

My thoughts reverted to Gortyna. But the only thing I could do with the little Graean was to pursue a policy of watchful waiting. If the thought happened to strike her to take advantage of the domestic religious laws she might cause serious trouble.

Well, time to worry about that when it came.

As for Helen, I regarded her still as my friend. A lover of fun, her jest had ended more gravely than she had intended— that was all. Accustomed as she was to the ways of the men of Sparta, she could not regard my seizure of Hecamed as a very serious offense.

When I finally finished with my reflections and arose to return to my rooms, it was near the middle hour of night. Quiet reigned throughout the palace.

At the door of my rooms I was filled with a sudden fear that Hecamed had taken advantage of my absence to flee, remembering as I did the evident impression of my parting words. I entered with a beating heart.

My fear was groundless. The room remained exactly as I had left it; the lamps on the ebony stand had burned nearly empty. As for Hecamed, she sat on the marble bench in the embrasure of the window; I verily believe she had not moved so much as a finger throughout my long absence! But as I approached and stood before her I saw that there were tears on her lashes, and a whitish streak down each velvet cheek.

"Why do you weep, Hecamed?" I asked; and my tone was gentle against my will.

"I ask your pardon," she said proudly, without looking up; "my tears are not for you."

"I did not flatter myself that they were," I retorted. "I take an interest in you because you are my property; I would not have you lean and ungraceful."

Crossing to extinguish one of the lamps, I added: "The hour is late."

"Yes." After a short pause Hecamed continued, as one who speaks unwillingly: "Your servant was here and questioned me."

"Thersin? What did he want?"

"Nothing; there was no message."

"That is well." I crossed again to her side. "Come, Hecamed; the hour is late; it is time we should retire."

She rose to her feet with an apparent effort, while there came into her eyes an expression of fear not pretty to look at; the look of a hunted animal. I took her hand—it was cold and lifeless—and led her within the next apartment. Then through a door to the left into another room, where I lit a lamp placed in a niche in the wall.

When I turned to look at her by its light, I saw drawn lips, eyes narrowed to a thin slit, hands tightly clenched at her sides.

"I am sorry," I said quietly, "that I have nothing better than this to offer you, though in truth with hangings of *serica* and benches of ebony arranged to your taste it will not be so bad. The couch has been unused, save when my friend Cisseis, or some other, has spent the night with me. Henceforth it is yours. Good night.''

And without giving her time to answer me, without even looking at her face, I left the room, closing the door behind me, and sought my own apartment.

CHAPTER XII

THE TEMPLE OF THAMYRIS.

WHEN, LOOKING BACK, I REFLECT ON THAT FIRST week which Hecamed spent in my rooms as my slave-girl, I am moved to unrestrained mirth. How was I harassed and worried by a thousand cares and anxieties which at this length of time appear wholly ludicrous! These, in addition to the everpresent fear that she would flee from the palace; for I had not given her a number on the household roll, and she was therefore as free to go and come as King Priam himself.

I had considerable difficulty in concealing the truth from the friends who came to visit me. If they had ever discovered the real state of affairs they would have laughed me out of Troy: as it was, one sight of Hecamed was sufficient to cause them to shower me with congratulations.

"For another Hecamed," declared Evenus, "I would battle with the entire Greek army single-handed."

This expressed the universal opinion of her charms. At these felicitations I indulged myself in a private smile at my own expense, and with it felt my heart contract with a pang of grief.

For Hecamed remained stony and hostile. Never a smile appeared on her ripe lips, that were made for smiles; never a glance for me save of dislike and contempt. Often, coming upon her unawares, I surprised her weeping; once I attempted to offer her my sympathy, but I did not repeat the experiment. I began to think she had spoken truly when she said she hated me, though I could not but believe that she had looked kindly on me at our first meeting in the tent of Nestor. Had she not assisted me to escape? But that, I reflected, may have been to spite the Greeks, who had killed her father and made her captive.

My duties as kesten were at this particular time anything but onerous. I spent a small portion of each morning arranging the order of feasts and sacrifices for the day. In the afternoon I attended the meeting of council; and that was all.

I must add that I was being somewhat annoyed by the antagonism of Oileus, Priest of Thamyris. He had not forgotten that I had transferred the annual sacrifices of Argive Helen from his temple to that of Mulciber, nor had he forgiven me for it. There was no way in which he could really harm me, but his underhanded attempts to discredit me with King Priam, and his efforts to stir up dissension among the priests, were distinctively annoying.

I had about decided, in fact, to ask the king for his removal.

The siege progressed as usual; that is to say not at all. It appeared that the Greeks had been genuinely disheartened by the repeated success of Hector and Æneas in repelling their troops. It was well known that they had expected Troy to surrender before their attacks within the first year. It had gone over nine years, and they were further away from victory than they had been at the beginning; besides, there appeared to be no hope of getting Achilles back to the field. For the most part they contented themselves with sitting in their tents eating salt-cakes.

As Cisseis put it to me one evening:

"If they don't hurry up Helen will die of old age, and there'll be nothing left to fight for."

I had not seen Helen since the day in her rooms when Gortyna had turned her jest into a matter only too serious. She had not appeared even at the morning gathering on the Scaean Towers. Several times she had sent a messenger to inquire after Hecamed, and on each occasion I had returned word that the daughter of Arsinous was as well and happy as an exile could be expected to be.

That message, I knew, would reach the heart of Helen.

One day—the fifth of the moon, I remember, and the seventh that Hecamed had spent under my roof—I was walking leisurely through the grounds of the palace after leaving the daily meeting of council. Old Antenor had been more wordy than usual that afternoon, and I was smiling at the memory of his heroic phrases. Then my thoughts turned to Hecamed, bringing with them the ever-recurring fear of finding her gone on my arrival. At that I hastened my step.

As I did so I heard my name called softly, in a woman's voice, from behind.

Turning, I saw Helen heavily veiled and attended by Æthra and Clymene, evidently out for a walk in the evening air— for she wore a loose mantle, and could not, therefore, have been in the town. I halted, waiting for her to approach.

As she reached my side, passing almost close enough for me to have reached her by stretching out my arm, I saluted with a bow. To my surprise, she took no notice of me; but just as I had decided that she meant to pass without a word or look, she turned her head sharply toward me and said, barely loud enough to reach my ears:

"Beware of Gortyna."

Then she passed on, before I had recovered sufficiently from my surprise to answer.

My first impulse was to run after her and ask for an explanation of this strange warning; on second thought I decided against it. "If she had wished to tell me more," I said to myself, "she would have done so."

Besides, it would have necessitated entering the lodgings of Paris, where I would have run the chance of a meeting with

Gortyna. For of course Helen could not have entered into a conversation with me in the public grounds.

What could the warning mean? Did Helen know of some specific intent on the part of Gortyna; some particular injury intended for me? Or did she merely intend to advise me that Gortyna was seeking revenge? That much I knew already. And I knew that Gortyna was capable of anything.

Suddenly, seized with a quick thought, I turned on my heels and ran back to the palace as fast as I could go; past the sentry at the entrance, down the corridors, and up the stairs to my apartments.

But my fear was groundless. Hecamed was safe. She sat in her own room, on a marble bench by the window, gazing pensively out at the terraces and plants of the garden.

At the noise of my entrance she rose to her feet and stood facing me.

"Has anyone been here?" I demanded, all out of breath.

Hecamed seemed surprised at the question. "No one," she answered shortly.

"That is well." I went to the door, then turned back again. "Hecamed, hereafter when I am out you must keep the outer door securely locked. It is—there are—I have enemies, and I fear an attempt to steal my treasure."

"Your treasure?" Hecamed looked around indifferently. "Is it here? Why do you not remove it to the vaults?"

I smiled. "I mean you, Hecamed. You are my treasure. I cannot very well remove you to the vaults, though you would no doubt be pleased to go."

"As you will. You are my master."

"I know; there is no need to remind me of it. I would speak of something else. This day I have spoken with Polyxena, daughter of Priam: she is my friend. I told her of your loneliness, and she has promised to come to see you."

"I do not care to see a daughter of Priam, or any friend of yours."

"I know; that is all very well. But will you receive Polyxena if she comes?"

"If it is your order."

"Answer me! Will you receive her?"

"Yes."

"That is well. Another thing. Cisseis will sup here tonight. Will you sit with us?"

"Yes, if it is your order. I would prefer not."

"Then we shall do without you!" And, exasperated beyond endurance. I strode out, slamming the door behind me.

This was the nature of my relations with Hecamed at the end of seven days. Not exactly a paradise.

Entertained as I was that evening by a call from my friend Cisseis, I entirely forgot Helen's warning to beware of Gortyna. But when he had gone, and I had retired to my couch, it returned to my mind, and I lay awake for an hour wondering what she had meant, if anything. Then my eyes closed in sleep.

The next morning Hecamed and I breakfasted together. I had insisted on her attendance at this ceremony from the beginning, though I certainly got little pleasure out of it. Not a word would she utter throughout the meal, save in answer to a direct question. There would she sit, peeling fruit, with her eyes on her plate, calm, indifferent, cold, disdainful—it was maddening! This morning she was even worse than usual; I verily believe she had not spoken a word since we had taken our seats.

Suddenly a knock sounded at the outer door. Thersin, having gone to answer it, returned to say that Smanus, a religious messenger, would speak with me.

"Bid him enter," I replied, thinking that the fellow was come on business. In my capacity as kesten I often received messages in this manner from the various priests.

"What is it?" I asked as Smanus entered. He came forward, half timidly, I thought, holding the end of his official girdle in one hand and a scroll of parchment in the other.

He asked in a shrill monotone:

"Are you Idaeus, kesten of King Priam, son of Dares, the priest of Mulciber?"

"You know it well," I replied somewhat testily, for the fellow had seen me many times before.

"It is part of my office," he explained apologetically. "The question must be answered."

"I am Idaeus. Proceed."

At that he took a step forward, unrolled the parchment, and began reading from it in the same shrill monotone, so rapidly that I could barely catch the words:

"Summons from the Domestic Council of Troy by authority of Priam, Most High King of Men. To Idæus, son of Dares. That having in his household in the royal palace of Troy an allowance of one slave-girl by the laws of the king; and having filled it by promise, agreement, and consent with Gortyna, a woman of Graea, in the household of Paris, son of Priam, under the account of Argive Helen of Sparta; and having therefor substituted the person of Hecamed, daughter of Arsinous of Tenedos, which constitutes a violation of said promise, agreement, and consent; he is hereby directed to appear this day before the Priest of the Temple of Thamyris and submit himself to the will of the gods."

He finished, rolled up the parchment, bowed, and turned to go.

"Smanus," I cried, recovering from my amazement as he reached the door, "who is the author of this? Whence came this summons?"

He halted. "I know not. It was given me on my round at the Temple of Thamyris."

"Is it signed by the priest? Let me see."

Approaching, he handed me the parchment, which I unrolled. At the bottom of the summons, in bold characters, was the signature; "Oileus."

That was enough; I dismissed the messenger with a piece of silver and a wave of the hand. When he had gone I turned to Hecamed:

"Well, I am in for it. This is a pretty mess."

Overcome by curiosity, she could not forbear the question:

"What is it? I couldn't understand a word he said."

I explained. "It is the charge of Gortyna, the serving-woman of Helen. You know her. She accuses me of having violated an agreement."

Hecamed's eyes had narrowed to a thin slit. "Well?" she asked in a low voice.

"Well—I am ordered to appear before the priest of Thamyris, who is Oileus, my enemy—no matter why. The gods will speak through him—what a joke! The decision is as good as rendered already. Gortyna will win her case."

"And that means?" She raised her eyes to mine.

"That means, my dear Hecamed, that you will probably have your wish—to be free of me. Being a bachelor lodged in the palace, the word of the priest is my law. Being my enemy, he will decide for Gortyna; and hereafter, instead of an unwilling slave, these rooms will hold an unwilling master."

The expression of joy which I expected to see on Hecamed's face did not appear. Instead, she clasped her hands tightly before her on the table, gazing at me as though she did not understand.

"You say I am to leave you?" she asked in a voice that trembled. It trembled—so I believed—at thought of the freedom that was soon to be hers; and, drinking in her beauty, I was overcome by the fear of losing her. Not caring to show my emotion, I rose abruptly from my seat without answering her question and went to my own room.

I wasted no time in idle conjecture. This was a fact, to be dealt with as such; I understood now only too well what Helen had meant by her warning.

The thing was plain enough. Gortyna, being a member of Helen's household, had doubtless been aware of my transference of her mistress's annual sacrifice to Venus and the resultant enmity of Oileus. She had, therefore, arranged that her complaint should be presented at the Temple of Thamyris, knowing that Oileus would be only too glad of the chance to be revenged on me.

With a strict admonition to Hecamed that no one should be admitted, save either Cisseis or Polyxena, in case they should call, and having given similar orders to Thersin, I departed for the palace to see if it were possible to do anything in the matter.

The difficulty was that I had not time to turn around; at midday I must answer the summons at the temple, and there remained but two hours in which to act.

I sought Orchomen; he was not to be found. I despatched messengers in search of Evenus, Cisseis, Hector, and Antenor; then, as the minutes flew by and I heard no word from any, I decided to make a direct effort in my own behalf and play my only card. Ascending the great stairway to the floor above, on which were the apartments of Priam and Hecuba, I demanded to be introduced at once to the presence of the king.

I found him seated on a raised dais in the inner salon, with Cassandra at his side, watching a group of Lydian dance-girls. That did not please me, for with Cassandra around he was almost certain to be irritable, what with her unpleasant way of speech.

At my approach she arose; the king dismissed the dancers with a wave of the hand, and we found ourselves alone.

"Well, Idaeus, what would you?" he said, turning to me with a frown.

"The exercise of your authority, O king," I replied boldly, advancing.

"In your affairs, or those of your office?"

"The latter."

"Speak."

I cleared my throat. "You know, O king, the complaints I have had to prefer against Oileus, priest of Thamyris. You have agreed with me that he is ill fitted for his office; I come to demand his removal."

"What new sin has he committed?"

"None. That is, nothing tangible. But you have said that my advice on all such matters is final with you; I thought it unnecessary to draw up a list of the charges."

"You thought aright. But why do you seek me now and at this place? This is a matter for council."

"I would not wait. The matter requires expedition; his offenses are flagrant; I would have him removed instantly." And not daring to mention my own perplexities, for Priam would never have consented to such a step for private reasons, I pleaded with him to exercise his authority without waiting for the approval of council, and despatch a captain of the guard for the instant removal of the priest.

I had my labors for my pains. Professing astonishment that I would dare to suggest such a high-handed proceeding, the king declared it to be impossible. I interrupted him:

"Is anything impossible to Priam?"

"Well—at least impracticable. I will not listen to it. Do not speak. I do not care to hear you further. Why are you so impatient? I shall present the matter for consideration to the council this day, and they may be depended upon to act with all possible speed. It was not well to disturb me for such a matter, Idaeus; I hold it against you. You may go."

Perforce I went. As I descended the steps of the palace a glance at the clepsydra showed me that it lacked not much till midday. Hastening back to my rooms, I found Cisseis waiting for me, and felt myself heartened by the very sight of his friendly countenance.

"What is this?" he cried, advancing to greet me. "Hecamed tells me you are in trouble."

In a few words I acquainted him with the situation.

"I am afraid there is no help for you," he declared, when I had finished. "If it is already in the hands of the priest, there is an end. I know Oileus; he is a villain; that's certain."

"You know Oileus?"

"Yes; slightly. I know his brother better; I was with him at the school. Epistrophus his name is. I believe he is associated with Oileus in the temple."

I was seized with a sudden idea. "Exactly how well do you know this Epistrophus?" I demanded. "Is he your friend?"

"Rather. We are members of the same secret order."

"You could ask a favor of him?"

"Certainly. But let me tell you this, Idaeus; no one is going to obtain favor or mercy from Oileus through his brother or anyone else. He is hard as iron."

"I know; but hear my plan. The time is short; we must act speedily. Go to Epistrophus and tell him you are my friend, and would have him intercede with his brother Oileus in my behalf. Tell him that Hecamed is distasteful to me; that I despise her. Say, also, that I love Gortyna, but fear her passion—for we must not expect him to swallow too big a dose. Say that if I were to keep any slave-girl, my choice would be Gortyna; but that my real wish is to be rid of both of them. And bid him go to Oileus and request him to render a decision in accord with my desires."

A smile of appreciation appeared on the face of Cisseis.

"That is capital," he declared. "Really good. But do you think Oileus will take the bait?"

"Let us hope so. At least, it is the best we can do. Hurry, or you will be too late. I will follow soon after you. Having seen Epistrophus, you are to meet me at the door of the temple and embrace me before the eyes of Oileus. Now go."

As soon as he had departed I made ready to dress for the street, for the Temple of Thamyris was at the western end of the town, some distance from the palace. My mind was anything but easy. In fact, I believed that Hecamed was lost to me; for the strategy which I had entrusted to Cisseis was weak, and held little chance of success.

My idea, of course, was to lead Oileus to believe that my desires were the exact opposite of what they were in reality, and thus mislead him into a decision favorable to me. I really held but slim hope of catching the sly old fox.

Having finished my preparations, I went to Hecamed's room to warn her once more not to allow anyone to enter during my absence. What was my surprise when she met me at her door, heavily cloaked and veiled for the street!

"Where are you going?" I demanded in astonishment.

"To the temple with you," she replied, quite as though it were a matter of course.

I gazed at her in amazement, wondering by what channel this strange fancy had entered her head. When I told her that it would be extremely improper for her to accompany me, she seemed not to understand; though, as I was aware, the laws of Tenedos were the same in this particular as those of Troy.

"But I want to go!" she exclaimed, as though that settled the matter. I had no time to waste in argument, and, com-

manding her strictly to remain in the apartments till I returned,
I took my departure.

I was so busy with my thoughts that the walk to the temple
seemed short, indeed. At the door Cisseis met me, true to his
word, and embraced me fervently.

"The trap is set, but the bird is cunning," he whispered in
my ear as we entered the temple together.

The Temple of Thamyris, one of the oldest in Troy, was
also one of the most impressive. Even I, scoffer as I was, had
never been able to enter it without a sense of exaltation and
awe. Its gray, dim interior had always appealed to me to be
far more effective than the brilliant whiteness of the Temple
of Apollo; the lofty, slender columns, disappearing in the
vague light of the upper vault, seemed to be lifting one's soul
to a higher world.

Everything was of the gray stone of Anticus, even to the
altar of the priest, set high above the heads of the worshipers
and suppliants at the farther end.

Immediately beneath the altar, on a level with the floor of
the temple, four or five men sat facing the door. One of these
was a clerk of the Domestic Council, whose duty it was to see
that the will of the gods was conveyed accurately to the Trojan
police; another of the men was pointed out to me by Cisseis
as Epistrophus, brother of Oileus. The others were strangers
to me, but I took them for under officers of the temple.

Standing back of the altar, so that his head and shoulders
were barely visible above its rail, was Oileus, the priest. As
Cisseis and I sought a bench at one end of the temple toward
the front, I saw his beady little eyes glittering triumphantly
upon me.

I returned his gaze with one quite as steady.

We had no sooner seated ourselves than a bell rang out
sonorously somewere in the rear. On the instant the four or
five men on the bench—with the exception of the clerk, who
commenced scribbling on a roll of parchment as though his
life depended on it—sprang to their feet and raced to different
parts of the temple. One ascended the altar; two others began
uncovering certain little ebony urns, from which the smoke of

incense curled lazily upward; still another filled a golden cup to the brim with sacrificial wine and drank of it with an air of deep solemnity.

Suddenly the voice of Oileus sounded:

"That Idaeus may earn the favor and mercy of the gods— for his sacrifice."

As he spoke, Epistrophus approached the bench where I sat with Cisseis, holding out his hand. I opened my purse and handed him six pieces of gold. This was to pay the costs of the case.

As though the jingle of the coins had been a signal, the attendants suddenly raced forward to the foot of the altar and began what appeared to be an intricate system of calisthenics. I soon understood what they were about, when great columns of smoke began to ascend from various points beneath the rail. The columns swelled, increasing in number and volume until the entire front of the altar and the head and shoulders of the priest were completely hidden from view.

The smell was something fearful.

Then the attendants knelt and began in unison a weird, uneven chant. I don't see how they were able to open their mouths; I should think the smoke of the incense would have choked them. Their voices swelled, filling the temple; the smoke curled around the lofty pillars in snaky circles; everything was confusion to my bewildered senses. And all the time the little clerk kept writing on his parchment for dear life.

This continued for a long while, during which the figure of Oileus, the priest, remained invisible, communing with the gods. I had begun to think they had visited their wrath where it belonged and stifled him in the smoke, when suddenly the chant ceased and I heard his voice raised in a sonorous monotone:

"To Idaeus, son of Dares; the will of the gods!"

After that a short silence; then the voice sounded again, louder than before:

"Because Idaeus now hath wrongly done,
  No one alone is his, but two in one."

As the echoes of the last word died away, the attendants rose to their feet and began to turn down the covers on the smoking urns. At once the veil that hid the altar began to disappear; soon it was gone entirely. The head and shoulders of Oileus were again visible; he stood exactly as he had stood before, looking down at me with his little, beady eyes all aglitter.

"Idaeus," he said, speaking now in his natural voice, "you have heard the will of the gods. Do you desire an interpretation?"

I knew well that this question was a mere matter of form, and that I would get an "interpretation" whether I wanted one or not. I answered simply:

"Yes."

Oileus cleared his throat. "The will of the gods is plain," he declared in a tone of satisfaction. "The first, that you have done wrong, which is the justification of your punishment for the violation of your agreement with Gortyna. The second, that no one is yours—that is, that you deserve neither Hecamed nor Gortyna for your pleasure. The third, which is the mercy of the gods, that you shall have two in one—that is, that both Hecamed and Gortyna shall reside in your bosom for their own content; and you are hereby charged to harbor them equally, and preserve their life and happiness."

I rose with a smile; Oileus, at least, should not see my vexation. "It is well," I said, turning to go. "The will of the gods shall be obeyed."

Together, Cisseis and I sought the door of the temple and passed out into the street. It was a little past midday, and the sun was shining brightly; the songs of birds and the shouts of children sounded from every side. Turning eastward at the first corner, we set our faces in the direction of the palace.

"Well, our ruse succeeded—in a way. Without it you would have lost Hecamed. Lucky dog! To have two beautiful slave-girls all for your own!" Cisseis chuckled maliciously.

I did not reply. I was too busy wondering what in Pluto's name I was going to do with Hecamed and Gortyna both on my hands!

CHAPTER XIII

I Take Another Slave.

CISSEIS LEFT ME AT DOREON SQUARE TO GO TO HIS OWN home, and I returned to the palace alone. My state of mind was anything but simple; I do not know if I was more glad or sorry at the "will of the gods." On the one hand, I was not to lose Hecamed; on the other, Gortyna had gained her point, and I knew well that the little Graean would do her best to turn everything upside down within five minutes of her arrival.

So vexed was I, and so ill pleased with the uncomfortable situation I saw before me, that I would gladly have rid myself of both of them.

Knowing that Gortyna would waste no time in the matter, I half expected to find her already at my rooms when I arrived; which of course was absurd. Thersin unbarred the door in answer to my knock, and I had no sooner entered than Hecamed came running from the inner rooms, her face alight with eager curiosity.

I answered her question before she had time to put it into words.

"Well, my dear Hecamed, you are not to leave me."

She stopped short. "Not—not to leave you?"

"No," I smiled. "It is 'the will of the gods—only we cheated them a little in the matter—Cisseis and I. You are to remain with me. . . . Oh, I know it grieves you, but you are wrong. If it had been otherwise, what could you have done? Where have gone? A girl of Tenedos, even the daughter of Arsinous, would have a sorry time of it alone in Troy."

"Think you I have no friends?" Hecamed retorted. "Argive Helen would protect me, if none other. Besides, anything would be preferable—to this."

But in spite of her words, her disappointment did not appear to be as keen as I had expected. Her face certainly did not glow with pleasure, but neither was it black with gloom. She appeared, indeed, to regard the matter with something of indifference, which was more distasteful to me than open hostility would have been.

I thought to move her by telling of Gortyna's coming, and began:

"But that is not all. Although Gortyna did not win, she did not lose. Come; lead me to your room; we can talk better there."

"I cannot."

"What! You cannot?"

"No. Polyxena is within. Tell me here."

"Polyxena! She came, then?"

"Yes; shortly after your departure. She is a very sweet girl; we have become friends. But what of Gortyna?"

"I will tell you of that later. Come; lead me within; I would talk with Polyxena."

"No! Tell me!"

"Hecamed, you have often reminded me that you are my slave."

At that her face flushed rosy red and she bit her lip in vexation. "Signs not at all discouraging," I thought as I followed her to the inner room; for she had turned without a word, nor did she look to see if I followed her.

Polyxena greeted me graciously, inviting me to a seat beside her. This daughter of Priam had always appeared to me to be the most lovable of all the royal family, though that is, in fact, faint praise, and she deserves heartier. Simple and unaffected, yet never forgetful of the dignity suitable to her high station; possessed of a saving sense of humor (unlike her sister Cassandra), frankly human in her likes and dislikes and the expression of them; such was her character.

As for her appearance, no praise of mine could add to her fame. All the world knows of the lustrous brown hair, the shapely limbs and figure, the liquid, sparkling eyes that were destined to lure a mighty hero to his death.

When, a few days before, I had requested her to be kind enough to pay a visit to Hecamed at my rooms, I had been not a little puzzled by the willingness—nay, the open eagerness—with which she had granted the request. Reminded of it now by the apparent good friendship so quickly developed between the two girls, I resolved to solve the riddle if possible.

"Polyxena," I began abruptly, after we had talked for some time on various subjects, "I do not know if Hecamed has thanked you for your visit. Perhaps she does not even know that thanks are due. Will you allow me to offer them?"

"Gladly would I, good Idaeus, if they were necessary," replied the daughter of Priam.

"Do you think me lacking in politeness?" put in Hecamed. "I have told her of my gratitude."

"That is well," I replied. "You must know, Polyxena, that I am aware of your kindness. There is much amusement at the palace; it is a sacrifice of your pleasure to thus give the day to the relief of Hecamed's loneliness. That you are bored is certain."

"On the contrary, I am much amused," declared Polyxena. "Your opinion is not complimentary to Hecamed, which is wrong. I find her conversation more pleasing than any amusement at the palace."

"Which is not surprising," put in Hecamed, forgetting herself sufficiently to smile at me. "I happen to possess a fund of information on a subject in which Polyxena is keenly interested. She has asked me no less than a thousand questions, and about whom, do you think? About Achilles!''

During the latter part of this speech I observed Polyxena, out of the corner of my eye, making frantic signs to Hecamed to hold her tongue. But Hecamed, looking at me, had not observed them, and the cat was out of the bag.

Polyxena's eagerness to visit Hecamed had been due to her interest in Achilles. Which, after all, meant nothing.

I turned to the daughter of Arsinous with a smile:

"You should be able to answer the questions, since it was Achilles that made you captive. I no longer insist on giving Polyxena our thanks; I only hope that the pleasure she finds in your conversation will persuade her to visit us often."

Polyxena, turning to answer me, was interrupted by the voice of the servant from the doorway:

"Sir, the Lord Paris asks admittance to your rooms."

I rose half way to my feet in surprise. What in Pluto's name brought Paris to visit me? Then, reflecting that he had no doubt come to summon Polyxena and escort her to the afternoon feast, I instructed Thersin to bid him enter.

A moment later he appeared in the doorway. A single glance at him showed me the purpose of this unexpected visit, for he did not wear the military costume which had come to be the universal dress for Trojans since the beginning of the siege. Instead, a chiton of the finest embroidered linen, girt at the waist, hung halfway down his thighs, while his shoulders were covered with a magnificent purple chlamys. His hair, close cut at the top, was shiny with oil and perfume; at his side was a chased scabbard of gold, at the mouth of which appeared the jewelled hilt of a sword.

His limbs likewise were anointed with fragrant oil, and soft sandals of *serica* protected his feet from the hard marble.

In short, he was dressed for battle—the only kind of battle he was ever energetic enough to enter. His intentions were perfectly plain. Having heard much gossip in the palace and at the clubs concerning the beauty of Hecamed, he had decided to see for himself, no doubt with the purpose of honoring her with his attentions if she proved worthy of them.

He stood motionless in the doorway, in a studied pose of

elegance. First he looked at me, bowing ever so slightly in recognition of my invitation to enter; then he shifted his gaze to Polyxena, smiling at her with an air of brotherly condescension; finally he allowed his eyes to fall on Hecamed.

At sight of her he started and took a step forward; I thought for a moment that the start was one of recognition, though I could not guess where he could possibly have seen her, for she herself had told me that she had not seen Paris during her stay overnight with Helen. Then I realized that his movement had been merely an unconscious tribute to Hecamed's beauty, and I said to myself:

"This gay young dog will bear watching."

In a moment Paris had recovered himself and advanced across the room with an easy, graceful step, saying airily: "You are well fixed here, Idaeus—quite a pleasant spot. Sister"—turning to Polyxena—"I have been looking for you; Cassandra said I might find you here. Have you discovered a new friend?" And he turned a bold gaze on Hecamed.

I stepped forward. "Hecamed, this is Paris, son of Priam and husband of Helen." That dug him: I saw him send me a swift glance. "Will you be seated, sir—there, beside your sister? Hecamed, have Thersin bring wine and cakes." Then, as she rose to summon the servant, I seated myself on a bench near the royal visitors.

Whatever the nature of Paris's business with his sister, it could not have been very important. He remained over an hour, drinking my best wine, mostly with his eyes roving impudently over the face and form of Hecamed.

In spite of my annoyance, I could not help but admire him. In the first place, he was undeniably handsome—exceedingly so; and in the second, he was the best-dressed man in Troy. That purple chlamys alone must have cost a small fortune.

What increased my annoyance was the fact that Hecamed returned his gaze with one fully as interested; she seemed to be fascinated by his magnificent appearance and elegant speech.

Polyxena was plainly embarrassed; no doubt she knew her brother as well as anyone else. Several times she attempted to

drag him away on one pretext or another, and ended by suc-
ceeding. He departed with an assurance even greater than that
with which he had entered; slapping me familiarly on the back,
paying series of broad compliments to Hecamed's beauty, and
laughingly telling his sister that she must not fail to seek his
company whenever she intended a visit to the rooms of Idaeus.

When they had gone and Hecamed and I found ourselves
alone together, I led her back to her own room to finish my
recital of the events of the temple. She would seem to have
forgotten all about it, for her first words were:

"So that is Paris!"

"Yes," I replied, looking at her curiously. "What do you
think of him?"

She shrugged her shoulders. "I don't know—I haven't
thought. He is very good-looking, but a little too effeminate
and insufferably conceited. I don't blame Helen for running
away with him; at least, he is an improvement on Menelaus."

"Do you disregard morals entirely in your judgments?"

"Yes—I don't know—let us talk of something else. Oh—
I forgot! You had something to tell me about Gortyna. What
was it?"

"Something not very pleasant," I replied. "As I said, if she
did not win, neither did she lose."

"Why do you speak in riddles? Tell me."

"Well—it is 'the will of the gods' that I take Gortyna to
be my slave."

Hecamed's eyes opened wide. "But *I* am your slave! Akh!
Am I—"

"To be free? No; did I not say you should remain with me?
You are to be my slave, and Gortyna also. Will she not be a
good companion for you?"

"Akh!" Hecamed's eyes blazed. "A companion for *me?*
For the daughter of Arsinous—she, a little Graean peasant?
Even if you are my master, you have no right to insult me
thus!"

At that I hastened to tell her that I had jested; that it was
"the gods" who had insulted her, not I.

"I know well, Hecamed, that she is not a fit companion for

you. But what can I do? I am ordered to receive her, and I dare not disobey. If you had but listened to my pleadings to become my wife; if you could care for me, Gortyna would be your slave as well as mine.''

Hecamed's face had resumed its old expression of sullen hostility.

''When is she coming?'' she asked coldly. Then she burst forth in sudden passion: ''And you think I believe all this! You have arranged it all! Did you not admit that you made love to her? It is I who shall be *her* slave! I hate her—I *hate* her! And I despise you more than ever!''

She rose to her feet, trembling from head to foot. I also arose, and was searching for a way to answer her, when I was interrupted by Thersin's announcement from the doorway that someone had called to see me. I turned to ask who it was.

''I know not, sir. Some woman. She will not give her name. She says that you will know who it is.''

''I do know—wait—what is she like?''

''Small; rather young,'' replied Thersin. ''Of the lower classes, sir. Black hair and olive skin, with snappy eyes.''

''Very well. Show her in here.''

Thersin disappeared with a bow. A moment later the form of Gortyna appeared in the doorway.

She made a curious picture. Evidently she had lost no time in answering the official summons, for she wore nothing but a scanty mantle that reached barely to her knees. Thick sandals were on her feet, but she had not stopped to put on either headdress or veil; her hair fell in a tangled mass about her shoulders.

In her right hand she carried a bundle wrapped in a dirty old mantle; odds and ends of feminine apparel stuck out from it on every side. In her other hand was a large wooden cage containing a black Graean parrot.

She set the cage carefully on the floor, threw the bundle down beside it, and turned to me with a grim smile.

''Well, Idaeus, your Gortyna has come,'' she remarked.

As though it had been waiting for the signal, the parrot suddenly began to flap his wings and cry in an ear-cracking falsetto:

"Idaeus! Idaeus! Idaeus!"

CHAPTER XIV

ON THE SCAEAN TOWERS.

THE FOLLOWING MORNING I AWOKE WITH A START. Something was happening. What was it? Shaking myself and rubbing my eyes to get the sleep out of them, I suddenly realized that someone was calling my name over and over, shrilly, desperately:

"Idaeus! Idaeus! Idaeus!"

"It's that confounded parrot," I muttered angrily to myself; and, turning over, tried to compose myself for another nap.

But the cries continued unabated and ended by thoroughly awaking me. Tumbling out of my couch, I started for the little room in the rear which I had assigned to Gortyna; then, perceiving that the cries came from the front, I started back again.

As I passed the door of Hecamed's room she poked her head out to inquire in a frightened voice what the matter was. At my reply that I had no more idea than she, she came out dressed in nothing but a gauzy chiton and followed me to the front. The noise apparently came from the main hall. We hastened thither.

Our alarm speedily gave way to mirth at the sight that met

our eyes, though in truth it was somewhat heartless to laugh. The cries came from the lips of my servant Thersin.

He lay on the floor of the hall, doubled up into a knot with his hands covering his face for protection. Over him stood Gortyna, belaboring his back, his shoulders, his feet—every projecting point of his body—with a heavy girdle of hide. With every blow she vented her breath in a grunt of satisfaction, muttering:

"Monster! Wretch! Thessalian dog!"

When I could get my breath I called to her to stop at once, for she was half killing the poor fellow. She paid no attention to me, but continued to lay on with the girdle. Approaching, I seized her arm and jerked her back.

"What would you, Gortyna? What is the meaning of this?"

She stood silent in my grasp. Thersin rose to his feet, rubbing himself with both hands. Tears were in his eyes. He stood regarding me mournfully, while his jaw moved regularly up and down; he was actually frightened out of speech. Suddenly Gortyna jumped forward out of my grasp, brandishing the girdle on high. Thersin, with a scream of terror, took to his heels and disappeared within.

"In heaven's name, Gortyna, what is the meaning of this?" I demanded again.

She turned to face me:

"He insulted me."

"Insulted you? How?"

"I will tell you," said Gortyna with a sudden air of engaging candor. She paused to scowl at Hecamed quite as a matter of duty, then continued:

"He—that little Thessalian man—was carrying the lamps to the rear. I was coming through the hall to take Zamus out for some air—"

"Zamus? Who in Pluto's name is that?"

"Don't you know? My parrot." She pointed to where the cage sat in a corner. I had not noticed it before.

"Very well, Gortyna, but you know what I told you last night. You must positively get rid of that parrot today. Go on."

"I was coming through the hall, and how could I know he was coming the other way? Maybe I was running—I know I was in a hurry, for Zamus was talking very loud and I feared he would awaken you. So I ran right against the little Thessalian. He said that one of the lamps stuck in his eye. Was that my fault? And then—he called me a long-haired Graean whelp!"

"Not a very complimentary remark," I observed, preserving my gravity with difficulty. I dared not look at Hecamed. If either of us had laughed I suppose Gortyna would have begun on *us* with the girdle.

"—So I beat him," Gortyna finished calmly.

And before I had time to open my mouth to reply—for, insults or no insults, I did not intend that my rooms should witness a repetition of the scene that had just taken place—she turned on her heel, picked up the parrot and disappeared in the outer corridor, slamming the door behind her.

I turned to Hecamed. She was plainly making an effort to keep a straight face, no doubt because of the fact that nothing tends so quickly to put people in sympathy with each other as for them to join in mirth. Looking at her, I forgot Gortyna; and she, becoming aware of something curious in my gaze, suddenly realized that she was standing before me dressed only in her chiton.

A deep, rosy blush suddenly overspread her face and neck; her eyes fell in confusion; and, turning abruptly, she retreated hastily to her room.

Finding myself thus alone, I returned to my own room to bathe and dress, having first sought out Thersin in the rear to discover the extent of his injuries. I found him anointing his back with some cheap oil of so fearful an odor that I made my escape as soon as possible, holding my nose with my fingers.

Not satisfied with her achievement of the morning, which would have been considered a day's work by anyone but a Graean peasant-girl, Gortyna soon found a fresh opportunity to make trouble.

It was at the breakfast table. Gortyna had returned from her morning walk, without the parrot; I never found out how she disposed of it. Hecamed and I had taken our seats at the table and Thersin had served the fruit, on little golden plates that were a present from my father, when Gortyna walked in, drew up a chair and calmly seated herself between us.

"What does this mean?" I demanded, when I could speak for astonishment. "Is it your place to sit at table with your master?"

"If I am your slave, so is Hecamed," returned Gortyna composedly. "The order from the temple is that we be treated equally. If she sits with you, so do I. It is the will of the gods."

"Gods or no gods, you do not sit here!" I cried, thoroughly exasperated. "Did I not tell you last night that you shall eat with Thersin in the kitchen? Begone, or I will beat you as you did beat him, only not so lightly!"

She ended by obeying, though with exceeding ill grace. After she had gone I looked at Hecamed with a twinkle in my eye, hoping to find her likewise amused, but she gave no sign, refusing to meet my eyes.

As usual, the meal was begun and finished in silence. Several times I tried to draw her into conversation, but she replied either in monosyllables or not at all. I ended by observing somewhat sharply:

"It seems to me, Hecamed, that you exaggerate your humor wilfully. What is your grievance against me? Have I not atoned for whatever wrong I may be guilty of? Have I not been patient with you? It cannot be that you are jealous of Gortyna, since you see in what esteem I hold her."

"Jealous!" she exclaimed scornfully, no doubt glad to have the word. "Do you think it possible that I could be jealous of anyone for you?"

"I do not pretend to say; I am only seeking to discover what your grievance is."

There was a short pause, during which she appeared to hesitate. Then she replied:

"I have no grievance, Idaeus, save that you seized me and made me your slave. Is not that enough? Have I not said I despise you? Must I say it over and over, that the truth may enter your dull brain?''

"These are strange words from a slave to a master," I said, feeling my face grow hot. "It is well that my love for you holds my arm at my side."

"If you do not strike, it is only because I am the daughter of Arsinous," she replied calmly. "Besides, if you ask a question I must answer it."

I had begun this conversation with a definite purpose in view. My friends were beginning to wonder why I did not appear with Hecamed in public. A little more, and they would discover the true state of affairs; I would be made ridiculous, and no one fears ridicule more than I. I had been waiting for Hecamed to swallow her dislike; it appeared now that I might wait forever, and in vain. I decided to try persuasion once more; if that failed, to exert my authority.

I faced her with a question:

"Then here is another for you to answer. Will you go with me this morning to the Scaean Towers?"

She raised her eyebrows in quick surprise. "But that is not possible, is it? For me, a slave?"

"Yes. In your case it is possible, for I have not placed your name on the roll. You see, I trust you; you are in reality as free as I am. There will be quite a gathering on the Towers; Æneas and Hector are to take the field this day, besides many others. The sight would amuse and divert you."

There was a silence, during which Hecamed was plainly struggling between her desire to go and her dislike of my company. At length she said, as though unwillingly:

"Why should I deny the truth for you? I would like to go; I admit it. But I will not."

"How! You will not?"

"No." And she started to rise from her chair as though the thing were settled.

I leaned forward, motioning her back to her seat. "Not so fast, my dear Hecamed. My desire is that you accompany me to the Scaean Towers. Once more I ask, will you go?"

She replied firmly: "No."

"Very well," I retorted. "In that case, I am forced to command you. This is my order: that you be prepared, at the end of the second glass, to accompany me through the streets."

"And if I do not?"

"You know the punishment for a disobedient slave. Nor am I to blame if you persist in a refusal so senseless and without reason."

Hecamed turned suddenly pale. "Punishment! You would not—you would not *dare!*"

"But I would. I owe it to myself as well as to the other masters of Troy. There is no reason for your refusal to accompany me."

Hecamed's face had gone from white to red.

"No reason!" she exclaimed in a voice suddenly full of tears. "You say there is no reason! Very well, I shall accompany you. I shall go with you to your fashionable gathering at the Towers; and do you know what I shall wear?" Her voice broke; she was near weeping with anger. "I will wear that dirty old white chiton and my only himation—full of holes! You have not bought me a stitch of clothes since I came to you!"

And with that she rose abruptly from her chair with blazing eyes and ran out of the room.

Completely overcome, I sank back in my seat. Great Olympus! It was true! I had not furnished her with so much as a pair of sandals. The poor girl must be absolutely without—well, without everything—and had been too proud to say a word about it! Of course, I had not wilfully neglected her; it was simply that the idea had never entered my mind.

Overwhelmed with contrition, I followed her to her own room, where she had taken refuge, and laid a purse of gold on the bench beside her.

"Forgive me, Hecamed," I entreated earnestly. "You know I would not purposely slight you. Here is my purse, filled with gold; take it, and procure what is needful. I implore your forgiveness."

"I hate you!" she cried, without looking at me. Her hands

covered her face; she was crying softly. "Take your old purse—I don't want it!"

I cajoled, pleaded, and threatened; at length she uncovered her face and looked up at me through her tears.

"Is it your order?" she demanded, and it was easy to see what answer she desired.

"It is my order," I replied, concealing a smile.

"Then—I will go," she said, still pretending reluctance. She added quickly: "On one condition: that you will accompany me. I do not know the customs of Troy; I should be frightened."

"Accompany you? Where?"

"To the bazaars. Where else?"

Now, if there is one thing I dislike more than another, it is pushing my way through a crowd of women in a bazaar. I said so, ending with a flat refusal; but Hecamed was immovable.

"I shall not go without you," she declared with the firmness of a woman who has made up her mind. "Why, I am even unacquainted with the Trojan dialect!"

It ended in my surrender.

A little later, therefore, we set out together, turning our faces towards the central part of the city. I had suggested taking a chariot, but Hecamed declared that she preferred to shop afoot.

"At any rate," I observed, "we shall have no difficulty in finding everything we want at Meneon's, so there will be little walking to do."

"Meneon's!" exclaimed Hecamed in scorn. "That's just like a man. They haven't a piece of imported goods in the place. We shall go to Thestis Brothers."

And to Thestis Brothers we went. Luckily we were early enough to avoid the crowd; still I found it sufficiently annoying. We hopped around from booth to booth; a chiton here, a fibula there, *toenias*, *zosters*, himations without end. Of sandals we ordered a dozen pair, and Hecamed absolutely insisted on hunting-boots, though Jove only knows when or where she intended to wear them.

We finished up in the headdress shop, where I was driven

half insane by Hecamed's frantic insistence on my opinion and advice.

"This petasus is pretty—yet—I don't know—I believe it covers too much of my hair—don't you think so, Idaeus? Try it on the other side. There! No, that won't do. Let me see that *ampyx*—no, not that, the one with the amber rings. Idaeus, what do you think—Idaeus, look at me! After all, I think I shall take a *kydaris*. And of course I must have a *stephane*; I always look well in a *stephane*. Great Juno! You must have had this over from the beginning of the siege. Idaeus, isn't it *awful?*"

And so on, ad infinitum, till my head whirled and I staggered onto a bench. At length, however—long after I had given up all hope—the performance was ended. Hecamed smiled at me in perfect good humor and sat down beside me while we waited for the clerk to bring the bill. He appeared, after an interminable wait, to announce calmly that it amounted to one hundred and sixty-five *distateronae*!

"Are you sure it is correct?" I demanded in astonishment.

"Perfectly, sir. You may check it yourself."

I turned to Hecamed.

"This won't do at all. Why, I only get eighty *distateronae* a month. 'Tis the sixth of a year's salary!"

As a matter of fact, my statement, though true, was not the whole truth. In addition to my salary as kesten, I received an allowance of one hundred *distateronae* a month from Dares, my father. But I thought it unnecessary to mention the fact.

Hecamed took the bill from the hands of the clerk and went over it carefully, item by item. Then she looked up to declare calmly:

"I am sorry; there isn't a single thing here I can do without; not one."

I sighed. "At least," I suggested tentatively, "you can wait a while for the hunting-boots. And that purple embroidered *zoster* is surely unnecessary."

"The hunting-boots!" cried Hecamed. "Why, they are perfectly stunning! And as for the *zoster*, Helen has one exactly like it, except that there are tassels on the ends, and I can put them on myself.''

Which did not appear to me to be a particularly convincing argument, but I was nevertheless forced to yield. I paid the bill in full, emptying my purse, and, ordering the articles to be delivered at once at my rooms in the palace, we departed.

On the way out of the store Hecamed chanced to spy some fancy girdles displayed on a counter and started for them with a rush. I got her away only by declaring on my word of honor that I had absolutely no more money.

Worn out by the hated exercise, I insisted on riding home and hailed a public chariot. Hecamed, too, was heated with the fray, but the light of victory was in her eyes.

''Now,'' I observed, sinking back onto the seat with a sigh of relief, ''I shall expect you to be a little more amiable.''

Hecamed looked at me as though in surprise. ''And why should I be amiable?'' she wanted to know. ''Because you have clothed your servant—that is to say, performed your duty? Akh!''

I subsided, speechless.

And so, after many trials and much preparation, we went to the Scaean Towers. We arrived late, for several reasons.

To begin with, Gortyna flew into a rage when she discovered that Hecamed's wardrobe had been so lavishly filled; it required five pieces of gold and as many wholesome threats to quiet her. Then came the question of choosing Hecamed's attire. So undecided was she among her unaccustomed wealth that we never would have got started if I had not set my foot down firmly and given her just the fourth part of a clepsydra more to dress.

When I observed the result I felt almost repaid for the trouble and expense I had been put to. Hecamed was one of those women who know how to wear a thing, no matter how foreign it may be, the minute they see it.

She came forth attired in a white himation embroidered in *serica* of pink, at the bottom of which could be seen the folds of a pink chiton. Her sandals were also pink, with straps of the same color; on her head was a Persian *kyrbasia*, with its high embroidered point reaching above my shoulders. Her beautiful white arms were bare, save where the straying folds of the himation endeavored, vainly jealous, to cover them.

"How do I look?" she asked, in a tone which plainly intimated that she had already answered the question to her own satisfaction.

"You are perfection itself; a mark for the envy of Venus," I replied with unfeigned sincerity. Indeed, she was beautiful; a pang of desire shot through my breast as I thought that she was mine only in name. "Come; lower your veil; it is time we started."

As I have said before, we arrived late at the Scaean Towers, though our charioteer urged his horses through the streets at top speed. Assisting Hecamed to dismount, I led the way through the great portals of red and yellow stone to the winding stairway within.

"Good heavens!" panted Hecamed when we were half way up, "will this never end? I can't go a step further!"

We finally reached the top together, all out of breath. As we stepped onto the broad platform the sound of many voices reached our ears. Then down the Passage of the Seven Pillars, and we found ourselves on the Towers.

It was a scene of animation that presented itself to our gaze; I had almost said a scene of gayety. Seated on the marble benches, placed here and there in groups of three and four, were all of the most prominent and fashionable men and women of Troy.

Priam himself was on the ebony throne at the edge of the parapet, surrounded by his councilors, peering out across the plain toward the battlefield. Seated at his right was Argive Helen, no doubt for the purpose of pointing out whatever Greek chieftains might come within the range of vision; on his left was Cassandra.

At one side was a group composed of Paris, Aethra, Clymene, and Polyxena; near the center stood Queen Hecuba, surrounded by her waiting-women. On her face anxiety stood with heavy feet, as it always did on a day that Hector took the field. For that one thing I have always admired the queen; she had sense enough to see that Hector was worth all the rest of her sons put together.

Moving through the various assembled groups, with here and there a bow to acquaintances or friends, Hecamed and I made our way to the outer edge of the Towers. On every side I heard whispers and saw glances in our direction; I felt a mean satisfaction in thwarting their curiosity by directing Hecamed to keep her veil lowered.

As yet the plain, stretching away from the gates far beneath us, was empty; the warriors had not yet appeared. Away to the east, at a great distance, was the dim line of the Grecian camp. We amused ourselves for some time by trying to discern the tent of Nestor, where I had seized Hecamed, but found it impossible.

"After all," said Hecamed, with her eyes strained toward the camp of the enemy—hers as well as mine—"I have much to thank you for, Idaeus. You rescued me from worse than death."

I drew closer. "It is only right that you should thank me, yet it makes me as happy as if it were undeserved. Does your hate begin to falter? Will you smile on me, Hecamed?"

"Akh! Nay. You know I am here only by your order. But come; Polyxena beckons; I would speak with her."

I tried to get her to talk with me further, but she would not listen, and we moved across to where the daughter of Priam stood talking with her brother Paris. Aethra and Clymene had gone to answer the summons of their mistress; Orchomen had joined the other two.

"Ah!" he cried as we approached, "can I believe mine eyes? Is it Idaeus with the fair Hecamed? My friend, how are you?"

"I am glad to see you, Hecamed," said the daughter of Priam. "My! What a beautiful *krybasia*! Did you get it in Troy? Come; sit by me. Why do you not raise your veil? 'Tis the custom on the Towers."

Hecamed hesitated, embarrassed. "I—I—the truth is, Idaeus has forbidden it."

Polyxena looked at me in surprise; Orchomen burst out laughing; Paris took a step forward, saying boldly:

"What! Would Idaeus deny us a glimpse of the lovely Hecamed? That is ungenerous; we must teach him better manners!"

And before I could either speak or interpose he had stretched out his hand to the veil and jerked it up, disclosing Hecamed's face, rosy red, to the view of all.

CHAPTER XV

AN ALARM FROM THE FIELD.

S O QUICK AND UNEXPECTED HAD BEEN THE MOVE OF
Paris that I had no time to forestall him. But on the instant I sprang forward with upraised arm. If it had not
been for the intervention of Orchomen there would have been
a pretty scene, in which I would inevitably have got the worst
of it, for one does not strike the son of a king with impunity.

Orchomen, however, rushed between us before my arm fell,
calling to me in a guarded tone:

"Hold, Idaeus; would you ruin yourself?" Then he turned
to Paris:

"It is you who should learn better manners. For shame!"

"I meant nothing by it," said Paris, evidently realizing that
he had gone too far. "I meant no harm. Besides, if anyone
should be offended it is the lady."

"That is for me to say," I retorted, my face white with
anger. "I take offense where I find it."

Paris did not even look at me, but kept his eyes fastened on
Hecamed. "It is well to be officious in your own cause," he

said nonchalantly. "And I swear—Hecamed, tell me, are you offended?"

All eyes were turned on the daughter of Arsinous. She was returning the gaze of Paris with steady eyes, yet in their depths was a hint of laughter. "There was no offense," she said at length; "or if there were I forgive you, Paris."

At that Orchomen burst again into laughter, and a smile appeared on the lips of Polyxena, while Paris sent me a mocking grin. As for me—well, if Hecamed had been alone with me at that moment, I verily believe she would have got the oft-threatened beating. To tell a man who had just snatched off her veil that there was no offense, after I had opened a quarrel with him! It was done to spite me, perhaps; but then Paris was the sort that always appeals to women. . . .

That ended the matter; I could not very well continue a quarrel on Hecamed's account when she denied that there was reason for one. I drew aside in a huff; Orchomen joined me, leaving Hecamed talking with Paris and Polyxena. We wandered off to the eastern parapet; I was silent, with a gloomy brow, while Orchomen rallied me on my discomfiture.

"What, Idaeus! The fair Hecamed denies your protection? Perhaps she denies your valor. Let her apply to me; for a smile from her lips I would take every man in Troy under forty and hurl him from these Towers to the Grecian camp. But—ah! Perhaps she means to protect you from the wrath of Paris, the great warrior."

"Your wit totters, Orchomen," I observed drily. "Try silence; it better suits your tongue; speech betrays you."

"As you will," he returned cheerfully. Then he added, suddenly serious: "But I advise you to keep an eye on Paris. Warrior or no warrior, he manages somehow to play the very deuce with women. I don't know what they see in him, but you cannot deny the fact. Did you see the look in Hecamed's eyes as she gazed at him? Beware!"

"Akh!" I exclaimed scornfully, "do you think I fear that popinjay?" And I turned my back on the group of three on the other side to show my unconcern.

At the same time I acknowledged to myself that it might be

matter for uneasiness, for I had indeed seen the look in He-camed's eyes of which Orchomen spoke. Did I interpret it aright? That Hecamed did not love me I knew well, but would she. . . . But nay! I shrugged my shoulders and pushed the thought from my mind.

"I think we shall see something soon," Orchomen was say-ing. "The time is passed; they should have appeared—see! They come! The gates are opened! Ah! Hector goes today in his chariot—and there is Æneas, with those horses he got from your father. He certainly got the worst of that bargain."

Everyone on the Towers was crowding to the edge of the parapet to get a glimpse of the warriors, who were emerging from the gates almost directly below. Hector was in the lead, as usual. Following him were some three hundred horsemen, with twice as many archers on foot. Then came Æneas with an even greater body of troops.

It could be observed, even at so great a distance, that the son of Anchises was uneasy, which was probably on account of the horses of which Orchomen had spoken. They were in fact pretty poor specimens.

Behind the two leaders came other princes and chieftains with their troops; soon the plain was overspread. The ladies on the Tower were waving the borders of their mantles with a graceful enthusiasm developed through nine years' steady practice; the men were saluting their comrades and sending them words of encouragement.

The scene, which had been animated, was now even bois-terous; everybody was talking and shouting at once. King Priam bent forward from his ebony throne, pretending to in-spect the troops as they left the gates; it may be doubted if his dim old eyes were able to perceive them at all. Queen Hecuba stood near him, resting her hand on the stone entab-lature; tears were in her eyes, but she was waving her mantle bravely and calling to her son Hector.

Suddenly, not ten paces from where I stood, I caught sight of a flash of pink. Leaning forward, I saw Hecamed standing beside Paris, resting her hand on his arm. On her other side was Polyxena; all three were laughing and talking together.

Then my attention was called away by Orchomen:

"See, here comes Evenus. I would not be surprised if he excelled them all today, for his men are clamorous for revenge of the death of King Rhesus. It would seem that their spirit has actually been communicated to their horses; see how they snort and prance about! Jove! I wish I were with them! I shall go out tomorrow."

"And leave your dance-girls?"

"I would leave a thousand dance-girls—a wife—even your Hecamed, for the smell of battle. Who would not?"

By this time the troops were assembled in order. The general was riding up and down the line in his chariot; messengers were running to and fro in every direction; one approached Hector, who turned to the trumpeter at his side. The next instant the martial sound rang out over the plain, and at the first note the army surged forward like the sweep of the Scamander flood.

The shouts on the Towers and along the walls were redoubled; many of the soldiers could be seen twisting their heads for a glance—possibly their last one—of weeping wives and laughing children.

Soon, as they drew out of earshot, the shouts died away. Those on the Towers began to leave the parapet and gather again in groups around the benches. But soon they were called back by a new cry:

"The Greeks! The Greeks have left their tents!"

So often had they observed that thin, almost imperceptible line, as of a dark cloud gathered along the horizon, that they could see it almost before it was visible. It was the cloud of dust raised by the Grecian troops as they rushed forward in their march to the field.

Though this scene, down to the last detail, was by this time an old story to the inhabitants of Troy, they showed as much enthusiasm, and almost as much excitement, as if it had been the first sally of the siege. It was more the thrill of suspense than anything else, for there was always the possibility that something unusual would happen. On this occasion it appeared to me that the faces of all were tense with expectation to an unaccustomed degree; the very air seemed fraught with great events.

Orchomen and I remained at our vantage point, near the edge of the parapet, towards which everybody rushed again at the sight of the Greeks advancing.

The Trojan army sped swiftly over the plain; the enemy moved as swiftly to meet them. Suddenly both sides halted, just when it seemed to us on the Towers that the next step would bring them together. We could see the archers in the rear, maneuvering for position; the foot soldiers rested on their lances; we guessed at the fact rather than saw it, for the distance was great. The horsemen were ranged at the front in three rows, with the brazen points of their weapons glittering in the sun; and at the head of the line were the white chariots of the leaders, some at rest, others racing up and down in front of the troops.

For some time they remained thus facing each other, while everyone on the Towers held his breath in momentary expectation of a general conflict. To us it appeared that the two armies were separated by less than the space of a strong javelin, but in reality they were still a considerable distance apart.

Suddenly a murmur of disappointment was heard on every side; the Trojan body had parted in several places and begun to deploy to right and left; all hope of a general conflict was ended.

Soon large open spaces were discernible between the several brigades as they moved to take up their respective positions; the archers had retreated some distance to the rear to entrench themselves behind the foothills. Through the open spaces it could be seen that the Greeks were employing the same tactics, dividing their forces to defend each avenue to their camp threatened by the maneuvers of the Trojans.

"Akh!" It was Paris's voice, raised loud enough for everyone to hear, in tones of disgust. "Akh! And I suppose you call that generalship! There's great Hector for you! If he had only called a general charge before they began to move—he had plenty of time—he could have broken their lines and torn their camp to pieces before they had time to turn around. And instead of that he sends all his veterans to cover the wings and leaves nothing in the main column but a lot of clerks and apprentices! How can you expect to do anything with that kind of tactics?''

''I suppose you would have done much better,'' someone observed sarcastically. Orchomen and I stood on tiptoe to see who the speaker was, but could not discover him.

''At least,'' retorted Paris, ''I would not play into the enemy's hands with every move.''

''Indeed you would not,'' the other returned. ''You prefer to stay within the walls and play with your wife's waiting-women.''

Bold words these to a son of Priam! The women giggled behind their hands; the men laughed outright.

Hecuba ended the controversy by turning to look at Paris with the words:

''Be silent; the censure is deserved. When you have proved your merit to be one half that of your brother Hector, we shall allow you to criticise him.''

All eyes were by this time turned on Paris, but it was difficult to bring discomfiture to that brazen countenance. For an instant his face was clouded by a frown of annoyance, then turned to Hecamed with some remark that caused her to smile up at him, as much as to say, ''Let them talk; I at least understand you.''

I tried to catch her eye, but without avail, and soon Orchomen called my attention back to the field.

Action had begun, but in the trifling, half-hearted manner that had prevailed since the beginning of the siege, save on the rare occasions when one or another of the warriors had really started something. Skirmishers could be seen here and there roving over the field, followed by a cloud of dust.

As I turned on hearing my name called by Orchomen, two of these parties had met in the center of the open space between the two armies. There was a sudden, sharp impact and the flash of swords and lances; the cries of the soldiers came faintly to the Towers. For some time nothing was to be seen but a surging, struggling mass, moving first towards one line, then the other. At length they separated, gathered up their dead and wounded, and retreated in opposite directions.

Suddenly the troops under Æneas, at the extreme right, were observed to move swiftly forward. At the same time the left wing of the Greeks began to swing out to cover the approach, and reenforcements hastened towards them from the middle. Æneas halted, faced about, and returned to his original position without striking a blow.

"That's what he calls watchful waiting," observed Paris scornfully; but no one paid any heed to him.

It began to appear then that the day would be marked only by unimportant skirmishes and maneuvers for position. Those gathered on the Towers returned to their benches, discoursing of this and that, or walked up and down the promenade in the rear. I noticed that Helen had left Priam's side, and, looking around curiously, discovered her seated with Polites and young Caminus at one of the tables against the northern parapet. At the next table but one sat Hecamed, Paris, and Polyxena.

The voice of Orchomen sounded behind me:

"Come, let us find someone, and to the tables. What do you say to Cassandra? She is ever amusing. And Alopé; she has a pretty face. Do you seek my sister; I will go for the other."

The daughter of Priam accepted my invitation graciously, and, joined by Orchomen and Alopé, we made our way to a vacant table. I purposely seated myself where I would be in plain view of Hecamed, with my back turned squarely toward her; this to indicate that her antics with Paris did not concern me.

There we sat for a long time, eating spiced cakes and drinking wine with cheese. As Orchomen had said, Cassandra was always amusing. She was pleased on this day to forget her habitual gloom and pessimistic attitude on life, and entertained us hugely by poking fun at those who had laughed openly at her prophecies, calling them "unbelievers."

"And it must be admitted," she declared with a laugh, "that everyone in Troy is an unbeliever."

"Excepting us, I hope," put in Orchomen.

"No, not even excepting you. What of your dance-girls?

Did I not say, dismiss them before another moon if you would avoid the Athenian money-lenders? You know the result.''

Which—as they say in Thrace—was enough to hold Orchomen for a while.

The afternoon wore away. We loitered about the tables and benches, vainly seeking diversion. Now and then a call from someone would send us all to the parapet, but it would be nothing more exciting than a meeting between two bands of skirmishers. As time passed even these alarms were disregarded, and no more attention was paid to the field than if it had been a sheep pasture.

I was standing by one of the marble pillars—Alopé and Cassandra had gone with Orchomen for another drink—when I felt a soft pressure on my arm. Turning, I saw Hecamed, who had approached silently from behind.

''Are you alone, Idaeus?'' she asked softly.

I replied in a gruff tone, ''So it would appear,'' and drew my arm away from her hand. Then, not wishing to seem childish, I added with a smile that I had left the others to amuse myself with my own thoughts.

''You are fortunate to be able to amuse yourself,'' she replied, and I could not tell if there were sarcasm in her voice. ''Come, will you not walk with me? Or do you prefer the company of that little Alopé?''

''If I do, it matters not to you. Why do you say, 'little Alopé,'? She is nearly of your size.''

''Akh!'' Hecamed snorted in contempt. ''Why, she has high heels on her sandals, and still reaches barely to your shoulder. I wonder what you can see in her.''

''As much, perhaps, as you see in Paris.''

''Paris! I never met him till the day before this.''

''I know, and are doing your best to make up for lost time. Confess it; he fascinates you.''

''Well—'' Hecamed hesitated, regarding me with a speculative eye. ''At least, he is better-looking than you are.''

''No doubt,'' I returned drily.

''And he wears such beautiful clothes!''

''He does indeed.''

"And he talks so prettily of my eyes!"

I turned to face her. "If pretty speeches are your desire, he is the man to go to," I said scornfully. "I am glad you have been amused. But let me tell you something. You are mine. Do not forget that. It was I who took you from the Grecian camp; it is I who shall keep you; not even a son of Priam shall take what is mine. Be warned."

With that I turned sharply on my heel and left her.

By now the middle of the afternoon was passed, and those on the Towers were beginning to grow weary. Nothing had happened or was likely to happen; still they remained, hoping for some unusual event to relieve the monotony, for they dared not seek diversion otherwise till Priam gave the word to depart.

But even that dim hope was smothered when two swiftly moving chariots were seen returning towards the city, and the cry was raised on every side:

"Hector is returning! Hector and Æneas have left the field!"

A few minutes later they were in plain view, and soon the chariots had reached the gates and passed within. There was another wait—no doubt they were having difficulty to force their way through the crowded streets below—then all eyes were turned on the doors leading to the Passage of the Seven Pillars as the forms of the two heroes were observed at the other end.

In another moment they were on the Towers. Neither had seen actual battle that day, but one would never have guessed the fact from their appearance, covered as they were with sweat and dust. Everyone crowded forward to meet them; Æneas was carried off to a table by some friends, while Hector pushed his way straight to the throne of King Priam, looking neither to right nor left.

Hecuba ran to his side and stood near, clinging to his arm while he spoke to the king:

"Priam, my father, I have left the field with wise Æneas to join you in council, leaving the troops in command of Evenus. Nothing more is to be expected today; the Greeks, unsupported by the mighty arm of Pallas, fear to advance, and Apollo withholds his word from us. Therefore have we returned.''

Then, turning to his mother, Hector continued in a tone of anxiety:

''But where is Andromache? Did she not come to the Towers?''

''No, my son,'' replied Hecuba, ''your wife hath stopped at home. You know her fear of the conflict; she is not to be reproached.''

''I know, but I would speak with her.''

Then he was led away by Orchomen and Cassandra to one of the tables to refresh himself with wine, while Priam sent messengers about in search of the councilors. One approached me, to say that the meeting of council would be held at the end of the clepsydra.

I had just turned to go in search of Hecamed, thinking to return home with her before attending the meeting, when my eye was caught by some unusual appearance of commotion on the field. The entire middle column seemed to be rushing straight at the Grecian line; they were so enveloped in a cloud of dust that it was difficult to discern the movement.

''The field! The field!'' I shouted.

The call had been heard so often that afternoon that few paid any attention to it. Old Antenor and Polites came forward and stood at my side; one or two others approached.

For a moment they gazed in silence, then Polites turned to repeat the call in tones of great excitement:

''The field! The field!''

At that they began to leave the tables and move forward, hastening their steps as they saw that something was indeed afoot. There was no longer any doubt about it; the middle column of the Trojans was in the thick of conflict. The shouts of the soldiers could be plainly heard, ever increasing in volume; right and left of the middle other troops were closing in.

Almost instantly the Towers was in confusion and uproar. Everybody crowded to the eastern edge, talking and shouting all at once. Priam was gesticulating excitedly to the messengers, instructing that the councilors who had already retired should be instantly recalled. Hector came running forward, calling out that he had given Evenus strict orders not to engage in battle; that it must be the Greeks who had attacked.

At all events, it was quite evident that someone had started something. The commotion on the field had increased all along the line; we could see the archers, in the rear, draw their bows and release the deadly shafts. The entire Trojan force was in motion; the din of conflict came roaring across the plain.

Suddenly I heard the voice of Hector quite close to me; I turned to see him standing with Æneas beside the throne; not far away was Hecuba.

"It is Achilles," the son of Priam was saying. "I am sure of it; no other Greek would do this. Come, Æneas—come!" And he turned to go.

Hecuba sprang forward and seized him by the arm. "Hector! My son! Nay! Spare me—your mother! If it is Achilles, do not go!"

"If it is Achilles I must go all the more," replied Hector, shaking her off impatiently. "Come, Æneas! Polites! Orchomen! Men of Troy! Will you see Hector meet the great Achilles?"

He rushed off, followed by Æneas, pushing aside those who stood in the way. The whole assemblage, hearing the name of Achilles, was whipped into a frenzy of excitement. Cries of encouragement were heard on every side; several of the women ran forward to press Hector's hand. He, heeding no one, made rapid strides to the doors, disappearing in the Passage of the Seven Pillars; behind him strode Æneas and one or two others.

Above all the voices on the Towers that of Queen Hecuba was heard, upraised in a great cry of grief and fear:

"Hector! My son! Hector!"

CHAPTER XVI

THE SCOURGE FALLS.

A S A MATTER OF FACT—THOUGH WE DID NOT LEARN IT till somewhat later, when Hector returned by twilight with the Trojan forces—it was not Achilles who had led the charge of the Greeks, but his friend Patroclus. The story is known to all the world, but I trust it will not suffer by repetition, and I shall be brief.

The Greeks had that day sent a deputation to Achilles, begging him to take the field. He had refused. On this Patroclus had offered to array himself in the armor of Achilles, thinking to affright the Trojans by the very sight of the dreaded helm. The Greek chieftains, rendered desperate by their recent losses and humiliation at the hands of Hector, had accepted this proposal. And it was Patroclus, encased in the armor of Achilles, who had led the charge and caused all the commotion.

What happened on Hector's return to the field is equally famous. Menelaus had slain Euphorbus with a dart that pierced his throat; his retreat had been covered by Patroclus. Then Limnius fell; some said by the hand of Apollo, which of course was absurd. It was Dardan, son of Panthus, that slew the Greek.

At this moment Hector arrived, riding like a whirlwind, and stood above the corpse of Limnius.

In another moment he had slain Patroclus and piled his body on top of their chariots to rescue the body; Hector withstood them single-handed, with the strength of a hundred.

They retreated; Hector tore the armor of Achilles from the corpse of Patroclus and put it on himself.

This final humiliation filled the Greeks with new fury; they returned to the attack. Then it was that Hector showed the strength of his heart. Hippothous and Lethus he slew; he beat back Ajax with heavy stones, knocking him twice to the ground. Grasping a dart from the hand of a soldier, the son of Priam let it fly at the fallen Greek; it missed, but struck Schedius in the throat and killed him.

Then Ulysses, supported by Phorcys and Periphas, came to the rescue in their chariots; and Hector, alone as he was and wearied, was forced to give up the corpse. He retreated in good order, leaving the naked body of Patroclus on the ground; nor did the Greeks venture to follow him.

By that time dusk had fallen, and Lycomedes, speeding forward, took Hector into his chariot and turned the heads of his horses for Troy. The troops, headed by Æneas, followed. It was nearly dark when they reached the gates, but the messenger who staggered breathlessly up the steps of the Scaean Towers found an anxious multitude awaiting the news.

We were all disappointed when we learned that it was not Achilles who had fallen, but we rejoiced at the death of Patroclus and the others. Everyone shouted the name of Hector and proclaimed his greatness; even Paris was caught in the general enthusiasm.

I was standing at the edge of the throng with Hecamed on one side and Polyxena on the other; feeling a pressure on my arm, I looked down to see Hecamed's eyes blazing with excitement.

"Ah, Idaeus," she exclaimed, "how I would love you if you were Hector!"

"It would be a different story," put in Polyxena, almost screaming to make herself heard above the tumult, "if Achilles had himself taken the field."

This observation, coming from a daughter of Priam, struck me as so curious that I forgot to reply to Hecamed's none too flattering remark. Instead, I turned to Polyxena:

"I verily believe you would rejoice to see your brother killed, if it were by the hand of Achilles!"

She had no chance to reply, for Orchomen arrived at that moment to conduct her to the palace. The crowd was already thinner; people were beginning to depart. Turning to Hecamed with a warning to wrap her mantle closely about her throat, for the night air was chill, I passed her arm through mine and led the way to the Passage of the Seven Pillars.

Soon we were in our chariot on our way to the palace. We sat in silence as the horses plunged through the narrow streets, crowded with men, women, and children rejoicing at the triumph of Hector. Really, it is no wonder that the man had become so insufferably conceited; the people of Troy idolized him and sang his praises from morn till night. Nor would I detract any from his deserved glory; it was hard won and sat well on his great shoulders.

Arrived at the palace, we made our way down the corridors and up the stairs to my rooms. Entering, Hecamed threw herself wearily onto a bench.

"Olympus!" she sighed, "What a day! I am tired and hungry. I feel as if I would like to rest for a year."

"It is easy to see that you are not a woman of Troy," I smiled. "They go to the Towers every day, and are but freshened by the event. Besides, have you not been delightfully entertained? What of the fascinating Paris?"

"Akh! He talks too much. I am weary of him also. Where is Thersin? I would have some wine."

I raised my voice. Footsteps were heard approaching from the inner rooms. But it was not Thersin who entered. Instead, Gortyna appeared in the doorway, wearing a chiton of flaming colors. She stood there, smiling at us foolishly.

"Bring some wine of Lemnos," I said peremptorily, for the

very sight of her was displeasing to me. "Or—stay—bring it later to Hecamed's room and serve us there."

Gortyna stood gazing at me stupidly, quite as though I had spoken in some foreign tongue. Finally, "You say—you say—you want wine?" she stammered, grinning and blinking her eyes.

"I said so. Wine of Lemnos."

"Memlos?"

"No! Idiot! Lemnos!"

"All right—all right." She turned, swaying slightly, and disappeared down the hall with a mincing, unsteady step. It was really funny; I could not repress a laugh.

"In the name of Pallas, what ails her?" Hecamed demanded in astonishment.

"Nothing much," I replied, "except that she is dead drunk. She probably got a quintum of cheap wine when she was out this morning, and you see the effect. Come; go to your room and make yourself comfortable; when you are ready, call, and I will attend you."

Which goes to show how closely one can approach a catastrophe and yet feel no premonition whatever, contrary to the belief of those who depend on religion for their guide.

I had bathed and anointed myself with oil of Ciletus and joined Hecamed in her room, after calling to Gortyna to fetch the wine. Soon she entered, bearing my largest and finest golden vessel on a cheap wooden tray, together with cups and a plate of cheese.

I addressed Hecamed. "Will you pour for me?"

She did so, while Gortyna went after cakes, still with her gait of a sailor in a storm. As I raised the cup to my lips I gazed at Hecamed over the rim, thinking how lovely were her eyes filled with languor, and her skin fresh and rosy from the bath.

"I drink to your charms," I said, and leaned the cup to my lips.

The next instant I sprang to my feet, throwing the cup onto the table with a bang and depositing on the floor what I had taken into my mouth.

"Great Bacchus and Holy Olympus!" I cried, jumping up and down in wrath. "What has this Graean devil brought us! Do not drink, Hecamed; it will kill you. Gortyna! *Gortyna!*"

"Are you mad?" cried Hecamed, setting down her cup without tasting. "Or are you also drunk?"

At that moment Gortyna appeared in the doorway with an immense platter of cakes. She took a step forward, stumbled on the threshold and fell to the floor; the platter flew from her hand, scattering the cakes in every direction. There she lay without moving, grinning amiably up at me and muttering:

"Somebody tripped me—that's what. Somebody tripped me. I'd like to know who tripped me."

I shook my fist at her in fury. Hecamed burst out laughing.

"Of course it's funny!" I shouted. "Very funny! You did not drink of it! Gortyna, what is that stuff you brought us to drink? Answer me! You peasant wench! Get up! Get up, before I lay my hands on you!"

She arose to her hands and knees, then slowly pulled herself to her feet, while her face took on an expression of profound gravity. She maintained her equilibrium with some difficulty, but did succeed in standing upright as she declared with great firmness:

"Somebody tripped me."

Clearly, nothing short of a beating would bring her to her senses. Seized by a sudden fear, I strode quickly past her, out of the room and down the hall to the pantry.

The worst was realized. There on the table stood the jars that had contained the wine of Lemnos—my last four—all empty! And beside them stood an empty cask that had contained a Thessalian liquid, used by Thersin for cleaning the walls and floors. This it was that Gortyna had carried to us in the golden vessel!

I turned and rushed back to Hecamed's room.

"Wretch!" I cried, advancing on Gortyna with uplifted arm, "no wonder you are drunk! You have guzzled my wine of Lemnos to the last drop! Four jars of the precious liquid in your miserable body!" I verily believe the look with which I regarded her had in it more of envy than of anger.

"Idaeus!" cried Hecamed, springing to her feet. "You would not strike! For shame!"

"No fear," I replied sorrowfully, letting my arm fall. "It would be an insult to the cargo she carries. Gortyna, leave us—if you can walk."

She staggered out, mumbling something to herself; Hecamed resumed her seat; I went to the pantry in search of wine of Pramnius, which would at least allay my thirst.

"But where is Thersin?" asked Hecamed when I returned. "After all, it is his fault and not hers."

"How so? This is Thersin's afternoon off. He cannot very well watch during his absence."

"At any rate, Gortyna knows a good thing when she sees it." And Hecamed began to rally me so sharply on my childish outburst over nothing more important than the loss of four jars of wine that I was glad, soon after, to seek the solitude of my own room.

Great vines of Bacchus! As though wine of Lemnos came from the public fountains! It is a fact that several times during the siege the price went as high as five *distateronae* a jar. I was so upset by the occurrence that I would have gone to bed supperless if Hecamed had not positively insisted that I join her over a slice of turned meat and some steamed herbs.

The following morning I awoke early. And to talk of the weakness of man—but let the tale speak for itself. After bathing and dressing myself, and after finishing with the barber, who butchered me, as usual, with a dull razor, I went in search of Hecamed. Instead, I found Thersin, who informed me that the daughter of Arsinous had gone for an early morning walk in the palace grounds.

"Alone?" I demanded.

"Yes."

"But did you not warn her—"

"Yes. She said she would go no further than the second walk."

None too well pleased with this information, I returned to my room to prepare some rolls of parchment for the order of sacrifices, after instructing Thersin to bring me a cup of *girzos*.

A few minutes later, hearing a step, I looked up to find Gortyna standing on the threshold. I suppose I must have frowned, for her manner was apologetic, even timid, as she said hurriedly:

"I have brought your *girzos*."

"Why did not Thersin fetch it?"

"He was busy; he sent me."

"Very well, put it there on the table."

She crossed the room with the quick, firm step of youth; I watched her with something like amazement. "Is it possible that this is the Gortyna of yesterday?" I asked myself, for she appeared quite pleasing to the eye.

Depositing the cup on the table, she started to leave; at the door she turned, hesitated, and finally spoke:

"Idaeus—I would ask you—you are not angry with me?"

Then, before I had time to answer, she continued rapidly:

"I mean about your wine of Lemnos. I am truly sorry. You had gone with Hecamed to the Scaean Towers—I was furious with disappointment—I scarcely knew what I did. That you do not love me I know, but will you forgive me?"

To see the fiery Gortyna thus humble and pleading for pardon was of itself diverting—and besides—I looked at her flashing eyes, her bare white arms, her dark-tinted cheeks—

"Forgive you?" I said. "Gladly. Come here, Gortyna."

She came forward slowly, gazing at me as though in an effort to read my humor. The gauzy chiton she wore revealed every line of her graceful, supple form; she moved with that natural ease, wholly unconscious and wholly admirable, that is seen only in wild animals and peasants. And how her eyes sparkled!

"Come, Gortyna; do not be afraid of me." I drew her down on the bench at my side. "I would talk with you. Tell me, have you a lover?"

She smiled, showing her pearly teeth, and replied simply: "No."

"None? You do not really expect me to believe that?"

"It is true. I have belonged to Argive Helen since my youth.

I have never looked on any man with favor. Never, that is, till I saw you.''

''But that is of necessity. I am your master.''

''Yes, but I forced the office upon you.''

''Then you do not hate me?''

She did not answer in words, but turned that her eyes might rest in mine. They did not flash then; they were half closed, dreamy, inviting, through the heavy lashes. And suddenly—I know not how it happened—my arm was across her shoulders and her hand was in mine.

''I am your slave,'' she murmured, ''your willing slave, Idaeus. Ah! Gortyna is not cold. Would you taste of her fire? You know the girls of Graea—well, was I not selected by Helen, the woman of love, from their number?''

She leaned towards me, resting her cheek on my shoulder. The blood raced through my veins; I passed my arms around her and held her close; she pressed tightly against me.

''Your willing slave,'' she whispered.

I know not what madness it was that possessed me, to be thus making love to a peasant slave-girl as though she had been the daughter of a king. But was it madness? Was it even weakness? Those who are acquainted with the customs of Troy in this particular will surely find it difficult to blame me, however I may blame myself. Even Hector, whose morals were held up by the priests themselves for the emulation of youth, was known to have disported himself with dance-girls when the loving embrace of his faithful wife Andromache awaited him at home.

And I sought nothing with Gortyna but harmless amusement. She rested her cheek on my shoulder; I passed my arms around her. That was all. What man would have done otherwise? If it still be said that I was weak, I can only reply that I soon paid for my weakness. For though—I repeat it—I merely sought harmless amusement, I soon found that another could not be so persuaded.

The other was Hecamed, who, returning from her walk and entering the rooms silently, came upon me as I sat holding Gortyna in my arms. Indeed, I believe—and I blush to confess it—that my lips were pressed against those of the Graean.

I looked up, hearing the rustle of footsteps, just in time to see Hecamed turn from the door, no doubt with the intention of departing in silence. Thrusting Gortyna from me, I sprang to my feet in confusion.

Hecamed must have heard my sudden movement and the cry that came from my lips, but she turned not nor halted.

I turned on Gortyna, crying: "Wretch! You have ruined me!" Then I hastened down the hall after Hecamed. She had gone into her own room, closing the door after her.

I approached and knocked on the door, at first timidly, then loudly. There was no answer. Again I knocked. Still no answer.

"Hecamed," I called, "I would speak with you."

After a considerable pause her voice came:

"To what end? Go to your Graean slave-girl."

Nothing makes a man more angry than the realization that he has made a fool of himself. So I began pounding on the door and calling in loud tones:

"Open the door! Hecamed, let me in! I would speak with you!" Then, as there was no answer, "I command you, let me in! Would you deny your master?"

At that I heard her footsteps crossing the room; the bars were withdrawn and the door flung violently open. By the time I stepped inside Hecamed had retreated to the further end of the room, where she stood regarding me with eyes flashing with contempt.

I adopted the method of candor.

"Hecamed," I said, advancing towards her with outstretched hand, "I wish you to know that I have done you no wrong. You have seen my weakness; it was no more. Gortyna came to my room to bring me a cup of *girzos*; something she said or did—I know not what—fired my brain; she came close to me—"

"But why do you tell me all this?" Hecamed interrupted.

"You know—I wish you to understand—"

"I do understand. I need not say that I am not surprised to learn that Idaeus finds pleasure in a drunken peasant."

"Hecamed—"

"You think perhaps that I am jealous. Nothing is further from my mind. It is but contempt, and wonder that you have attempted to convince me—"

"That I love you? I do love you. You know it. It was no fault of mine that you discovered me with Gortyna."

"I suppose it was mine. I should have waited longer before returning from my walk."

"Then—you will not forgive me?"

"I forgive you nothing and hold nothing against you. I am indifferent."

"At least you know that I love you?"

"Of course." Hecamed laughed scornfully. "And Helen, and Gortyna, and every woman. It is no wonder you hold hate for Paris. You endeavor to emulate him, and find yourself still surpassed."

I pleaded and cajoled, ending with threats, but she would not be moved; and I was under the disadvantage of knowing her to be in the right. That made me angrier still and loosened my tongue in fury, but Hecamed listened to all unmoved, until I began to think that she was in fact indifferent to me.

At length, thoroughly exasperated, I ceased all effort at explanation and broke in suddenly with a curt demand that she prepare herself to attend me to the Scaean Towers. She refused flatly.

"You refuse to go?" I shouted, beside myself.

"I do," she returned calmly.

We stood tensely silent for a moment, gazing into each other's eyes; hostility blazed between us. No doubt she read my thought, for she took on an added air of defiance as she repeated firmly:

"I will not go. Do what you will, you shall not force me to attend you."

"Do you know what it means to disobey your master?" My face was crimson with wrath.

She merely nodded, without taking her eyes from mine. Her cool impertinence, her persistent obstinacy, her open con-

tempt, were more than I could bear. Turning sharply, I called
to Thersin to bring me my hunting whip.

Evidently he knew what I intended, for when he appeared
in the doorway with the whip in his hand his face was filled
with fright. But not so the face of Hecamed as I advanced
towards her with determined step. Her eyes met mine squarely,
with a depth of hate that I shuddered to see; it was with an
effort that I kept my own from wavering.

"Uncover your shoulders," I said in a voice hoarse with
passion.

She did not move. Reaching forward, I grasped her chiton
at the throat and tore it roughly away, revealing her shoulders
and arms halfway to her waist. Then I raised the whip on high.
My arm descended; and then, quite as though it were torn from
my grip by some unseen hand, the whip dropped from my
nerveless fingers to the floor, brushing Hecamed's body as it
fell.

I sank onto a bench, quivering with emotion. She stood as
before, without taking her eyes from me, but her face had gone
white as death.

"You see—you see—" I stammered, stretching out my
arms towards her.

She laughed aloud. "I see," she said in a voice as harsh as
my own, "I see that it takes more of a man than you will ever
be to strike the daughter of a king."

"It is false!" I cried. "I cannot strike you, Hecamed; I
cannot; but it is love that stays my hand, not fear."

"Akh!" She did not move; her voice no longer trembled.
"Have done with your lies! You have bared my shoulders;
there is your whip; use it, or leave me."

Somehow I got to my feet. I do not know if I said anything.
Leaving the whip lying on the floor where it had fallen, I
turned abruptly and left the room.

CHAPTER XVII

ON THE BATTLEFRONT.

I HAVE MANY TIMES REPROACHED MYSELF FOR MY CON-
duct of that morning. Of all the faults of man I hold indecision to be the worst, perhaps because it is my own
greatest weakness. Having sent for the whip, having raised it
I should have brought it down; that is the argument of my
brain; that my heart failed me is not matter of gratulation,
though the event proved my fortune.

After the scene with Hecamed I left my rooms without waiting for breakfast, stopping only to put on my chlamys and to
leave orders with Thersin concerning the household. On my
way through the hall I found myself suddenly face to face
with Gortyna.

"Are you displeased with me?" she began softly, in insin-
uating tones; but I pushed her aside without answering and
continued on my way. She followed me with her voice, but I
stayed not for words.

For some time I walked around the palace grounds; the object of my thoughts was Hecamed, but there was nothing definite about them. I did not know if I loved or hated her; I

knew only that I could not exclude her from my mind.

At length, however, another thought did succeed in forcing an entrance: the thought that I was hungry. I had tramped throughout a clepsydra. But I swore to myself that I would starve to death rather than return to my rooms then. In the first place, I did not desire to see Hecamed; in the second, I hated the sight of Gortyna; and lastly, there was not a drop of decent wine in the place.

I turned and started for the outer gates, saying to myself:

"I shall breakfast with Cisseis."

A short walk brought me to my friend's house, and soon after I was seated at table with him. He would talk of nothing but his regret at not having been at the Towers the day before, saying that he had been detained at his father's office on business. Said he:

"That is why you find me up at so early an hour this morning. I am determined to miss nothing today, for I believe that something is really going to happen."

"It would be a surprise to me," I remarked scornfully. "You know how it has ever been. Yesterday there was some real fighting—that must be admitted; but the result will be that they will rest for a month."

"I do not agree with you," returned Cisseis. "One thing you have forgotten: the death of Patroclus. He was dear to the heart of Achilles, and do you think Achilles will be content to remain in his tent after viewing the corpse of his friend? He will not, or I am much mistaken in him. Mark my words, this day will see Achilles on the field; you know what will happen then."

"That is just what I do not know," I said with a smile, "nor anyone else. But if your surmise is correct it will be something worth seeing."

"And it is to be regretted that we shall miss it."

"How is that?" I looked at him, not understanding. "Shall we not be on the Towers?"

"Yes," returned Cisseis, "but that is not what I meant. Nothing can be seen from the Towers but clouds of dust, and nothing is known till the arrival of a messenger. It is much better—Hear me: will you go to the field with me this day?''

My first impulse was to accept with enthusiasm. The excitement of battle was what I needed to drive my own troubles from my mind; and besides, I would not for the world have missed the long-expected encounter between Hector and Achilles. It was on my tongue to say yes, when I suddenly remembered my promise to my father to remain within the walls save when sent in my capacity as kesten. I had told Cisseis of my promise before; now I reminded him of it.

"I know," was his answer, "but will you go if I persuade your father to release you from your vow?"

To that I agreed eagerly. Immediately Cisseis leaped to his feet and began calling in the slaves for orders. A chariot of the finest, with the fleetest steeds, was ordered to be in readiness at the end of the third clepsydra to conduct us to the field; his armor was to be polished and made ready; two other chariots were ordered, one to take him to my father's house, the other to return with me to the palace.

"Why all the excitement?" I wanted to know. "It is long before the warriors will leave the gates."

"Well, we shall be ready for them," returned Cisseis. "Here, Pausinus, take my plume. Nay, not that—fool! That is my brother's *kausia*. I leave the armor to you. Come, Idaeus—nay, stay—did you say you have no wine of Lemnos? Pausinus! Clymen! Here, take twelve jars of the best red and put it in the chariot of Idaeus."

"Cisseis, you have saved my life; I thank you!"

"That's all right; the old man has a cellar full of the stuff; it doesn't cost me anything. He was wise enough to stock up at the beginning of the siege. Ah! There are the chariots!"

We moved out to the street. "Play strong on the 'duty to Troy' thing." I said, springing into the chariot to see that the precious jars were safely bestowed. "My father is influenced by that every time."

"I know," called Cisseis, jumping into his own chariot. "Never fear; I will get his permission. Where shall I come? To your rooms?"

I thought for a moment. "Yes. I shall have to go there for my armor. I shall await you."

"All right. Expect me at the end of the third clepsydra. Forward, Clymen!" And off he went.

A moment later we followed him, but only as far as the first corner. He continued straight ahead on his way to my father's house; I turned to the right, towards the palace. Arrived there, I dismounted, calling for some slaves to carry the jars to my rooms.

Giving the wine into the charge of Thersin, who informed me that Hecamed had kept to her room since my departure, I made ready to put on my armor.

It seemed that nothing could go right that day; I was unable to find a clean military chiton anywhere, being forced at last to tear off the bottom of one of my ordinary garments. Then I found that the armor had grown dull, having been left overnight near an open window through which the rain entered; Thersin and Gortyna rubbed their arms half off before they got it polished.

At length, towards the end of the third clepsydra, everything was ready. Buckling on my greaves, curets, boots, and gorget, and taking my casque and shield under my arm, I walked down the hall to Hecamed's door and gave three sharp knocks on the panel.

There was a short pause, then her voice sounded.

"Come in."

I entered, closing the door behind me. The daughter of Arsinous was seated on a bench near the window with some embroidery in her lap. The face with which she greeted me was utterly expressionless—the face of one who has buried every feeling to be recalled only by the will. This was what I had expected, and still it angered me to see it, suggesting as it did that my presence meant nothing more to her than the presence of her master.

I advanced to the middle of the room. As I came into the light I fancied I detected a shadow of surprise flit across her face, no doubt at sight of my armor.

"I am sorry to disturb you," I said quietly, "but it is necessary to tell you that I am going to the field, and shall not return till the end of the day. You know my orders that no one is to be admitted during my absence; I have repeated the same orders to Thersin. In addition, I would prefer that you should not go out without his attendance, but that is merely a request; it is your privilege to disregard it. Good-by.''

I bowed, backing towards the door; Hecamed inclined her head, but said never a word. I was certain then that I was indeed indifferent to her. If it were otherwise, I thought, could she send me away in silence, knowing that I went to encounter the dangers of the field? It was on my tongue to plead with her for a kind word, but pride restrained me.

There remained the necessity of obtaining leave of absence from the king. On my way to his apartments I chanced to meet old Antenor in the corridor, and he, delighted at my purpose of going to the field, promised to arrange that I should not be missed at council.

''Ah, my lad,'' said he, laying his trembling old hand on my shoulder, ''you will see a glorious sight this day.''

When I asked him what he meant he repeated Cisseis's speculations on the probability of a meeting between Hector and Achilles. For my part, I doubted that even the death of Patroclus would bring the sulky Greek from his tent; not so Antenor.

''Would that I were young again!'' he sighed. ''Ah! My old frame will no longer sustain the weight of armor. Strike a blow for Troy, Idaeus; you are not a hero, but you are at least a man.''

I left him to go in search of Cisseis, whom I found waiting for me at the palace gates in a snow-white chariot drawn by black Thessalian horses. With this I was ill satisfied, for men like Cisseis and me, who do not pretend to be great warriors, should not allow themselves so brilliant an equipage; it is in bad taste, and invites ridicule. I said as much, but Cisseis merely laughed at me, so overjoyed was he at the prospect of a day of strife.

I took the reins; Cisseis sat in the quadriga. I think I had never seen the streets of Troy so crowded as they were on that morning. We were forced to go at a snail's pace to avoid trampling women and children underfoot. Everyone wore an air of expectation; evidently they all looked forward to the same event. The name of Hector, coupled with that of Achilles, was heard on all sides; it was easy to guess from the tenor of their remarks which they thought would be the victor.

As we halted at a street corner, unable to proceed through the throng, I overheard one man saying to another:

"The fact is this fellow Achilles is greatly overrated. I've never seen him in action, but I have a friend whose uncle was not far from Tenedos when the town was taken, and he says that Achilles is a good runner and that's about all. He may do for the Olympic games, but wait till Hector gets after him."

Which, absurd as it may seem, is fairly typical of the sentiment that prevailed throughout Troy. The reason was that they were completely crazy about their great Hector. Not that I would endeavor to detract from his fame—he was undoubtedly a good man on the field—but it cannot be denied that he was thought in some circles to be somewhat of a mollycoddle.

He disapproved of dancing. He did not belong to a single fashionable secret order. He drank only when he was thirsty.

Finally, with great difficulty, we succeeded in getting as far as the gates. There a vast throng was assembled; at one point I found it necessary to descend from the quadriga and lead the horses through, clearing a road with the butt of my lance. Excitement ran high. For some reason or other everyone seemed to have worked himself into the belief that that day would see the end of the siege.

Once through the gates, a disappointment awaited us at the outset. The first piece of news we heard was to the effect that Hector had not appeared, and that the troops were to be led by Æneas. No one seemed able to explain Hector's absence; they merely knew that he wasn't there. One rumor had it that he was waiting for a new suit of armor which had been promised by Apollo; another, that Andromache and Hecuba had locked him up in the nursery at his home, refusing to release him till he gave his word not to go to the field.

To this day I do not know the truth of the matter.

Not caring to ask a favor of Æneas, with whom I had never been on friendly terms, I sought out Evenus and requested a place beside him at the head of the Thracians. He was plainly reluctant, probably because he wanted all the glory that happened to come in his direction, but he ended by giving his consent. Cheers came from the soldiers as I urged our horses to the front of the line; they were not sorry to have another chariot to cut a path for them through the ranks of the enemy.

Suddenly the word was passed, and the army moved forward. On the instant a tumult sounded, it seemed above our very heads; we looked up to see the Scaean Towers alive with waving mantles and loud with the shouts of two hundred throats.

"That is the best place to be this day," I remarked to Cisseis, pointing with my free hand to the Towers, "if Achilles comes forth and finds not Hector to stay his revenge."

The only answer he gave me was the one word: "Forward!" As I had often observed, give Cisseis a goodly lance and a seat in a quadriga, and he forgets the meaning of the word discretion.

We crossed the plain somewhat slowly in order not to tire the foot soldiers. Which precaution appeared to me to be totally unnecessary, for as soon as we reached the field Æneas deployed the forces in the form of a semi-circle, instructing them to await further orders before making any advance. That meant a day of inaction; it began to appear that Cisseis and I had had all our trouble for nothing.

The Greeks had left their tents and taken up their positions before us; a good archer with a strong bow could easily have sent a shaft among them. The faces of those in front could be plainly seen. At a point near the center of their line was a group of chariots; the chieftains had dismounted and were talking together at one side. Ajax was easily recognizable by his great size; Cisseis also pretended to distinguish Agamemnon, but I was not so sure.

A messenger arrived suddenly to say that Æneas ordered the attendance of all the captains at his station in the middle, and Evenus allowed us to accompany him. Soon all the Trojan chieftains were gathered together, whereupon Æneas asked for opinions concerning the advisability of an assault.

Polites spoke in favor of it; Hyrtacides advised delay. Then Pylaeus arose, and so potent was his tongue that his first sentences fired everyone with the desire for glory. Things began to look brighter; I nudged Cisseis, but a glance showed that he was paying no attention to the argument. Instead, his gaze was riveted afar on the Grecian line.

"What is it?" I asked curiously, turning.

I needed no answer. Some unusual commotion was taking place in the group of Grecian chieftains; they were pointing to the rear, towards their camp, and gesticulating excitedly; some shouts were heard.

And as I looked, I saw a chariot speeding towards them from the direction of their own camp. It came nearer, glistening in the sunlight, followed by a trail of dust; the horses plunged like centaurs and seemingly without effort, so easy and swift was their motion.

It was the horses—great, powerful beasts—that first took my eye. Where had I seen them before, or heard of them?

Then suddenly I knew. They were Xanthus and Balius, seed of the Harpy—the steeds of Achilles!

I turned to call to Evenus, but my words were drowned by a sudden deafening clamor from the Greeks. They had recognized their hero and were welcoming him. Our council of war was forgotten; everyone was gazing across the field. By now the chariot had stopped, and Achilles himself had sprung to the ground. The other Greeks ran forward to meet him, redoubling their shouts.

We stood gazing at them across the field, struck with sudden wonder and amaze. Rumor then had spoken truly; the death of his friend Patroclus had drawn swift-foot Achilles from his tent. But there was no Hector to meet him. We were not cowards—at least, most of us were not—but on every Trojan's face was written plainly the thought, "Where will that dreaded lance first strike?"

The admiration which I now hold for Æneas—in spite of my dislike for him—proceeds directly from his action on that day. While the rest of us were still wonde-ing what to do, he did.

Calling a herald, he directed that the purple standard be raised before our line. Then, without even stopping to tell us of his purpose or seek our advice, he put on his helm, caught up his lance and stepped forth alone into the open space between the two armies. It amounted to a direct challenge to Achilles for a single-handed combat of champions, and I repeat that it was a brave deed!

The challenge was no sooner given than it was answered. We saw Ajax arguing with his comrades for the privilege; vain and boastful as he was, he might have known they would not allow such a slight to be put upon his great cousin at the moment of his return. They restrained him; and Achilles, with his lofty helm shining on his head and the famous javelin, which no other Greek could wield, in his hand, stepped forth to meet the challenger.

We looked on in breathless suspense as the Greek and Trojan neared each other, shaking their weapons threateningly. For my part, I expected an instant attack, but I might have known better. It had been long since Achilles had issued one of his famous defiances; it was natural that he should not let this opportunity escape.

They halted, still some fifty paces apart, and Achilles spoke:

"Why do you stand thus alone, O Son of Venus? Have you the courage to change blows with me? Has someone promised you all of Troy, with Priam's throne, that you should thus boldly front me? You shall be hard put to win the prize. Once, I think, my javelin drove you in terror from the field; do you not remember that day on Mount Ida when you were so anxious to get away you left your oxen behind? Then it was Jove and the other gods that saved you; today they may not assist you; I would advise you to fly ere your soul flies. Fools are wise too late!"

But Achilles was badly mistaken if he thought to beat Æneas at that game. The Trojan could give him three extra dice at the gentle art of making speeches, and he immediately proceeded to do so:

"Hope not that words can childlike terrify my stroke-proof breast, Achilles. I can use tart terms as well as you, but our stock was too gentle to bear fruits so rude. Fame sounds your worthiness from famous Peleus; I myself affirm my sire to be great-souled Anchises; Venus is my mother. By the light of these, unworthy boasts and dares do not befit us, though my cousin Hector might answer you in kind. Why paint we, like women, the face of conflict with our words? A man's tongue is voluble, and pours words out of all sorts every way. Such as you speak you hear. Have done with talk. It is your steel, divine Æacides, must prove my proof, as mine shall yours."

He finished; and on the instant upraised his lance and sent it hurtling through the air. Achilles, caught off his guard, interposed his shield barely in time; the lance pierced two of the plates and hung suspended, while the force of the blow sent the Greek to his knees.

He was up immediately, drawing back his javelin; the next moment it was whistling through the air with tremendous force.

Æneas held his shield firmly in front, disdaining to step aside, but his temerity came nearly proving his ruin. The javelin came straight through, but was so turned by the fold of hide that it went towards the ground, grazing the Trojan's shoulder and forcing the shield from his hand, leaving him without protection.

At that Achilles drew his sword and rushed forward, roaring like a lion.

For a single instant Æneas was observed to falter, then, springing aside with the agility of a panther, he caught up a stone from the ground, larger than a man's head, and set it rudely gone straight at the oncoming Greek.

In attempting to dodge Achilles slipped and fell; as he went down he hurled his sword at his opponent in blind fury. Æneas caught the sword as it came whirling through the air, without pausing in his advance.

Achilles was thus left unarmed. There was nothing to do

but surrender or retreat. Choosing the latter course, he turned
and ran swiftly towards the Grecian line, shouting for his chariot. Not caring to engage in a fruitless pursuit, Æneas halted
and gave the signal for a general charge.

As the purple standard came to the ground we started at top
speed for our respective positions. The soldiers had grasped
their weapons and leaped to attention. Cisseis sprang into the
driver's seat of our chariot; I followed, getting my lance and
sword in readiness; Evenus was already mounted. At the first
word from Æneas the reins were loosened and the horses
plunged forward.

We met the men of Ephyr and Syma. Just at our right was
the Greek center, led by Agamemnon and Achilles, who
seemed to have buried their animosity in the common cause.
I did not fear Nereus with his men of Ephyr; their long javelins
were so unwieldy that we were upon them before they were
prepared for us.

Cisseis urged the horses straight forward, nor did they wa-
ver, from the course. I struck right and left with my sword,
leaning far out of the quadriga. The men of Ephyr were completely overwhelmed by the suddenness of the attack.

All at once I felt the chariot swerve to the right. Glancing
up in surprise, I saw that Cisseis had altered his course and
was bearing directly toward the center! I shouted to him in
desperation, but words were useless in the universal uproar.
Intoxicated by the smell of battle, Cisseis was wilfully carrying
us to sure destruction, but I could do nothing save take a firmer
grasp on my lance and trust to luck.

Our horses plunged forward, knocking down all in their
path. The Trojans leaped aside, cursing; the Greeks sprang at
the bridles, only to be trampled underfoot.

One did succeed in getting a hold, but he soon fell with a
dart through his breast. It was the prettiest stroke I had ever
made, and gave me confidence. Others hurled their javelins at
us as we passed, but none came near.

At last Cisseis reached the goal he sought. The sight that
confronted us might well have brought the heart to the boots
of a stronger man than myself. On the side of the Greeks,

Achilles and Agamemnon were backed by other champions and the men of Eubœa; the Trojans, led by Æneas, Iphition, three sons of Priam, and other heroes, were fighting in hot desperation to hold their own. The press was so great that our chariot was perforce halted.

Cisseis sprang to the ground, catching up a lance; I followed him. The next instant we were in the thick of the fight.

It raged with most violence about Achilles. At the moment we sprang forward I saw Iphition fall with his skull cleft in two by a brazen dart. A dozen others rushed towards the mighty Greek; he, undaunted, sent his lance through the breast of Polydore, beloved youngest son of Priam, whose hot and inexperienced blood thus sent him to his death.

"Forward!" roared Cisseis above all the rest, maddened by the fall of Polydore.

But no man, no number of men, could withstand Achilles or force him back an inch. Demoleon, son of old Antenor, was his next victim, brought down by a crushing blow of the sword on his head.

The others hesitated momentarily; Achilles bounded forward, whirling his sword like a circle of flame.

Othryoneus, the lover of Cassandra, tumbled backwards with his body cleft half in two; Demochus, Philetor's son, and Dryope were laid low with two lightning strokes. Springing over Dryope's body as he fell, I found myself face to face with the Greek.

There he stood—Achilles the mighty, the invulnerable—not five paces away. His massive shoulders were slightly stooped. He had thrown away his shield; his left hand was empty, but in his right he gripped the famous shining sword. His eyes of lightning flashed mercilessly; his terrible face, dark with thunder, seemed to fill the sky; it was covered with sweat and grime, and his armor was stained with the blood of his enemies.

My heart was in my throat; somewhere in my mind was the thought, "My time has come."

I have said I am no hero. With a great sob of fear and rage I hurled myself forward, straight at the terrible face, praying for strength.

CHAPTER XVIII

※

I TAKE MINE OWN.

B UT CISSEIS WAS AHEAD OF ME, BRANDISHING HIS
lance. The strength of Cisseis was twice my own, but
Achilles parried the blow with ridiculous ease.

Still Cisseis pressed forward; the sword of Achilles flashed
and my friend fell back into my arms with his head hanging
to his body by a mere thread of skin, while his blood spurted
all over me.

Again the sword flashed, but I was dragged to the ground
by the weight of Cisseis, and it passed harmlessly over my
head.

That was enough for me. Besides, I had a duty to perform,
and I lost no time in setting about it. By a superhuman effort
I threw myself backward, dragging Cisseis with me; another
effort and I was out of danger.

I did not stop to see the fall of Mulius, or Echeclus, or
Deucalion, or Rhigmus, or Areithous; all that was told me
afterward. With the head of Cisseis under my left arm, and
dragging his body along with the other hand, I somehow made

my way to our chariot, which by a miraculous chance stood where we had left it.

With the din of the conflict ever increasing about me, and with a last glance at my comrades pushing on against Achilles in desperate fury, I threw my bloody burden into the quadriga, leaped onto the driver's seat, caught up the reins and turned the horses' heads toward Troy.

I did not stop till I reached the entrance of the great marble house on Ida Street, where I had breakfasted so pleasantly with my friend but a few short hours before. They tried to stop me at the gates; as I passed through the city a thousand voices pleaded for news of the battle; women and children scattered in all directions before me, barely missing the horses' thundering hoofs. I halted for no one.

As I leaped from the chariot the door of the house was thrown open and Lymetus, the aged father of Cisseis, appeared on the threshold, supported by Clymen. Seeing that I was alone, and perceiving the anguish in my countenance and the blood on my armor, he threw up his hands to heaven, crying: "Cisseis! My son!" and dropped senseless on the marble floor.

With the assistance of Clymen I carried him up to his room, where we left him under the care of slaves, while we returned to the chariot for the body of Cisseis. I was reminded of another day when I had returned from the field alone after leaving the dead body of my brother Phegeus to the mercy of Diomed, and tears came into my eyes at that memory coupled with this new misfortune.

At the same time I was conscious of a feeling of gratitude for my own escape; it was at that moment that the thought first entered my head that my life was under some special protection. Not of the gods; I would not be thought guilty of that absurdity; but there is such a thing as Fate.

Having promised Clymen that I would either come myself or send one of my friends to look after Lymetus and arrange for the burial of Cisseis, I left to go to the palace. The chariot I placed in Clymen's charge; it was so covered with blood and grime that I preferred to walk rather than ride in it.

Arriving at the palace, I started for my own rooms on the second floor.

Would to heaven I had reached them! But I was stopped in the main corridor by a captain of the guard with the information that King Priam, who had heard of my return from the field, commanded my instant attendance at the Scaean Towers. Thither I betook myself, still wearing my bloody armor.

My entry created a sensation. Everyone crowded around me, demanding news. Them I disregarded, pushing my way through the throng till I found myself before the throne of Priam.

"I am come from the field, O King—"

He interrupted me:

"Has Achilles appeared?"

"Yes."

A murmur of excitement came from the multitude; they pressed closer, eying me in breathless expectation. At the command of the king I recited the morning's events. But there was one thing I could not bring myself to. I forbore mention of the death of Polydore, youngest son of Priam. That unwelcome task I left for other lips.

When the king had finished with his questions others came, and still others; their insatiable curiosity could not be appeased. All applauded Æneas for his defiance of Achilles and thanked the gods for the lucky chance that had brought him out of it alive.

Polyxena in particular would not let go of me.

"How did Achilles look? He would have killed Æneas, would he not, if he had not slipped and fallen? And none were able to withstand him? Was he not glorious as a god? Had I noticed whether he wore a band of pink ribbon around the sleeve of his armor?"

Thus ran her eager queries. I thought she would never have done.

Then I found myself besieged by Helen and her waiting-women, who sought news of the men of Sparta. Them I had not seen; not even Menelaus. That explained, Helen waved Æthra and Clymene aside, then approached me in a half mysterious manner and asked in a low tone:

"Was Paris on the field?"

A little surprised, I answered in the negative. I had supposed that Paris was somewhere in the crowd on the Towers, and said so.

"No," returned Helen, "he has not been here this day. He dressed early in his armor, saying that he expected to take the field; are you sure of his absence?"

"Yes. You know it will be a cold day when Paris goes to battle."

"I know . . . yet—he said—"

But the doings of Paris held no particular interest for me; I dismissed him with the thought—though I did not venture to give it expression—that he was probably somewhere with some wench. Besides, I was anxious to return to my own rooms, and as soon as possible I excused myself to Helen and went to Priam to get permission to leave.

This received, I lost no time. Again making my way through the crowd I entered the Passage of the Seven Pillars, descended the winding stairway and returned to the palace.

Thersin unbarred the door in answer to my summons. I was startled at first at the appearance of fright and uneasiness on his face; then, thinking that it was no doubt caused by my own bloody appearance, I passed within, making for my own room.

There I prepared to take off my armor, when the thought struck me that it would not be a bad idea to show myself to Hecamed thus covered with the marks of battle. A childish thought, perhaps, but one which need not shame a man to avow.

I called to Thersin.

"Is the daughter of Arsinous within her room?" The question was a mere matter of form; I had no idea but that she was there. To my surprise, however, he answered:

"No, sir."

I looked at him quickly; his tone appeared to be filled with—what? Fear—uneasiness—hesitation—

"Where is she then?" I demanded.

There was a moment's pause, then he answered:

"I know not."

"You know not!" I fairly shouted. "What do you mean? That is impossible!"

"No, it is true," he answered, avoiding my eye. "She left a long time ago with a man. I know not where they went."

A suspicion of the truth flashed into my mind like a ray of burning light. I leaped forward, grasping Thersin by the shoulder; he shrank from my touch. Then, realizing that nothing would be gained by bluster, I released him and tried to speak calmly.

"You say Hecamed is gone?"

"Yes."

"Where is Gortyna?"

"In the kitchen."

"Did she see this man with whom—Hecamed—"

"No."

"Did you?"

"Yes."

"How long ago was he here?"

"About the middle of the second hour."

Thersin was answering my questions willingly enough; I began to doubt my doubt of him. I continued:

"You say you saw him?"

"Yes."

"Who was he?"

Thersin hesitated, glancing uneasily from side to side, and ended by stammering:

"I know not."

It was written all over his face that he was lying. I had no time for a cross-examination; every minute might be precious; I reached to the scabbard at my side and drew my sword.

"Who was this man?" I repeated sternly, raising my sword.

"I know not—I swear it—before Apollo—" Thersin fell to his knees.

I brought the sword down broadside on his shoulder. "Who was he?"

"I swear to Apollo—to—Venus—to all the Gods of Olympus—Master, you know I would not lie!"

"Fool!" I cried, "keep your gold or whatever bribe he gave you, but tell me who he was, or die!" Again I brought the sword down, harder than before, knocking him to the floor.

"It was—it was—" he gasped, for the blow had taken his breath. "Master, have pity! Pity! It was Paris!"

"Ah! Your tongue has untwisted itself! You do not lie? It was Paris?"

"Nay, master, Thersin could not lie to you. It was my lord Paris."

Truth was in his voice. I drew back and returned the sword to its scabbard. No need for further questioning; I knew what had happened as well as though I had seen it with my own eyes.

Still, there was a doubt; I nourished it in spite of myself. Turning again to Thersin, I put another question:

"Did she go willingly?"

"Yes," he replied promptly. "As far as I could tell. He came; I introduced him to her room, and a moment later they came out together; she was clinging to his arm."

This calm confession of his treachery maddened me; I raised my sword again to strike, and brought the sharp edge down. But it cut nothing but air; Thersin, dodging barely in time, had leaped to his feet and disappeared down the corridor.

I sat down on a bench to try to think. Thoughts came, but in confusion. What to do? The wise course—indeed, the only practical one—was clear: to do nothing.

Ordinarily, when one man takes another's slave, the result is a duel; but not in the case of a son of Priam. If he had seized her by force, it would have been a different matter; I could have demanded justice from Priam himself, and would have received it. But if she had gone willingly—

That brought thoughts of Hecamed—tender, womanish thoughts, if you will, but they had their result. She had, in fact, occupied the first place in my mind ever since I first caught sight of her face in the tent of Nestor; she had then given me reason to believe that I was not indifferent to her, and later she had incurred great danger for my sake.

That led me nowhere. But then came a vision of her slender

form in the arms of Paris—her sweet lips pressed against his—her arms around his neck—her whisperings in his ear—

I leaped to my feet, bellowing like a bull. Son of Priam or not, he should pay dearly for this ravishment! As for Hecamed, she had taunted me with the title of "master"; she should now be made to use it in good earnest! She should be a slave indeed!

My sword was at my side; stopping for no other weapon, nor even to put off my bloody armor, I left my rooms and the palace.

"It is folly to go alone; I shall get Cisseis," was my first thought, and then I remembered that Cisseis was dead. It was at that moment that I began to hate the Greeks with a genuine, deep hatred, though I did not at the moment realize it, other thoughts being uppermost in mind. And, in particular, Achilles.

There remained only to pursue my purpose alone, for there was no one whom I could count on as I could have counted on Cisseis. I hardly knew which way to turn. For one thing, I knew that Paris maintained bachelor apartments on Troad street; for another, I doubted that, shameless as Hecamed appeared to be, he could possibly have persuaded her to go there with him. And I was aware that Paris was quite daring enough, in an affair of this sort, to run any risk, however great, as far as he himself was concerned.

These speculation led my footsteps as I turned abruptly through the palace grounds, having decided first to try his lodgings. The bachelor apartments could be tried if the other failed.

Soon I was on the broad marble walk inside the great wall; another minute, and I was at the entrance of the lodgings of Paris.

My loud summons brought a slave immediately. He peered at me through the wicket, demanding my business. For a moment I hesitated, then said boldly:

"I would speak with Argive Helen."

The man looked at me in surprise.

"But are you not Idaeus, kesten of King Priam? You should know my mistress is at the Scaean Towers."

"So she is," I replied promptly. "I saw her there an hour ago, and she said then she would soon return hither. I am to confer with her concerning the sacrifies; I will await her in her rooms. Let me enter."

"But I know not—I am not sure—"

"Fool!" I cried, "would you insult the king? Admit me!"

He put forth a reluctant hand and slowly drew back the bars. The wicket flew open; I passed within and began to proceed down the long corridor. Behind me I heard the servant replacing the bars, then the sound of his footsteps running after me.

"I will show you the way," he said, so courteously that I could not very well object. But the courtesy was exaggerated; I told myself that I was on the right track as I followed him up the stairs—those stairs down which I had once rolled with Gortyna's fingers fastened in my hair—and along another corridor to the door of Helen's rooms.

There he left me, saying that he would tell his mistress of my presence as soon as she arrived, and with a last glance askance at my stained armor. No doubt he feared I would soil the tapestries.

I passed within; then, after sufficient time had passed for the servant to have reached the floor below, I again approached the door and stood listening.

No sound came from any direction; the corridor was deserted.

Moving as noiselessly as possible, what with my heavy boots and armor, I crossed to the other side and entered a hall leading in the opposite direction from Helen's rooms.

I had never been in the rooms of Paris, but I knew their location, having had their windows pointed out to me. According to my calculations, this hall should lead me directly to the door.

I realized fully that I was entering upon a dangerous business. To be caught thus prowling about the royal household—

but I tossed the thought aside. What matter, if I found He-camed? And I swore that I would find her.

It seemed to me that my boots made a fearful clatter on the marble floor, despite my efforts at caution. I stooped over and removed them. A few steps further I found myself before a door opening on the right of the hall. But it was closed tight, and its solid appearance gave no hope that any sound could come out or that I could get in.

I stood undecided; to burst open the door was all very well, but would it lead me to those I sought?

Suddenly, just as I had stretched out my hand to try if it were locked, the door began to swing open. I stepped aside noiselessly; it opened still further, and on the threshold appeared a man in the livery of a royal slave.

I acted before he had time to see me. Springing forward, I gripped his throat in my fingers with the strength of desperation; one gurgling rattle sounded in his throat, and that was all. The next instant I had borne him to the floor inside the door and closed it with my foot as silently as possible behind us. Then, using his girdle and the ends of his chiton; I bound and gagged him and carried him to an alcove behind a hanging tapestry.

Looking around, I saw at the first glance that I was indeed in Paris's rooms. The rich hangings, the golden vessels and ornaments, the elaborate jasper and ebony benches and tables, left no doubt on that score.

With a last hasty inspection of the man in the alcove to make sure he was secure, I crossed cautiously to a passageway leading to the inner apartments.

I began then to fear that I had come to an empty nest, for though I stood on the alert for some time I heard nothing. At length, convinced that the only other person in the rooms was the slave I had left behind me, I walked boldly through the passageway into the inner apartment.

At the door I stopped, struck by the astounding magnificence that confronted me on every side. Great vessels of gold stood on pedestals of ivory and chalcedony; the tapestries stood out like half reliefs on the walls, so heavy and rich was the *serica*. The room itself, finished throughout in *nero antico*, was indescribably splendid, but there was a touch of the effeminate south—an intangible something—

"A fit setting for the man." I murmured to myself.

Then I saw the man. Suddenly there was a stirring among the curtains over an alcove on the right; two or three cushions came tumbling out, and after them Paris himself. He stood supporting himself by the curtains, stretching to his full height and yawning; a superb picture. I stood waiting calmly till he should discover me, though a thrill ran through me from head to foot at sight of him, and unconsciously my hand stole to the hilt of my sword.

Paris walked to a nearby chest, took from it a bottle of perfume and sprinkled some over his head and shoulders. Then, stepping in front of a mirror, he tried some half a dozen different ways of arranging his pointed Phrygian cap. None seemed to suit; he tossed the cap onto a bench, turned lazily, yawned again, and then, catching sight of me, started violently and stopped short with an expression of the most profound amazement.

"Great Aphrodite," he cried, throwing up his hands, "is it an unlucky vision you send to plague me?"

I shall always regard that as one of my lost opportunities. It was evident that Paris, startled by my sudden unaccountable appearance in full armor, covered with blood, mistook me for a vision sent by Venus. If I had only had the wit to address him in the deep, solemn tones of an oracle I could have hoaxed him prettily, and no doubt could have also gained my purpose by delivering a command from the gods. But I was never distinguished by presence of mind; certainly not in this instance.

I stepped forward. When I spoke my voice trembled, though I like to think it was not with fear.

"You have to deal with no weak vision of your brain," I said, "but with a man of flesh. Do you not know me?"

Instantly the expression of terror left his face. "Ho!" he cried, "it is Idaeus himself! Idaeus, the great kesten!" Then, sternly "How do you come here?"

"That is unimportant; the point is, you see me," I retorted.

"And to what purpose?"

"You should know; I come for my own."

"I understand you not."

"You lie, Paris. Weak evasion will not serve. You have stolen Hecamed of Tenedos, my slave. I come for her."

He laughed mockingly. "You say I lie? Well, the last day of a man should be permitted amusement; you shall die for this outrage, Idaeus."

"If so, it will be after you. Come; time is short; where is Hecamed?" Drawing my sword, I took a step forward.

This action had the desired result. I knew that, despite his weakness, Paris was no coward; he could be depended upon to defend himself. As my weapon flashed from its scabbord he turned quickly, ran to the wall and took down a short Spartan lance.

That was my opportunity. The moment his back was turned I leaped forward, but not at him. My goal was a door at the further end of the apartment, which, I calculated, must lead to his bedroom.

My surmise was correct. As I burst through the door I heard a cry in a woman's voice within. I sprang towards the sound. Standing by a window, with eyes opened wide in terror, her fists clenched at her breast, was Hecamed.

One bound took me to her side.

"Come!" I cried in a tone of command, seizing her arm. Then, warned by her shifting gaze, I turned barely in time to see Paris dash through the door brandishing the Spartan lance and yelling in fury.

I had no desire or intention to commit murder, for it would have been nothing less. Releasing Hecamed's arm I held both hands high above my head. Paris halted, crying:

"Guard yourself, wretch, before I kill you!"

"That would not be so easy," I retorted. "Hear me, Paris. I do not fear combat with you, but it must be honorable. Your puny lance could not pierce my triple armor; you are unprotected; I would not slay you. Let me depart in peace with my slave; if at any future time you wish to meet me on equal terms, so be it.''

But he would not be put off. ''Guard yourself!'' he cried again, trembling with fury. ''You cheap scribe! You dirt of Dares! You palace bantam! Your armor will not protect you— guard yourself!'' And he rushed forward in mad folly.

A wild scene followed. Armed as I was it was impossible for him to injure me with his slender lance; my only task was to protect Hecamed from his indiscriminate thrusts and blows, and to avoid wounding him. A dozen times I could have run my sword through his throat or breast; he lunged forward blindly with no thought of defending himself.

Placing Hecamed at my back and commanding her to stay there, I slowly forced him back to the door, and through that into the next apartment. There I had more room and handled him with greater ease. By now he was panting heavily with his fruitless efforts; still he pressed the attack in desperation. His shouts had ceased.

I had nearly crossed the second apartment into the last, where I had left the slave bound in the alcove, when there suddenly began a tremendous pounding on the door leading into the outer hall. Simultaneously voices were heard without, demanding admittance.

At that Paris, fired with new zeal, lunged viciously with his lance; the point glanced off my helm, barely missing He-camed's throat.

That was too much for me; I sprang forward and dealt him a sturdy blow on the side of his head with the flat of my sword, knocking him to the floor. Then I flew to the door, dragging Hecamed after me, and drew the bolts. By the time I turned again Paris had scrambled to his feet and was upon us, bellowing in wrath.

I heard the door open behind me, and a voice sounded:

''Hah! Paris! Idaeus! I thought as much!''

It was Argive Helen, returned from the Towers. Paris drew back, dropping his lance, and I lowered my sword as she stepped between us; behind her were her waiting-women and three or four slaves. A single glance at Hecamed, and, understanding the situation, she turned her flashing eyes on Paris.

"For shame," she cried, "to turn your blows on a Trojan, when your brothers are united against the Greeks! You contemptible man! I speak not of the insult to *me*, your wife, that you should bring women into my very house." Then she turned to Hecamed and me with the one word:

"Begone."

"Hold!" cried Paris, stepping forward. "This is none of your affair, madam; these are my own rooms. It is you who are intruding; begone yourself, and let me deal with this fellow."

But he quailed and stepped back again before Helen's eye of wrath. It was Hecamed who spoke next.

"Madam," she faltered in a tone of timidity, touching Helen's arm, "I would explain—it was a message brought me here—"

"No doubt," Helen interrupted scornfully. "There is nothing to explain. Go with your master."

Paris again stepped forward, but a glance from the Argive queen stopped him. Seeing that further words were useless, I took Hecamed by the arm and led her to the door; the waiting-women and slaves fell to one side to give us passage.

An angry exclamation from Paris followed us, but I gave it no heed; a minute later we had reached the wicket below, and, passing through, found ourselves in the palace grounds.

CHAPTER XIX

A CONFESSION.

BY THEN IT WAS LATE IN THE AFTERNOON. AS WE
neared the palace the rays of the declining sun were
reflected from its shining walls and dazzled our eyes.
No one was to be seen; evidently Helen had left the Scaean
Towers, for some reason or other, before anyone else.

In silence Hecamed and I walked side by side down the
broad pavements, up the great staircase and through the corridors and halls to my rooms. What her thoughts were I could
not guess; her face was a study in blankness; there was even
no sign of her old hostility toward me.

Once, when she sent me a quick glance—it was at the door
of my rooms—there seemed to be an appeal in her eyes; but
that, I thought, was impossible. I set it down to fancy.

My own mind was made up. Two courses were open to me.
One, to make Hecamed in reality my slave; for it would have
been absurd to admit her again on the old footing. But a little
consideration showed me that it would be impossible for me
to treat her as a slave. I had never regarded her so.

Thus the only alternative was forced upon me; as I say, my mind was made up.

We entered, to find Gortyna in the hall. At sight of Hecamed the face of the Graean filled with an expression of surprise and hatred; it was quite evident that she had never expected to see her again. I gave it no thought at the time; instead, I merely asked her if Thersin had returned.

"He is in the kitchen," replied Gortyna sullenly.

I went to speak to him. At sight of me he cowered into a corner.

"Thersin," I said, "you are forgiven for your treachery for the sake of your services to my father; but if ever it is repeated I shall kill you as I would a snake."

Then I returned to the front, took Hecamed by the arm and led her into her own room, closing the door behind us. Gortyna had disappeared.

Motioning the daughter of Arsinous to a seat, I stood before her for some minutes in silence. I knew what I wanted to say, but it was difficult to begin. I sighed. How lovely she was! But that was not for me!

"So," I began in a calm tone—it was the first word I had spoken to her since we had left the lodgings of Paris—"so you show your contempt for your master by betraying him. Do not think I reproach you; I was fairly warned."

I waited for her to speak; then, as she remained silent, I continued:

"A great heat burns within me, Hecamed; if I am outwardly calm it is because I force myself to be so. I would be just to you. You spoke to Argive Helen of an explanation—a message. What did you mean?"

For the first time Hecamed raised her eyes to mine. "Why should I explain to you?" she demanded bitterly.

"For no reason," I replied; and I added dryly, "especially since you cannot."

She half rose to her feet, then sank back onto the bench.

"To be sure!" she burst out fiercely. "You see, I am already condemned. The practice of Greeks and Trojans alike—the smallest evidence will shatter a woman. Have you not already decided against me? Of what use would it be to explain? What use to say that Paris came, saying he carried a message from Helen? That I went with him because he said that Helen desired my presence? That, in short, he lied to me and deceived me?''

''Thersin said you went willingly.''

''I do not deny it. I did go willingly, thinking myself called by a message from Argive Helen.''

I looked at her half in doubt, not knowing what to say or what to believe. An answer came from elsewhere. Suddenly I heard a door open behind me, and, turning, saw Gortyna burst into the room with blazing eyes.

''You lie!'' she cried fiercely, glaring at Hecamed. ''There was no word of any message from Helen; I heard all: I saw you fling yourself into his arms; I heard your shameless promises. You lie!''

I gazed at her in astonishment. ''How do you know all this?'' I demanded.

''Walls have ears—and eyes,'' replied Gortyna.

Hecamed was staring at her, speechless; whether with discomfiture or mere bewilderment, I could not determine. At any rate, I did not want the evidence of an eavesdropper; taking Gortyna firmly by the shoulders. I pushed her by main force from the room, declaring meanwhile that if she repeated the offense I would beat her.

Then, closing the door and bolting it. I turned again to Hecamed.

''You heard the words of Gortyna—'' I began.

''Do you believe them?'' she broke in proudly.

''I know not what to believe. But I know what I mean to do, and that is what I would tell you. One thing you must understand, Hecamed; I do not complain of you. I would ask you a question: Are you in love with Paris?''

''Akh!'' she exclaimed scornfully, ''no more with him than with you.''

''You are sure? I have a reason for asking. But first I must explain why I sought you at his rooms. It was not to bring you here. It was not for love of you. I did it because I was your master and wished to prove myself so. Even Paris shall not humiliate me with impunity. But now that I have got you, and punished him, you are free to return. That is why I ask if you are in love with him. If it is your desire to go to him, to feel his arms about you, you may do so. I set you free."

"I have said I do not love him," said Hecamed quietly; but her face was pale as death.

"You have really as little love for him as for me?"

"As little—yea."

"Then I will not force you to go to him. But neither can I allow you to stay with me. I shall speak plainly, Hecamed. You cannot be my slave, for I love you as a wife. You do not need to speak; I know that you hate me for my love. No longer shall you live with me, to feed my desires and then deny them."

"But I do not—it cannot be—"

"Let me finish. It is, the question is, what to do with you? I cannot return you to Tenedos; the town is in ashes. To send you to the market is out of the question. Nor can I make you free in Troy; as a captive Greek you would be at the mercy of every man. There is one thing I have in mind; if it can be managed you will be safe. I shall know by the morrow."

I stopped; Hecamed sat looking at me with the expression of one who sees her world crumbling about her. I could not understand that; I had expected one of joy and gladness, with perhaps a little gratitude, for this was not a small thing I proposed to do.

"But why?" she stammered finally, "why must I leave you?"

"Have I not explained?" I demanded a little wearily. "I cannot have you stay to amuse yourself with hating me."

"But if—if I do not hate you?"

"You have told me of your hate too often to allow me to doubt it."

"But it was not—not today I told you."

I wheeled about with a short laugh, looking her squarely in the face.

"Do you love me, then?" I cried bitterly; then, as she

shrank back at my approach, I turned and strode rapidly from the room. The scene was becoming too much for me. Not satisfied with breaking my heart, she wished to play with the pieces. That would have been my thought if I had been capable of one so lucid.

Arrived in my own room, I at last rid myself of the soiled and bloody armor I had worn all day, and clothed myself in a chiton and mantle. It was the sight of the armor lying on the floor that took my thoughts to Cisseis; then I remembered my duty to Lymetus, his poor old father.

Glad of an excuse to get away, I left the palace, after telling Thersin that I would not sup at home that night.

At the mansion on Ida Street I found that the confusion of the morning had given way to black, unrelieved despair. The slaves sat about on benches, gloomy, disconsolate, sullen. Lymetus, still unconscious, was in his room under the care of physicians; I did not venture to enter. Instead, I had Clymen conduct me to the chamber where lay the remains of my dead friend.

The head had been skilfully joined to the body, and the whole cleaned and anointed; still the form, cold and stiff, did not appear as that of Cisseis. A glance sufficed; then, stooping to place a kiss on the clammy brow of him who had been my best and dearest companion, I left the chamber and the house.

I hardly remember what I did that night; the memory comes to me now as that of an indistinct, half-forgotten dream. For a long time I walked the streets, then I went to the home of Evenus for supper. I know that I was there late at night, when some of the warriors who had been lucky enough to return from the field on their own legs were relating their wondrous exploits to whoever would listen.

I was congratulated and commended for bringing the body of Cisseis home to his father, and it was then that I learned of the death of Mulius, Deucalion and others who had been in the circle around Achilles at the time of my departure. It was past the middle hour of night when I finally left to return to the palace.

The following morning I was up early, for there was much

to do. In the first place, I was determined to have done with Hecamed that day. To have her no longer in my sight in the intimate surroundings of my own rooms might bring me ease, I thought; to look at her beautiful large eyes, her laughing lips and cheeks, and to think that they were not for me, was maddening.

Still I found myself not early enough for my purpose. After a hasty and solitary breakfast I went to the west wing of the palace to seek an audience with Queen Hecuba. Much to my surprise, I was informed that she had already departed for the Scaean Towers.

"Does she wish to see Phoebus Apollo start his horses?" I demanded in astonishment.

"It is not Phœbus Apollo she would see," returned the waiting-woman, "but Hector. He takes the field today to meet Achilles."

I left to go to the stables for a chariot to carry me to the Towers. There was not one to be had; nothing remained but a few old broken-down Pylians in a forgotten stall. One of them I mounted; a pretty picture I must have made.

Arriving at the Towers, I found that Queen Hecuba was not the only early bird. The place was crowded; all of fashionable Troy was there—before the end of the second clephydra! Some who had evidently come without their breakfast were seated at the tables against the south wall, eating sweet cakes and fruit. Among others I saw Paris seated at a table with Helen and Polyxena; the two latter greeted me with smiles as I passed, but Paris turned his head in the opposite direction, pretending not to see me.

I had little fear that he would make a complaint concerning the events of the preceding day, for by doing so he would have exposed himself to the ridicule of all Troy.

I had meant to obtain an immediate audience with Queen Hecuba, but postponed it when I caught sight of her in a remote corner with Hector and Andromanche. Astyanax, Hector's little son, was on his shoulder; the boy and the warrior were laughing and playing with each other, while the two women regarded them with tearful eyes.

Hector was dressed in full armor—the armor of Achilles, which he had taken from Patroclus—except for his helmet and shield, which he had probably left in his chariot below. He was indeed a splendid man: I admired his great frame and powerful arms and legs, while alertness and courage shone from his eye, doubting if even the mighty Achilles could stand before him, notwithstanding the so recent proof of the Greek's prowess.

That Hector and Achilles would meet that day for the first time appeared certain. Achilles would undoubtedly take the field, having made up his differences with Agamemnon; Hector was going for the express purpose of meeting him. Trojan hearts beat fast that morning—except those of the champion's mother and wife, which scarcely beat at all. The mainstay of their hopes was going forth to do or die.

With my new hatred of the Greeks in my breast, I was as anxious as any other, despite the fact that my mind was taken up with my own troubles.

I loitered about for some time, talking mostly with Cassandra, whom I found near the throne of Priam. The old king's face wore a look of grief that verged on despair. His son Polydore had been killed the day before; many others had fallen; his favorite Hector was going forth to face the greatest danger.

To add to all this, Cassandra informed me that she had just finished repeating, for the hundredth time, her prophecy of evil; and when I reproached her for adding wantonly to her father's burden, she replied calmly:

"Do you think I myself am joyful? Was not my lover Othryoneus slain under yesterday's sun? I would not add to his burden, or mine; my desire is to persuade him to return Helen to the Greeks and thus lighten both."

She had the spirit of her race, as well as its beauty.

Suddenly there was a stir amongst the crowd: Hector was observed to leave Hecuba and Andromache and approach the throne.

"I go, sire, to fight for Troy," he said in a loud tone of boastful confidence.

Priam stretched out his hand. "Go, my son!" His voice

trembled with emotion. "Go, my son, and may Apollo smile on you and great Jove himself guide your arm!"

The warrior turned to depart, and the crowd, falling back on either side, formed a lane for his passage. Everyone was silent; only, from the remote corner, were heard the smothered sobs of Hecuba. Without another word, without even turning his head, Hector disappeared in the Passage of the Seven Pillars.

As soon as he had gone everyone crowded to the eastern parapet. Soon the gates, far below, were opened, and Hector issued forth, followed by his troops. Then Æneas, Polites, Evenus, and many others; as we looked the plain was filled. They wasted no time, but, forming ranks as speedily as possible, started the march to the field, with Hector in the lead in his chariot. Still it appeared that it would be some time before the action commenced, for we could see that the Greeks had not yet left their tents.

I took advantage of the interim by seeking out Queen Hecuba where she sat on a raised dias near the throne of Priam. On her lap was her little grandson, the offspring of Hector; at her side stood Andromache.

"What would you, Idaeus?" she asked, in a voice made kind by misery.

"A favor, O Queen," I replied, advancing to her feet. "I know you are worn with care; still you may find pleasure to lighten the cares of others."

"Speak."

"It is of my slave I would speak. She is Hecamed, daughter of Arsinous of Tenedos."

"Yes. I have heard of her."

"I would not have her longer in my house—no matter why. I know there is a vacancy in your entourage; I bespeak it for her."

"Is she a virgin?"

"Yes."

"On your word?"

"By Apollo."

"Then bring her to me at the palace tonight." The queen's

voice faltered; no doubt she was thinking of what might happen before "tonight."

"Then the place is hers?"

"Yes."

I made my bow with profuse thanks, and withdrew. For a little while I stood watching the maneuvers of the army on the plain; then, regretting the necessity, turned to go. The queen had told me to take Hecamed to her that night, but it was not my intention to wait till then. She could be left with the serving-women in the queen's apartments, and I felt that I would have no peace of mind till she was out of my rooms finally and forever.

"The death of hope," I said to myself, "is often followed by that of desire."

Descending again to the street, I mounted my scrawny Pylian steed and turned his head toward the palace. My progress was slow, for I moved in the face of a flowing tide of humanity. The whole city was going to the walls, their faces struggling between anxiety and hope. What shouts of gladness, I thought, what howls of joy would there be if a messenger urged his foam-covered horse through the gates with the cry: "Achilles has fallen! Hector has slain Achilles!"

At length I arrived at the palace; the journey had taken a full hour. The captain of the guard ran forward, thinking I brought news from the Towers; he looked at me as though I had been a madman when I told him that I had merely returned on personal business. That one should leave the Towers at all on such a day was beyond his comprehension.

In my rooms I found Hecamed alone. I had given both Thersin and Gortyna permission to go the walls; which was just as well, for they would have gone anyway. The daughter of Arsinous sat in her room with a piece of embroidery on her lap, gazing out through the window at the trees and flowers of the garden. A different scene, indeed, from the one I had just left!

She rose as I entered. I motioned to her to resume her seat. She remained standing.

"It is not right that I should sit in the presence of my master," she declared. And, fancying that I detected a note of sarcasm in her tone, I felt all the more ready for my task. I began abruptly:

"That would be pertinent, Hecamed, if it were not for the fact that I am no longer your master."

She looked up at me quickly, opened her mouth to speak, and then was silent.

"You have ceased to be my slave," I continued; "you are now a waiting-woman of Queen Hecuba. Only this morning she accepted you. I am come to conduct you to her apartments. Make ready."

I was prepared for some sort of protest; if for no other reason, merely because I knew that the proud daughter of Arsinous would object to being so summarily disposed of, especially by me. But I was startled at the look of distress and anger that flamed in her face.

"A waiting-woman of Hecuba!" she exclaimed. From her tone you might have thought I had asked her to become a public water-girl.

"I have said so." I replied curtly. "Make ready."

Then, thinking that perhaps she really did not understand, I explained:

"It is a place of honor, worthy of your name. You are not to be a slave. Your associates are three noblewomen of Troy; one is the wife of Demoleon, son of Priam. There is nothing to shame you."

"It is not that," said Hecamed in a tone which I thought decidedly curious. It was almost tearful. "It is not that; but I—I—must I really leave you? Am I no longer your slave?"

"Great gods of Olympus!" I cried in exasperation. In truth, her vagaries were like to set me crazy. "You hate me, and now you hate to leave me! You have heard my words. Make ready. I shall await you in my room. And by the way—it is a matter of no particular moment—you will of course take with you whatever is here. Pack it in a box, and I shall send it to you by Thersin."

I left her and went to my own room. "Verily," I said to myself, "a thought in the mind of a woman is as the Minotaur in the Labyrinth. It darts forth at the most unexpected places

and times, and you never know where it comes from." It was
evident that Hecamed was pursuing till the last her favorite
diversion of making a fool of me; well, all would soon be
over.

Thinking it would take some time for her to make her preparations, I got out my curets and greaves and began polishing
them up a bit. A long interval passed; I became impatient and
called to her to hurry up. Her footsteps sounded in the hall
and halted in the doorway of my room.

I looked up. There she stood, dressed in a light, flowing
chiton, just as I had left her; on her feet was a pair of thin
house sandals!

"In the name of Apollo," I cried, jumping to my feet,
"what have you been doing? Must I wait all day?"

She took a few short steps forward, then stood regarding
me in silence with the same curious look I had seen in her
eyes before. Finally she spoke, in a voice so low I barely heard
the words:

"I am come to tell you I am not going."

"How! Not going?"

"No. I cannot. Do not try to force me. I will not."

"But you will!" I cried, advancing.

"No," she repeated, and there was finality in her tone.
"You cannot make me go. Beat me; do anything you will;
you cannot move me."

Both her voice and the expression of her face told me it
was no mere whim that moved her.

"What new madness is this?" I demanded, knowing not
what to think. "What would you?"

"I would be your slave."

"But what—why—" I stammered in bewilderment. "You
hate me, and yet would be my slave!"

"Do I hate you?"

"You have said so many times."

There was a pause. When she spoke again there was a note
of timidity in her voice, but there was also a something, a
gentle raillery, that smote my ear with pleasantness. "Idaeus,"
she said, "you are a great fool. Do you think if I really hated

you I would have wasted so much of my breath in telling you so?''

''What—what—what—'' I was completely fuddled. ''What do you mean?''

''I mean—I mean—that I would be your slave, or—whatever you desire—''

''Hecamed!'' I cried in a voice of thunder, beginning to see that I had indeed been a fool.

''But—since you found me with Paris—and suspected me—''

''Hecamed!'' I repeated, while my heart beat like the hoofs of a warhorse.

''And I cannot leave you—surely you see I cannot—because I am yours—forever yours—''

The next instant she was enfolded in my arms. The blood raced through my veins. To have her so at last, and of her own will! I forgot the field, the Towers, the army at the gates—forgot everything but the warm form clinging close to mine, the arms around my neck, the head against my shoulder.

I kept whispering fiercely, ''Hecamed—Hecamed—Hecamed,'' quite as though each repetition gave me a dearer right to the name. She was murmuring in my ear:

''Idaeus—mine—mine! You do love me truly? You have no thought of Gortyna? Nor any doubt of me? Ah, I have suffered tortures that you should suspect me of wishing to leave you. You know I did not go with Paris of my will?''

''I know—I know but tell me.''

''How could I, when I love you and only you, with my heart and soul? I have prayed to Venus and Apollo—you have no thought of Gortyna?''

That was a foolish question, and I proceeded to tell her so, till she closed my lips by placing hers upon them. We stood thus, wrapped in a close embrace, for a long time; then I led her to a secluded bench and sat down beside her.

There were many important questions to which I demanded an immediate answer. For instance, at what day, hour, and minute had she ceased to hate me? Would she marry me at once? What was it about me that she admired most? Which did she think was the greater man, a philosopher or a warrior?

Though—I hastened to add—I was by no means unacquainted with the dangers of battle.

At the end of my catechism, the answers to which were perfectly satisfactory, she began one of her own. I did not think her questions so important as my own; nevertheless, I humored her. That done, we talked at length, Jove only knows of what. I could not repeat a word to save me, though I do remember that the discourse was punctuated with long silences here and there, by no means tiresome.

It was a remark of Hecamed's that finally brought me back to the realization that there were other people in the world beside ourselves. Somehow the conversation reached a point where she asked me if I had interviewed Queen Hecuba that morning at the palace. Thus reminded of the scene I had left behind me at the Scaean Towers, I jumped to my feet, telling Hecamed to dress for the street as quickly as possible.

"For what?" she demanded in surprise. "Not—for the temple?"

"No. I will tell you on the way. Hurry! Make ready!"

She disappeared, and soon after returned wearing a veil, mantle, and heavy sandals. By then I was all impatience; I preceded her hastily to the door and into the corridor.

"But where are we going?" she demanded again. "Tell me."

"To the Scaean Towers," was my reply, as we descended the great staircase. "To see if he who killed your father has himself been slain. Today Hector meets Achilles!"

CHAPTER XX

DEATH STRIKES TWICE.

IN THAT WHEREWITH I NOW ENGAGE MY STYLUS I SHALL endeavor to assume an impartiality that is far from my real feeling. But even if I should fail—or rather, if my prejudices cause my words to lean—it cannot be said that I am without justification. Some scenes, some memories, are burned into our minds so deeply that all thoughts to come are colored by them.

That I did not actually see the event itself does not lessen the force of the impression. Its effects spoke louder than any singing of a lance. Andromache lying in a dead faint with her little son Astyanax weeping over her, and her waiting-women, distracted, trying every remedy without avail: old King Priam tearing his white hair from his head, while tears coursed shamelessly down his withered cheeks; Queen Hecuba tearing off her veil and caul to beat her naked breasts and, screaming in anguish, to send a fearful prayer to heaven; all Troy raging in grief and despair; that was the scene on the Scaean Towers.

Hector was dead. Dead by the hand of Achilles; but it was foul chance had directed the blow. I have said I shall be impartial; but is it not plain to anyone who has heard the true story of that famous encounter that the Trojan, after proving his superiority over the Greek, was overcome by a hostile Fate?

In the first place, Achilles, not willing to exchange evenly, stood like a man of wood waiting for Hector to begin the combat. Again, it was pure blind chance that caused him to turn so that his shield took a glancing blow from Hector's lance, for any schoolboy knows that to parry thus intentionally is impossible.

But why multiply arguments? The main point is this:

Two days before, Hector had slain Patroclus, friend of Achilles, and taken his armor. This armor was in reality that of Achilles, worn by Patroclus in an effort to frighten the Trojans, as I have narrated. Thus Achilles knew of a certain weakness in the lower helm, unknown to him who wore it; for this he aimed, and thrust his lance through Hector's throat with such force that it came through the back of his neck.

But that, it may be said, was the chance of war. One had to die; the luck was with Achilles.

Very well. Granted. But, not satisfied with this doubtful triumph, Achilles still further proved himself less than a man. As Hector lay dying he cursed him; a Greek it was who reported these words:

"Now, Hector, the dogs and fowls in foulest use shall tear you up; your corpse shall be exposed to all the Greeks abuse!"

And Hector replied, half fainting:

"Let me implore you, Achilles, even by your knees and soul, do not inflict so foul a cruelty upon me. Return my corpse to Troy, that my peers may tomb it with sacred fire."

At that Achilles broke out with foul curses, saying: "Dog, urge not my ruth. I would to God that any rage would let me eat you raw, sliced into pieces; at least I'll deface you piecemeal with fowls and dogs."

Then, perceiving that his fallen foe breathed no more, the Greek proceeded to make his words good. With his sword he made holes through Hector's feet, between the heels and ankles; in these holes he made fast the ends of some cords of whitleather, and tied the other ends of the cords to his chariot. Then, springing into the quadriga, he urged the horses forward; and in this manner dragged the body to the Grecian camp, the head and shoulders bounding over the rough stones.

Reaching the camp, he drove thrice around the tomb of Patroclus.

It was at this moment that Hecamed and I reached the Scaean Towers. That scene of despair and anguish I have already described as well as I can; some future poet may do it justice, for it is beyond my power. Women wept and tore their hair; some, themselves in need of comfort, tried to comfort Hecuba and Andromache. Ucalegon, Antenor, Panthous, and others were gathered around King Priam, supporting his shaking frame in their nerveless arms; other men stormed up and down, breathing sorrow and swearing vengeance.

One I saw clenching the bare edge of his sword till the blood ran from his fingers; I remonstrated with him, grasping his arm; when he turned I saw to my surprise that it was Paris.

"Ah," he exclaimed, seeing me start back, "Idaeus, do not turn from me. Can you not forget my offense, petty in the face of our great grief? I am tormented with reproaches; I should be where my brother Hector is now."

"Your reproaches should be vows of vengeance," I replied. "For the rest, I forgive you." We embraced.

"Ah!" sighed Hecamed at my shoulder, and I saw that tears of sympathy were in her eyes. "I have hated the Trojans for bringing the Greeks against Tenedos; now that I see them suffer, I forgive them."

Soon I saw that people were beginning to leave; and indeed, nothing was to be done on the Towers, or anywhere else. Receiving assurance from Paris that the king and queen would be cared for, and seeing that Andromache was being attended by her waiting-women, I led Hecamed to the Passage of the Seven Pillars, and thence to the street.

The streets were still filled, but joy had fled. No more were heard their shouts of defiance and exultation. Already their grief was beginning to give way to fear; with Hector gone and

Achilles still thirsting for vengeance, what could Troy expect but defeat?

There remained Æneas, but there remained also Ajax and Ulysses. No longer did the citizens of Troy regard the siege as a holiday; no longer did I myself regard it as a joke.

Arrived at our rooms—I can no longer say *my* rooms—Hecamed and I found that neither Thersin nor Gortyna had returned. It was then only about the middle of the afternoon; there was absolutely nothing to do, for there would surely be no meeting of council that day. Some of the leaders might gather together to consider ways and means of recovering the body of Hector, but the presence of the kesten would not be required for that.

So Hecamed and I made ourselves comfortable on a couch in her room, with a bottle of Lemnos wine, which had been given to me by Cisseis, on a table before us. Is it a matter of reproach that, thus together, it was not long before we forgot everything but our own happiness?

But that is not strictly true; for, though happy, we were not gay. Our discourse was sober and grave, and free from caresses. I told Hecamed of my father's home, of my early friendship with Cisseis, which had ended only with his death, and of my brother Phegeus. In return she talked of Tenedos; the magnificent palace, destroyed by the Greeks, which had been her home; the narrow, crooked streets; the great factories renowned throughout the Troad.

She spoke also of a visit she had made to Troy when a child, and told of her awe and admiration of the great walls and lofty buildings.

"And even then," she finished, "you were no doubt playing in the gymnasium, or riding through the streets in your chariot. Perhaps you actually saw me! But I hope not; my provincial dress was scarcely calculated to please the eye of a fashionable and fastidious young Trojan."

"In any dress you are my Hecamed, and the most beautiful of women."

It is well that a lover's speeches need not be original in order to please.

Thus the afternoon wore away; it was dusk before we knew it. I had just started for lamps when I was called to the front by a summons at the door. It was Thersin, returned from the walls. Soon after Gortyna also arrived.

One task I saw before me which I anticipated with a considerable amount of disrelish. Therefore I decided to have it done with as soon as possible.

With that end in view I called Thersin into Hecamed's room to inform him of the new turn affairs had taken in the household. It took but two words; he bowed in acknowledgment of my command, then went to send in Gortyna.

The little Graean entered with a sullen face, probably having suspected the truth when her sharp eyes observed the amity between Hecamed and myself. We sat side by side on the couch; she stood looking down at us.

"Gortyna," I began, "I have sent for you to bow to your new mistress."

Then, seeing that she pretended not to understand, I continued slowly and distinctly:

"That you may not think me guilty of ill-treating you, I must explain that you alone have been my slave. The name of Hecamed has never been entered on the rolls. Tomorrow, at the Temple of Mulciber, she will become my wife—or soon after; therefore, your mistress. You shall remain in my household as the slave of Hecamed."

"That cannot be," said Gortyna, her eyes flashing. "It is the will of the gods—"

"I care for no gods," I interrupted. "I make whom I choose my wife, and you are my slave. You should know I am none too well pleased with you; you have too great a fancy for listening at holes and peeping through cracks. I would advise you to watch your behavior and guard your tongue, or I will beat you; if that does not serve, you shall go to the public market. Do you know that your friend Oïleus is no longer a priest?"

Gortyna's face was a study. A wiser observer than I might have read her every thought in its expression; and even my dull eye could see the struggle that was taking place in her mind—a struggle between the rage of hatred and the cunning discretion of a peasant.

She saw that to give vent to her feelings would prove disastrous; and, strong as they were, she subdued them. Her eyes, that flashed with malevolence as she turned them on Hecamed, were suddenly lowered; when she raised them again the fire had disappeared and in its place was sullen submission. So shrewd was she that I thought the transformation genuine; I did not guess that the fire smoldered beneath.

Yet I might have known. A Graean dies, but never kneels.

"You will do well to heed my words," I continued, speaking more kindly when I saw, or thought I saw, that she bowed to my will. "Henceforth the orders of Hecamed are to be considered as my own; you shall obey her in all things, and attend her wish. I await your submission."

Gortyna bent her head forward; her eyes were downcast. "I will obey," she murmured.

"Very well; that is all. Tell Thersin to serve supper as soon as it is ready."

When she had gone I sighed with relief, glad to get out of it so easily.

After supper I asked Hecamed to get on her wraps, saying that we would go for a walk in the palace grounds. The fact was, I had a project in mind, and no small one. I think it had been hovering in the back of my brain for some time; the events of that day had brought it forward and decided me to attempt its execution.

This I told Hecamed as we descended the great staircase of the palace, ending with the announcement that it was my intention to pay a visit to Argive Helen.

Hecamed halted abruptly. "But—am I to go with you?"

"To be sure. Why not?"

"For no reason—only—have you forgotten Paris?"

"Akh! That matters nothing." I took her by the arm and started forward. "As for myself, I no longer fear him, since you are mine; and as for Helen, never fear but that she has forced the truth from his lips. She will receive you as a friend and sister exile."

In which surmise I proved to be correct. Indeed, Helen not only received Hecamed graciously; she seemed delighted to see her, declaring that no one else in Troy ever called at her rooms, presumably because they could not forgive her for having been the cause of the siege.

"In which particular we are little better than they," I observed, "for we come only to ask a favor."

"At least, you do not stay away," smiled Helen. "But what is the favor?"

Thinking to surprise her, I announced proudly that Hecamed and I were to be married on the following day. "For once, daughter of Zeus and Leda, you have been blind. Hecamed's heart is mine."

"Pooh!" retorted Helen. "I knew it all the time. But how can I help you?"

"We would have you go to the temple with us."

"I will do so gladly."

"We thank you. It is not required, but still we desire it. And no public attendance can be expected at such a time."

"I know; I am happy to be needed by someone. More, I shall order sacrifices to Venus in your name."

"You know my opinion of that," I smiled, "but I would not offend you."

"You do not. Skeptic! Come, Hecamed; do you know you are marrying a man who denies the gods, yet knowing that I am the daughter of Jove?"

But her eyes were twinkling with mischief, and I made no protest. Leaving them together, I strolled aimlessly about the room, examining the bric-a-brac and tapestries. Among other things, I wondered that Helen did not think to order wine, for the walk had made me thirsty, and I knew that Paris had the second finest cellars in the city.

Should I broach my project to her? That was the question I was trying to decide. (I do not mean the project of ordering wine.) There appeared, on consideration, to be little or no chance of its success. I hesitated. But what harm to try? She could do nothing worse than refuse; time to think of the remaining difficulties if she consented.

Thereupon I approached the window where the two women reclined on a heap of cushions and asked Helen pointblank if she were strongly averse to returning to Sparta.

"Why do you ask?" she returned, looking up with a quick glance of surprise and interest.

"Because I would know."

She sat up straight. "Idaeus, you have an idea buzzing in your brain. I see it in your eyes. Come; tell me."

So I told her. My project, in two words, was to attempt once more to end the siege by returning Helen to the Grecian camp. That the Greeks would acquiesce was at least possible; many of their heroes had fallen and many more would fall before they could hope to batter down the walls of the city. As for the Tojans, it was enough to say that we had lost Hector, for by that loss we had been weakened greatly.

I should, perhaps, confess that in the conception of this plan I was not entirely disinterested; that is, I was thinking not only of the welfare of Troy, but also of my own fame. The frame and spirit of a warrior had been denied me. I could not hope to distinguish myself on the field. But what if I, alone and unaided, succeeded in accomplishing by diplomacy what all the heroes of the Troad had failed to achieve by force of arms?

The glory of the deed would make me immortal; I would be greater than Æneas, than Ulysses; my name would be shouted all over Troy, and the echoes would go down to posterity.

One difficulty was removed on the spot, when Helen agreed to return willingly, and to send a message to Menelaus whenever I was prepared to take it. It was in a tone of sadness that she declared this willingness.

"I would be sorry to depart from Troy," she finished, "but better that than see the city destroyed before my eyes. As well Menelaus as Paris; they are two of a kind; and my consolation is that I shall again behold Sparta."

"The main difficulty," I suggested, "is to get the consent of the Greek chieftains, especially Ajax and Achilles."

"True; that is your part. Indeed, I fear it is impossible. You can but try."

Soon after that we left to return to the palace.

"It will be necessary to use great caution," Helen whispered to me at the door, "that no word of our purpose reaches the ear of Paris."

We went out into the moonlight. How peaceful seemed the night! The grounds were deserted; in the whole length of the walk we met only two men, and they were members of the guard. The white palace, ghostly in the silver light, added to the atmosphere of mystery about us; the whisperings of the leaves, tossed to and fro by the night breeze, sighed of the city's sorrow.

"Cynthia guides our footsteps," said Hecamed, with the intention of arousing me out of silence; but I was too busy with my reflections to give time to a harangue on superstition. Arm in arm we walked past the spreading portals of Hector's lodgings; we stopped to gaze for a brief moment in silence, thinking of the monster grief that had spread his black wings over the once happy roof.

Gortyna opened the door of our rooms in response to my summons, saying that Thersin, exhausted from the excitement of the day, had retired. This did not please me, but I made no comment. Gortyna herself appeared to be anything but exhausted; there was an alertness to her step and a quickness in her eye, as she helped Hecamed with her mantle, that made me wonder if she had been at the wine again.

By which thought I was reminded of my own thirst, and I turned to ask Hecamed if she would join me at some refreshment in my room. Her assent given, I called to Gortyna to bring us cups and a vessel of wine of Lemnos.

"Unmixed, and neat," I added; "I will have none of your watery stuff, and let it be cooled."

"Do you know," asked Hecamed as we seated ourselves side by side on a bench, "that I have a quarrel with you?"

"Nay," I smiled, "nor am I much affrighted at the prospect. What is the quarrel?"

"That you should undertake to return Argive Helen to the Greeks. It means no happiness for me. If you are successful, so great will be your name that your pride will scorn poor

Hecamed; if you fail, I may lose you as Andromache has lost Hector.''

I assured her, in a manner that proved quite satisfactory, that I could never occupy a place so high that there would not be room for her beside me. "And as for failure, let us not consider that, but pray for success.''

"But if you should meet misfortune, Idaeus, 'twould break my heart.''

"You do love me, then?''

"Ah! You know it.''

"Dearly?''

"So dearly that with you I forget everything—even Tenedos—everything.''

"And you are willing and happy to be my wife?''

"Yes.''

After that we sat silent, close, each with his own thoughts, though they were probably the same. "Tomorrow," whispered Hecamed suddenly. It seemed to me that the word had come from my own lips. "Tomorrow." I repeated, kissing her hair.

The sound of footsteps came from the hall. Gortyna entered, carrying a vessel of wine and cups. Placing them on a table, she turned to us:

"Shall I pour for you?''

I nodded an affirmative, rising to place our bench near the table. A grunt came from Gortyna as she lifted the heavy golden vessel. Hecamed, going to her own room—to fix her hair, she said—returned soon and took her seat on the bench.

What happened then was almost enough to convert me to a belief in the protection of the gods. Ordinarily my senses are dull, even when my brain is quickest. But as I raised my head after adjusting the bench I surprised something in Gortyna's eyes that put me instantly on the alert. A flash—a gleam—it was like a streak of lightning in a black sky, ominous and eloquent of danger.

It was directed at Hecamed, and thus my observation of it escaped her. The thought leaped into my mind:

"The little Graean is up to something.''

Still I would not have guessed her purpose if it had not been for what followed. Hecamed and I sat side by side on the bench placed at one end of the table—an unusual position, but I did not care to put myself to the trouble of pulling up another bench. Gortyna, having filled the cups, set one on a serving platter before each of us.

It was her manner of placing the cups that caught my eye the second time. I do not know if I can tell what I mean, so indefinite was the impression, so intangible. It was not that her hand trembled—on the contrary, it was quite firm—nor was it any perceptible agitation of her countenance.

Perhaps you will know what I mean when I say that to serve a person with wine is an operation which is ordinarily performed with perfect indifference, whereas the Graean placed Hecamed's cup before her in a manner which indicated that no other task in the world was of equal importance. Then, as she served me, her manner changed completely; she even spilled a few drops on the platter.

Suspicion leaped into my mind like a flame, and seemed at once to quicken my brain. For a single instant I was inclined to laugh at myself; the next I had decided on my course. At least, I would see—and I remembered the story of Asoné.

As Hecamed started to raise the cup to her lips I turned suddenly:

"Wait: I have an idea; shall we not celebrate our happiness by forgetting past differences? You shall drink with us, Gortyna, and pledge our future. Get another cup."

The Graean began to protest:

"Nay; I cannot drink with my master—"

I interrupted her:

"But if I request it? What, do you yet cherish your foolish hatred? Come; get the cup."

At that she departed, with a backward glance. As soon as she had disappeared through the door Hecamed turned to me, saying in a low voice:

"What nonsense is this? Would you raise her out of her place?"

"Silence." I whispered hastily. "I have a purpose; whatever

I do, show no surprise; watch yourself. And do not drink—''

I broke off abruptly as Gortyna reentered with the cup, which she placed on the table and filled; I saw with joy that it was exactly similar to the other two.

''Hold!'' I cried suddenly, just as Hecamed lifted her cup for the second time, ''you have brought no cheese! The wine of Lemnos must have cheese. Fetch some: you will find it on the second shelf in the pantry in the right hand corner.''

Setting her cup on the table, the Graean turned to obey. At the door she turned again to ask:

''The white or the brown?''

''The white,'' I replied.

Then, as soon as she had gone, I stooped over quickly, picked up her cup and put it before Hecamed, and put Hecamed's where Gortyna's had been.

''What do you—'' Hecamed began in astonishment; but a glance silenced her.

As Gortyna re-entered the door I saw her cast a sudden, swift glance at the table; a significant glance, I thought. Then she came forward, placing a plate of cheese on the table. Hecamed took some between her thumb and forefinger and sprinkled it on my wine and her own; Gortyna took none.

I lifted my cup:

''Will you pledge us, Gortyna?''

The Graean's eyes passed swiftly from me to Hecamed and back again, and I thought it strange that she made no greater effort to conceal their malignant and triumphant gleam.

''May the gods smile on you,'' she said finally; and we drank.

At least, two of us drank. I only pretended to do so, for I was by no means sure that my own cup was harmless. Hecamed drained to the bottom the cup that Gortyna had poured for herself; Gortyna emptied the one she had prepared for Hecamed.

''What is this?'' I cried, setting down my own cup still full. ''It tastes queerly. Are you sure this wine is unmixed?''

''You did so order it,'' replied the Graean, looking at me with quick eyes.

"I know, but did you so bring it?"

"Yes," she answered, "the jar was never opened till now. Do you think I would disobey you? It is one of those which you brought—*Akh! What is this? What is this?*"

She broke off suddenly, pressing her hands convulsively to her abdomen, while an expression of pain and fear shot into her face. Then I knew that I had guessed aright.

"What is this?" she screamed, in sudden anguish. Her hands fluttered above her head, then again she pressed them to her sides, while her body rocked to and fro like a sapling in a storm. "I am on fire! My insides are burning out! Akh! Gods of Graea—Idaeus, you fiend! You have done this! Help—I am tortured—curse you—curse you!"

She shrieked like a soul condemned to the shades; and even knowing that these sufferings were what she had intended for Hecamed, I could not help but pity her.

Suddenly she swayed and sank to the floor; the shrieks gave way to moans and unintelligible curses. This for a moment only; then there was a rattle in her throat, her limbs stiffened out with a jerk like a released bow-string, and she lay still.

Hecamed, sobbing, knelt at her side and gently lifted her head. But, ignorant of such affairs, I knew not what danger there might be in it, and I pulled her away. Then I myself stooped over the dead form of the Graean, crossed her hands over her breast, closed her eyes, and threw the corner of her mantle over her face. Hecamed's voice sounded softly behind me:

"It is the will of Jove."

CHAPTER XXI

WE DRINK TO REVENGE.

U NDER ORDINARY CIRCUMSTANCES GORTYNA'S DEATH, occurring as it did within the palace itself, would have created an immense stir. Hecamed and I would have been examined at length by an officer of the court; the funeral would have been plenteously attended by the morbid and curious; a searching investigation would have been instituted to ascertain the nature of the poison she had used and the place where she had procured it.

But at that time of great excitement and universal grief the death of the peasant slave-girl received not even a passing notice. I made no report of the affair whatever; Thersin had the body removed by the authorities, and that was the last I heard of it.

The following day Hecamed kept to her room. Her nerves had been painfully shocked by the occurrence; more, I suppose, at the realization of her own narrow escape than because of any feeling for Gortyna. It was horrible enough, but who will say that it was undeserved?

Early in the morning I sought the apartments of Priam. A

considerable crowd was already collected in the antechamber; Æneas informed me that no one had been permitted an audience. It was presumed that the king, prostrate with grief, was unable to see anyone.

Also, Æneas told me that Achilles had rejected all demands for the return of Hector's body. Rumor had it that the corpse was to be given over to fowls and dogs for insult; all Troy was in a rage; vows of vengeance were heard all over the chamber.

As the morning passed the crowd increased. No one was to take the field that day, and all the warriors who possessed the privilege came to the palace instead.

I saw Evenus for the first time since Cisseis's death, and had a long talk with him. Somewhat later Paris arrived with Lysimachus. Paris had some wild tale to tell of Apollo appearing to him in a vision to say that he (Paris) should be the one to take revenge for his brother's death.

At this some snickered behind their hands, but none laughed openly, for Paris did in fact appear to be a changed man since the day before. Æneas ventured to remark that if Paris really intended to become an instrument of vengeance it would be necessary for him to get on the other side of the walls.

Towards the middle of the day Rhemius entered the chamber breathless and covered with dust and sweat, to say that he had just returned from a scouting expedition to the Rock. He was at once the center of interest, and when he finished his recital the hall was filled with shouts of rage.

He had seen the body of Hector, still attached to the chariot of Achilles, dragged up and down the lines of the Grecian camp, while the soldiers spat at him they durst not face when he was alive. He had seen twelve Trojan youths of noble birth sacrificed at the tomb of Patroclus. Achilles had cut their throats with a dagger and scattered the blood over the ground; the bodies had been thrown to the dogs. He had seen the funeral games, where the Greek chieftains, from Ajax down to Menelaus, had engaged heartily in friendly contests of strength and skill.

"To think," stormed Æneas, "that they should play games

over the dead body of great Hector! Venus, my mother, where is thy vaunted protection? Apollo, where is thy favorite champion?'' Æneas was a great orator.

Meanwhile Rhemius had been conducted within to relate the news to Priam. As time passed and he did not return to the chamber, voices were lowered and men looked askance at one another; on every face was plainly written the fear that this last blow had been too much for the old king: we expected every moment to hear through the doors the dreaded:

"Aï! Aï! Aï!"

How surprised were we, then, when the door opened to disclose the form of Priam himself. He was bowed, indeed, and, unable to stand alone, leant on the shoulder of Rhemius for support; but in his eye gleamed a spark of the old proud spirit. At sight of him all faces were turned toward the door and every voice was hushed.

For a long moment he cast his eye over the throng in silence, then he spoke in a strong, clear voice:

"Men of Troy, you see your king bending under sorrow. Is it a pleasing sight, that you flock thus to my chamber? Are not your griefs enough at home? Would you see how miserable I am? You might know, ere you came, what such a son's loss weighed with me. But, O Troy! ere I see your ruin, let the doors of hell receive and ruin me!"

He stopped; every man trembled at his frown. Then suddenly he turned to where nine of his sons stood in a group: Helenus, Paris, Hippothous, Pammon, divine Agathones, Deiprobus, who had failed Hector in his time of need, Agavus, Antiphonus, and strong Polites. Thus he spake to them:

"Haste, you infamous brood, and get my chariot; I myself will go to the Grecian camp for the body of my son. O me, accursed man, all my good sons are gone; you that survive are base liars and common freebooters. All your graces are in your heels; as dancing companions you are excellent. Hence, you brats! Love you to hear my moans? Will you not get my chariot? Command it quickly! Fly!"

So terrible was his glance that none durst interfere, though all feared the event. Helenus and Pammon hastily left the hall to order the chariot; Paris would have spoken, but was silenced by a gesture. Not a sound was heard throughout the hall.

Then, struck by a sudden thought, I stepped boldly forward. This was a chance not to be overlooked. Priam, seeing my movement and my intention to speak, roared out:

"Well, you palace hanger-on! You nice fellow! What would you?"

Not to be balked of my purpose by his rage, I spoke loudly:

"O Priam, if you go to the Grecian camp, you must needs have a charioteer. I offer myself. I am no warrior; the Greeks are not incensed against me. I implore you, accept my services."

Others crowded forward, claiming the honor for themselves, but Priam waved them back.

"It is enough," he said, "Idaeus shall drive me. Ho! Agavus! Paris! Where is my chariot?"

Helenus entered, out of breath, to say that the chariot was ready. "It is well," said the king. "Diephobus, go within and direct the slaves with the presents. Make haste!"

I sprang forward to conduct Priam to the other chariot; Rhemius took his other arm. Following us came the slaves with the gifts which the king had ordered to be collected. There were twelve curiously wrought veils; twelve plain gowns; as many suits of wealthy tapestry; as many mantles; horsemen's coats; ten talents of fine gold; two tripods; four caldrons; a golden bowl which had been presented by the ambassadors of Thrace. It was evident that the old king held nothing too dear to rescue the body of Hector from disgrace.

We found the chariot, with four prancing horses, at the palace entrance. I sprang upon the driver's seat; others assisted Priam into the quadriga and placed the presents about his feet.

From above there suddenly sounded a piercing cry; it was the voice of Hecuba:

"My husband! Turn back from your folly ere it is too late! Think you that cursed Greek will honor age or pity woe? Turn back, my husband!"

But Priam, paying no heed to her, cried sternly:

"Drive on!"

I shook the reins; the horses leaped forward.

Many were trampled in our path that day. Through the streets we rushed, regarding none; soon we were at the gates, which opened at our approach. Then over the plain, past the mighty tomb of Ilus, past the very spot where Hector had been slain the day before; it seemed but a moment before we were in sight of the Grecian camp.

Having received instructions from Rhemius how to reach the tent of Achilles, I vowed that nothing should stop me till I had reached it. As well try to stop a whirlwind.

Half the time the horses were beyond my control; I lashed them into greater fury. It was chance, rather than the reins, that guided them to the center lane of the camp.

On they rushed, until I at length perceived the yellow banner described by Rhemius floating before a tent higher than the rest. Pulling lustily on the reins, I halted the chariot at its very entrance.

Leaping out, I assisted Priam to the ground and we passed hurriedly within. At the door I left him to enter alone, as he desired, and returned to stand by my horses.

Alcimus and Automedon, who were with Achilles when Priam entered, have since related what occurred at that memorable meeting; at the time I knew nothing of it. Alcimus appeared at the door to instruct a captain of the guard that I was not to be molested—for by that time a crowd of soldiers had gathered curiously about me—but he turned again and disappeared within.

After a long wait Achilles and Automedon emerged from the tent, carrying the body of Hector on a bier. It was frightfully mangled, but not beyond recognition.

They covered it with two of the cloaks of tapestry brought by Priam in the chariot; the remaining gifts they carried within the tent. Then they came out again to place the bier in the chariot.

Here, I thought, was my opportunity. As Achilles sprang from the quadriga after arranging the cloaks over the body of his dead foe I approached and touched his arm, saying in a low tone:

"I would speak with you."

He turned sharply:

"What would you?"

"A word. Speak lower. Will you carry a message for me to King Menelaus?"

"Akh! I am no errand boy. It is great Achilles you see before you. What is your message?"

"This," I spoke rapidly. "Helen would return to Menelaus; I have it from her lips. She mourns for your losses. If you will end the war she will return. Speak; your word is enough."

For a moment Achilles stared at me in silence. Then suddenly he burst into scornful laughter. "So," he sneered insolently, "the Trojans seek peace! No wonder; do you see the corpse of Hector in that chariot? That is how all Trojan dogs shall lie before a month; your city will be in ruins. Tell Helen not to mourn for our losses; soon she shall come to us by force of our valor."

He turned on his heel and entered the tent without giving me a chance to reply.

So much for my fine project! A sneer—an insult—and that was all. My lips were perforce silent, but my heart boiled in fury. At that moment I would not have treated with the Greeks if I could, and I reproach myself for ever having considered it.

I swore vengeance on Achilles. You will laugh to hear it; it is a wonder I did not laugh at myself; all the same, I swore it, and I was in deadly earnest.

It was then I first discovered what it means to hate from the heart, bitterly. As he himself had said of Hector, I could have torn him to pieces alive and thrown him to the dogs.

As I stood staring at the entrance of the tent with blazing eyes, the form of old Priam appeared, supported on either side by Alcimus and Automedon. I assisted him to mount the quadriga, where he stood beside the body of his dead son, then leaped to the seat in front and gathered up the reins. As I did so Automedon addressed me:

"Give your horses wings, if you would return your king safe to Troy. If Agamemnon learns of his presence in the camp he is as good as dead. 'Twas a daring venture."

I thanked him with a curt nod, and, needing no second hint, urged the horses forward.

Once more the wheels of our chariot thundered down the long line of the Grecian camp. But at the first opportunity I turned aside into the field, heeding Automedon's warning to keep far from the tent of Agamemnon. Again we raced over the stony and rutty ground of battle; again we reached the plain, and crossed it, and passed the tomb of Ilus. I did not allow the horses to slacken their pace till we reached the gates of the city.

Once within, I found it impossible to go forward. The citizens, observing the approach from afar, had gathered to welcome us: a mighty shout arose at the news that we had been successful, and they rushed forward to view the remains of their hero. But Priam would have none of them.

"Back, you recreant knaves!" he roared, while his eyes flashed lightning. "You would not follow him alive; now that he is dead you steal his air. Back!"

At that thundering command and imperious gesture they made a lane for our passage, and I urged the horses forward. They answered to the word as though fresh from stable, plunging through the streets like sons of Xanthus.

At the palace another throng awaited us, of women and children, warriors and kings. They fell back respectfully at our approach, until I motioned for assistance.

Some helped Priam to the ground and up the steps; others lifted the corpse from the chariot and bore it tenderly after the aged king. On all sides were heard lamentations and wails of grief. It was on that day that all Troy first dressed itself in black. Nevermore was any other dress seen within the walls of the city.

The fame of my exploit was in the mouths of all. They led me into an inner chamber as though I had been a mighty hero, and warriors vied with each other to serve me with wine and cakes. This I found not displeasing, but I was far from being lighthearted. My grand project had failed miserably; I had stood helpless while Achilles threw insults into my very face; and, worse than all, I saw clearly that the end of Troy was near, for who was left to withstand the mighty Greek?

I had vowed vengeance, but so had everyone else, and mere vows do not kill.

But it rejoiced us to hear from King Priam that Hector was at least to be permitted fitting obsequies. Achilles had consented to a twelve days' truce on the supplication of Priam, agreeing to keep all the Greeks within their camp for that period. On the advice of Æneas, however, guards were placed at all parts of the walls, day and night, for fear of a surprise. By that time we knew the wily Greeks.

Early the following morning the task of constructing the pyre began. Slaves were sent with wagons to the woods west of the city to return loaded with logs and fagots. At this they labored nine days, at the end of which time the pile had grown to the height of twenty men. On the morning of the tenth day everything was in readiness.

At the first opportunity I had reported to Helen the failure of our scheme. She expressed her regret, made a sacrifice of Venus, and speedily forgot all about the matter, though she had publicly declared over the corpse of Hector that he had been dearer to her even than her own husband.

Some took this to be a confession of a secret intimacy between them—shameful and false odium to cast on the dead hero! But in truth he had loved Andromache far too well to accept the embraces of any other woman, even Argive Helen.

I should, perhaps, defend her name also, in recognition of her kindness to me. She had not forgotten her promise to attend my marriage at the Temple of Mulciber. It took place on the third day after the return of Hector's body, and was indeed a royal event; for my exploit as Priam's charioteer had given me a dizzy prominence.

In addition to Helen were present Paris, Helenus and Deiphobus, sons of Priam; Polyxena and Cassandra, his daughters: Evenus, Æneas, Antenor, and many others. There was no joy in the festival, save that which reigned in the hearts of Hecamed and myself. At last we were united, and for that day our happiness drove all thought of the common sorrow from our minds.

But I was forced to leave her much alone during the days that followed, on account of the preparations for the funeral of Hector, and was therefore much pleased by the fact that Polyxena, who had apparently taken a strong liking to her, spent most of each day in our rooms or walking with Hecamed through the palace grounds.

A close friendship rapidly developed between the two; this I guessed at rather than knew, for Hecamed told me nothing of it.

On the ninth day the preparations were completed, and early in the morning of the tenth all Troy gathered before the great funeral pile, set up in Doreon Square. The body of Hector was brought from the palace in his own war chariot, drawn by four white horses; following, in other chariots and wagons—some afoot—were all who could gain a place in the procession. Everyone was dressed in black; the warriors carried empty scabbards; the women wore long, flowing veils that covered their mantles to their very feet.

Æneas, Deiphobus, Agavus, and Paris carried the body up the narrow ladder to the top of the pile, and left it there exposed naked to the sun. Then they descended, and Evenus and Pammon approached with the torches. Around the pile they went, touching each heap of soft fagots and soon the flames began creeping toward the top.

When at length the leaping tongues were observed to pass around the body and above it, ten thousand throats joined in a simultaneous moan of grief and despair. Then the throng began to disperse.

All day it burned, and all night, while guards were set to watch it. On the following morning the people assembled once more in the square, and the procession once more wended its way thither from the palace, Priam leading. The word given, a hundred slaves advanced with vessels of blackish wine to extinguish the flames.

That done, the four who had carried the body the day before

approached the table of stone and took therefrom the snowy bones. One by one they carried them to an immense urn of finest gold that stood nearby and gently cast them in. Then, lifting the urn into Hector's war chariot, they led the way back to the palace gates and through them to the burying ground in the rear, where a pit had been prepared.

None but relatives and members of the royal household were permitted to view the final ceremony. The urn was lowered into the pit with straps of whiteleather fastened to its handles; then all stood back while Andromache approached with the first stone. Her face was bathed in tears; at intervals a low moan came from her tight throat. The stone dropped from her nerveless fingers, clattering against the urn in the pit.

As it fell Andromache sank senseless to the ground.

Willing hands cared for her, while others threw in the remainder of the stones until the pit was filled. Then the women and old men returned to the palace, while the rest of us began the task of raising the sepulchre. Priam and Hecuba, unable to stand on their feet, were carried in by slaves.

To a great height the sepulchre grew, crowned at the top with a tower of whitest marble. Well pleased were we with our work; and well exhausted, too, when the end of our labors at length permitted us to rest.

The afternoon I spent with Hecamed alone in our rooms, but as soon as night came on we prepared to attend the funeral feast, which was to mark the end of the rites. Living as we did in the palace, we escaped the inconvenience of dressing for the streets, and also were enabled to start for the red chamber only after all the guests had assembled and everything was in readiness.

It was a brilliant scene that met our eyes. The company numbered over six hundred and included everyone of name and position in Troy. Priam, with Hecuba on one side and Andromache on the other, presided at the head of the great table, covered with snowy linen and alight with a thousand lamps. The lofty walls and pillars of jasper and *nero antico* shone and glittered like the tomb of Ilus in the sunlight; the rich gold of the tapestries gleamed like points of fire.

Hecamed sat between Evenus and Pammon; I was placed somewhat further down, with Polyxena on my right and Argive Helen on my left. Æneas sat on the other side of Helen; and as his conversation was continually amusing, she gave all her attention to him: I was forced to bestow my own on Polyxena.

The feast was sumptuous and splendid enough, but, like all such affairs, grew exceedingly tiresome toward the end. Half the men present had determined to make a speech, and most of them made good their determination. The longest was that of Æneas, though Deiphobus was a close second. I was grieved to see that Evenus also was inclined to try his own breath and the patience of the audience; I really believe that he would have won the palm from Æneas if I had not signaled to Hecamed to pull him back onto his bench. She did so, amid general laughter.

But everyone grew serious when the time came to drink to the soul of Hector, and the prayer of Priam, brief but eloquent, brought tears to the eyes of many. Amid profound silence we emptied our cups, all standing.

Æneas then opened his mouth to propose a unique ceremony. Leave it to his agile brain to think of something different.

"Men of Troy," he said, "we have drunk to the dead; let us now drink to the living, but with a different prayer. That the soul of Hector shall disport itself joyously in the fields of Elysium is our true desire; is it not also our desire that the men who slew him shall suffer the torments of Hades?

"Slaves! Fill the cups! Drink heartily! May the wrath of the gods descend on Achilles; may the prophecy of his end be verified by the event; may he suffer all that Hector shall escape!"

Applause sounded from all ends of the table. The cups were speedily filled. Again the company rose to their feet, and drank in unison to the discomfiture of the enemy.

I made some remark to Polyxena, and, receiving no answer, turned to repeat my question.

Then I saw that she had not heard me. Her eyes were set

straight ahead with that vacant, far-away expression which shows that the mind is elsewhere; and glancing down at the table, I saw that she had set her cup down as full as it was before, without tasting a drop.

CHAPTER XXII

PARIS DREAMS A DREAM.

I T IS NOT STRANGE THAT THE FACT OF POLYXENA'S LEAV-ing her wine untouched did not make a strong impression on me at the time. It might have been that she was not feeling well, or that she did not like the wine, which was of Pramnius—I have never been very fond of it myself—or merely that she had drunk as much as she could hold. It is only in the light of after events that the happening assumes importance.

Still, it did impress me somewhat, and as I walked to our rooms after the feast, with Hecamed at my side, I wondered if it might be taken as an indication of anything.

Hecamed had told me several times of Polyxena's liking for discourse of Achilles, but I had given the thing no serious thought, believing it merely the ordinary fascination for a somewhat silly girl of a great warrior whom she knew only by name. Polyxena had never had any opportunity of meeting the Greek, nor had she seen him except from the height of the Scaean Towers.

So I then believed; subsequent events altered that belief.

The following morning began the twelfth day, and with it hostilities recommenced. The Trojans, greatly freshened by their long rest, sought the combat with renewed vigor, but the same may be said of the Greeks. And whereas we were greatly weakened by the loss of Hector, they were equally strengthened by the acquisition of Achilles.

The first day's battle was a series of unimportant skirmishes. Achilles was pleased to display the abilities of a general rather than those of a champion, and amused himself by deploying his troops from one vantage point to another; but at no time did he approach within striking distance of the city's walls.

Towards evening, indeed, he made a swift and unexpected sortie, and it was then that Deiphobus was killed and Rhemius taken prisoner. A score or so of common soldiers also perished.

On the second day things were different. I went early to the Scaean Towers, leaving Hecamed at home, for she expected to come later with Polyxena.

At this time the Towers seemed deserted when one thought of the throng that had been wont to crowd them a little before. Priam and Hecuba no longer appeared, nor Andromache, nor Lysimache, nor Cassandra. All the men, with very few exceptions, went to the field. I myself had requested permission to do so from the king, but he refused, saying that it was necessary to have one capable charioteer left within the city.

I smiled at that; it was easy to guess where I had got that reputation with him.

I stood on the parapet beside Argive Helen as the troops emerged through the gates below with Æneas in command. To him a word of praise is due. Vainglorious and boastful as he was, he had respected the memory of Hector by leaving inviolate his assignments of the troops, and he had sent his wife Cheüsa to live with Andromache and console her. A manly and honorable action.

As I watched him ride across the plain, standing upright in his chariot, lance in hand, I thought certainly that he would never again enter the gates of the city. It was a safe guess that by now Achilles once more hungered for fight, and the son of

Anchises would most probably be the point of his first attack.

It was not so. Achilles indeed resumed his old violence, but he kept clear of the centre of the line. Was it because, coming at last to fear the prophecy of his end, and thinking it would most likely arrive at the hands of Æneas, he endeavored to postpone the event by avoiding him?

However that may be, the Greek confined his operations throughout the day to one or the other wing, leaving Ajax and Ulysses to meet Æneas in the middle.

Not that his efforts were fruitless. With my own eyes I saw my friend Evenus fall with the lance of Achilles through his breast. Soon after Agathones was caught between two lines of the Greeks and perished. Antilochus met his fate at the hands of Æacides. Then Achilles, rushing forward in his chariot, so obscured things with a whirling cloud of dust that details were lost to me.

Everywhere else the Trojans had the better of it. Æneas, leading his men single-handed, drove Ajax and Ulysses back. Many Greeks were killed in the retreat, including Meleager, Alcimus, Menestheus, and Scarphis; at one time it appeared that Æneas would force them to their very tents. But being summoned to the aid of Adrastus, who was sorely pressed on the right wing, the Greeks were saved from that humiliation.

Withal, the day's struggle proved clearly that the capture of Troy was only a matter of time. This on account of Achilles. None could stand before his attack, and it appeared that none could inflict injury on him.

You will say: "Of course not; he was invulnerable." That is, you will say that if you are superstitious enough to believe in silly tales.

I have always regarded that story of his being made invulnerable by being dipped under water while his mother held him by the heel as one of the best jokes I ever heard. I am perfectly aware that most people believe it, but then most people are fools. Perhaps they will change their opinion when they read my story.

To return. It seemed that Troy was doomed, and by the valor of one man. Sooner or later the might of Achilles would prevail. That was my thought as I walked slowly through the streets with Hecamed and Polyxena. We walked not of choice, but because horses had become so scarce in Troy that they were all employed in drawing war chariots.

When Hecamed and I reached our rooms we found that Thersin had supper ready for us. The meal was finished in silence, broken here and there by some inconsequential remarks from Hecamed, to which I gave little attention; I was buried in thought.

My hatred of Achilles had attained nearly to the dignity of a mania. He had slain my friends Cisseis and Evenus; he had slain Hector; he had spat insults in my face; his valor endangered the very existence of my native city. If I had believed sufficiently in any god to make it worth while to pray to him, I would have prayed that my frame be made bigger, my arm strengthened, my courage multiplied, that I might conquer Achilles the unconquerable.

After supper we went for a walk in the palace grounds. The night was soft and warm; a gentle breeze from the Scamander, bearing the perfume of its flowery banks, cooled our temples and pleased our nostrils. Quiet reigned on every side; the branches of the trees waved mysteriously in the fading moonlight. In the midst of her peril Troy appeared thus peaceful.

Hecamed began talking about a new mantle she and Polyxena had designed that morning; I found the subject distasteful, and said so bluntly.

"In the first place, I do not admire Polyxena's taste, either in design or color; secondly, the topic offends me by its triviality," was the way I put it.

"I suppose your mind is on great things," Hecamed smiled.

"Yes. I think of Achilles. I cannot drive him from my mind. Akh! To have him here, beneath me!" I ground my heel savagely into the turf.

We walked on in silence, reached the end of the grounds, and turned.

"That is another subject on which you disagree with Polyxena," Hecamed observed presently.

"What? What's that?"

"I say, that is another subject on which you and Polyxena think differently."

"You mean?"

"Achilles. She is crazy about him."

I snorted in contempt. "Do you give ear to her empty vaporings? She merely likes to speak his name because it is a great one, and famous. I would not believe her unpatriotic; she would be ready enough to pierce his breast with a dagger if she had the chance. It is nothing but the romanticism of a young girl."

"I think it is more," said Hecamed quietly.

"Well, you are mistaken."

At that Hecamed stopped suddenly to look at me. She opened her mouth, closed it again, and ended by saying: "Idaeus, it is you who are mistaken. I know what I am talking about. I tell you, Polyxena is genuinely in love with Achilles."

I grunted in disbelief. "And I tell you, it is impossible. Why, she has never seen him save on the field, encased in armor, with his face hidden by his helm."

"Has she not? I am not so sure." Hecamed appeared to hesitate for a moment, then added, "I am truly anxious for her; that is why I speak of it. Perhaps I should not tell you—"

"Why not?"

"Because . . . But I will, for I would save her from ruin. It is this. Three nights ago Polyxena not only saw Achilles, but was with him for a long time—alone."

I stared at her in amazement, wondering if she had gone crazy. "What mad tale is this?" I managed at last to gasp.

"It is no mad tale, but sober truth. Polyxena has met Achilles and loves him."

"Where?"

"I know not. But I am sure of the fact. She did not say so in so many words, but she betrayed herself and then half acknowledged it."

"But Hecamed! Do you know the importance of your words?"

"I know they are true."

"But this—this—" I stammered in excitement. "Tell me

everything she said. When did you talk with her? Tell me—but wait. We must not talk of this here. These trees have ears. Come.''

I led the way back to the palace, so swift in my eagerness that she could scarcely keep pace with me. Arrived there, we entered my room and I closed and bolted the door.

''Now,'' I said, seating myself beside her on a bench, ''tell me everything—everything!''

''But I have told you.'' Hecamed was apparently somewhat frightened at my elaborate precautions.

''Tell me what Polyxena said.''

''Well—'' She hesitated a moment, then continued: ''It was this morning, after you had left for the Towers. As you know, Polyxena came to see me here. I myself introduced the subject of Achilles, because it is all she will talk about, and I happened to say that his hair is not golden, as is Pammon's, but a sort of dirty yellow.

'' 'It is nothing of the sort!' Polyxena exclaimed, without thinking. 'It is the most beautiful golden hair I ever saw!'

''Then, seeing her mistake, she looked at me half-frightened.

''I demanded to know when she had ever seen Achilles. 'How can you know anything about his hair?' I asked. 'You never saw him with his casque off, and only at a great distance.' ''

Hecamed halted abruptly and glanced at me questioningly:

''But perhaps—I should not tell you—''

''Go on,'' I commanded, rough in my eagerness.

She continued more slowly:

''After that Polyxena didn't know what to say. Finally she declared that she had seen Achilles and talked with him. I laughed at her incredulously, saying, just as you have, that it was impossible. It made her angry to have me disbelieve her. 'What do you know about it?' she said. 'Do you think Achilles afraid to dare any danger? And do you know all of my movements? I am not always with you, am I? What of three nights ago, the night before the feast?'

''I exclaimed in horror, 'Polyxena, you wouldst not meet

the Greek at the very time the body of your brother Hector
was eaten with flames?'

" 'Do not speak of Hector,' returned Polyxena, and her eyes
filled with tears. 'I—I would forget him—if I may. We are
talking of Achilles. Him I would meet anywhere, at any time.
Tomorrow night—but no, I have said enough.'

"And that was all she would say."

Hecamed finished; I sat in silent amaze. How was this thing
possible? Did Polyxena go to the Grecian camp? Did Achilles
dare to enter the city? But that could not be: he would have
been surely discovered.

I ended by declaring:

"Hecamed, she was befooling you."

But Hecamed swore that Polyxena had spoken truly. "She
could not have been deceiving me. Truth was in her eyes and
voice: I felt it. I tell you that you should save her from her
folly, if there is any way it can be done. She said, 'Tomorrow
night.' That much escaped her lips; it must be that she intends
to meet him again."

It was hard to believe, but I ended by believing. For a long
time I questioned Hecamed in an attempt to get further information, but she had told me everything she knew.

My own memory brought its portion of proof. I remembered
that Polyxena had defended Achilles publicly on the Scaean
Towers: that she had refused to drink the cup of revenge proposed by Æneas at the feast. According to this tale, only the
night before that she had actually been with the Greek!

I do not know when it was that the thought which later gave
birth to a great event first entered my head. That night my
only sensations were astonishment and wonder at Polyxena's
cunning. This until, some time later, I laid myself beside Hecamed to go to sleep.

It must be that the idea stole into my brain in a dream, for
I awoke in the morning with the plot as fully developed as
though I had pondered on it for hours. Everything was provided for; every possible mischance anticipated.

My first impulse was to take Hecamed into my confidence
and ask her assistance and advice, but on second thought I

decided that it would best to deceive her. She was Polyxena's friend, and she would probably refuse to betray her even to save Troy or to get revenge on Achilles for her own misfortunes.

Accordingly, I approached the subject warily. It was at the breakfast table. Waiting until Thersin had left the room, I turned to Hecamed with a question:

"Have you decided on anything concerning Polyxena?"

"No," she replied. "I have been waiting for you to invent a way. You have understanding of these things; I am but an ignorant woman."

"This would be difficult, even for Æneas or Uylsses." I twirled my cap in my fingers regarding it speculatively. "Nevertheless, I think I can prevent her folly, if you can discover from her the place of meeting?"

"But that is the difficult part!" cried Hecamed.

"I know, but it must be done. She cannot be followed, for it is impossible to tell how she will leave the palace. She will certainly use one of the hidden entrances, and there are a score of them. Are you to see her this morning?"

"Yes. She comes at the second clepsydra. You must promise me one thing, Idaeus. No harm must come to her."

"I mean no harm to anyone," I replied, without raising my eyes. "I mean merely to protect Polyxena."

"Akh!" Hecamed's voice was filled with scorn. "Do you think to deceive me? I know very well what your wishes are. Whatever you do to Achilles will please me, but I fear injury to yourself and to Polyxena."

So much for my little strategy! I confess it was clumsy, but no harm was done. It appeared that she was only too willing to take advantage of Polyxena's weakness to bring about the downfall of Achilles. She defended herself by saying that if Polyxena were allowed to continue her course of folly, she would bring ruin on herself and obloquy on her name, and that we were in fact performing an act of kindness to the daughter of Priam.

For my part, I gave my word that no harm should come to

Polyxena. "I swear to you, Hecamed, that I will protect her at whatever cost. And as for myself—for I see your fear in your sweet eyes—you know I am made nine parts of prudence to one of daring. Have no fear; we shall be successful and lose nothing."

"But still—I am afraid for you—"

"You need not be. Akh! At thought of the opportunity to get revenge on the haughty Greek, I feel the blood of a thousand heroes in my veins! But easy; we must not forget that all is useless unless you can discover the time and place of meeting from Polyxena."

"I will do my best."

"More is impossible. When do you expect her?"

"I told you; the second clepsydra."

"Then I will leave, that you may be alone with her. Use all your cunning; if she suspects, there is an end of it."

"Depend on me."

With that I left her and sought the streets. Never, I think, had I been wrought to such a pitch of excitement and impatience. If only Hecamed could get the information we needed; if only, having received it, I could crown our project with success—ah, Achilles should pay dearly for his victories and insults!

One thing was certain: I must have a companion in my venture. To divide the glory was not to my liking; on the other hand, it would be the height of folly to attempt the thing alone. Who should it be? I cudgeled my brain.

Cisseis and Evenus were dead. Æneas would probably refuse to take a hand in it. Antenor was too old. Agavus and Orchomen lacked the necessary spirit. Paris—why not Paris? He possessed the skill I wanted; he was brave enough when aroused from his habitual sloth and lethargy.

I decided on Paris, and went in search of him.

Hastening to his lodgings, I was told that he had departed some time before. No one knew where he had gone. I returned to the palace for a horse, but none was to be had. Half walking and half running, I started off across the city towards the eastern walls.

I mounted the endless stairs of the Scaean Towers, only to meet with another disappointment. Paris had not been seen.

"Is it possible that he intends to take the field?" I wondered; and, again descending to the street, I sought the square before the Scaean Gates, where the troops were mustered.

I was just in time. Paris, in full armor, was in command of the men of Thrace. He was just mounting his chariot when I arrived, breathless and exhausted, at his side.

"What would you?" he demanded impatiently. When once aroused to action he was as impetuous as Ajax himself.

"I would speak with you," I replied taking his arm.

"There is no time. Wait till my return."

"But you may not return. What I have to say is of the highest importance. You will not regret it."

Seeing the resolution in my eyes, he jumped to the ground.

"Speak," he commanded.

I did so. "First, you must not go to the field today. You are needed—for something else. Give your command—"

He interrupted me:

"What nonsense is this? Is it a message from Priam? It is his taunts that have driven me!"

"It is no message from Priam," I replied, and I continued impressively, "Paris, you know me, do you not?"

"Yes—I know you."

"You know I would not speak gravely on light matters?"

"Yes. You are not a fool."

"Then do as I tell you. Do not go to the field. Give your command to another. Rest yourself today in your lodgings; do not stir; await me there. If you will do as I say, I promise you on my word that tonight you shall—*slay Achilles*!"

I expected him to be amazed, astonished; it would have been no wonder if he had thought me crazy. He was moved, but in a different manner. He leaned suddenly forward, seizing my arm in so firm a grip that I winced in pain, and demanded hoarsely:

"Are you sent by Apollo?"

It was I who was amazed. "What do you mean by that?"

I demanded in turn. "I am sent by no one, certainly by no god. But my words are true."

Paris, releasing my arm, drew back and passed his hand over his forehead as if to drive away some bewilderment.

"This is strange," he said slowly, "exceeding strange! I will tell you—last night Apollo appeared before me in a dream—or, rather, this morning, for it was nearly dawn—and said to me what you have just said: 'Tonight you shall slay Achilles.' The very words! It *must* be you are sent by him!"

I resolved on the instant to take advantage of his superstition.

"It is quite possible," I declared soberly, restraining an inclination to jeer at him. "It is quite possible, though I have not seen Apollo for some time. The point is, will you do as I say?"

"I thought it would be on the field," resumed Paris, still with a faraway look in his eyes. "That is why I have come forth; I thought Apollo meant I should slay him on the field. But since you have come to tell me—Decidedly, he must have sent you."

"There can be no doubt of that," I replied firmly.

"Then—I will do as you say."

So much for my confederate. Little I cared if it were a foolish dream that persuaded him to assist me. In fact—I may as well confess it—his tale of the appearance of Apollo made me certain of success. Not that I am the least bit superstitious, but it would have been foolish to have disregarded so pertinent and conclusive a portent.

Thus I left Paris filled with new confidence. He had agreed to obey me strictly; to go at once to his lodgings and there await further word from me. I had told him that I might not appear before the end of the day; he had replied that I would no doubt come whenever Apollo sent me. In his eyes I had become a direct representative of the god.

All the same, I was tortured with uneasiness. What if Hecamed failed to extract any information from Polyxena? I would be left in a pretty hole indeed, with Paris anxiously awaiting a message that would never come; besides, I had given him my word of honor that he should that night slay Achilles. Not to mention my own disappointment at the failure.

I returned to the palace—by the time I reached there it was the middle of the day—and, seeking my rooms, inquired of Thersin at the door if anyone had called. He replied that Polyxena had come some time before, and that she and Hecamed had gone together to the Towers.

"May she be endowed with the cunning of Ulysses and the wit of Pallas," I muttered, entering the hall.

Going to my own room, I went to a chest in the corner and took from it two arrows, slender and flexible, but of great strength. They had been presented by Rhesus of Thrace to my father many years before; he had given them to me.

Concealing them under my mantle, and instructing Thersin to stay within to receive Hecamed when she returned, I again sought the street.

Walking westward from the palace, I proceeded along Troad Street until I came to a lofty building of black marble on the corner of the square. Entering, I asked a slave if Polydorus was within.

"Yes. He is in his apartments."

"Send word that Idaeus, son of Dares, would speak with him."

A little later I was closeted with Polydorus. He was a little old man of about ninety with a flowing white beard, and had long been known as the quaintest character in Troy. Immensely wealthy, he never appeared outside of his apartments save when he drove to the country in a rickety old chariot to gather plants and herbs.

He was possessed of much curious learning—evil, some said—and was rather feared than liked by those who knew him.

"Polydorus," I said, advancing boldly to where he sat before a table heaped with curiously wrought vessels and cups, "are you a friend of Dares?"

He merely nodded, peering at me from under his eyebrows.

"And therefore of his son?"

He nodded again.

"I have come to prove your friendship. You have an opportunity to use your learning for the good of Troy. More I cannot say. This you shall do."

I opened my mantle, took forth the two arrows and laid them on the table.

"I do not know the names of your poisonous juices," I finished, "but whichever is the most deadly, cover with it these points."

Polydorus said nothing. He glanced at the arrows, glanced again at me, then arose and carried the arrows with him through some curtains to a room in the rear. Before the curtains had become still he appeared again; the points of the arrows glittered as though they had been dipped in some colorless shiny paint.

"Have care," said Polydorus in a thin, cracked voice, "that the juice does not enter your own blood. The tiniest scratch of your finger and you are gone."

I placed the arrows carefully inside my mantle and closed it. "You have earned the gratitude of Troy as well as my own," I declared, turning to go. But Polydorus was again poring over his curious vessels and gave me no answer.

Again I found myself on the street. Part of the afternoon yet remained. What to do? Suddenly I thought of my father. "This adventure is risky," I said to myself. "I may meet death in it." Accordingly I made my way to my old home, and spent a long time conversing with Dares. I said nothing, however, of the business of the coming night. I never saw him again.

It was dusk when I finally returned to the palace. I bounded up the steps three at a time bursting with impatience, for I had stayed with my father much longer than I had intended. Hecamed met me at the door.

"Are you alone?" I demanded in the first breath.

"Yes; except for Thersin, who is in the rear."

"You saw Polyxena?"

"Yes."

"And you discovered—"

"Everything. She meets Achilles tonight."

"Well?" In my excitement I grasped her roughly by the arm so that she winced. "Tell me—"

Hecamed glanced nervously to either side and the rear, then approached me on tiptoe and whispered in my ear:

"The middle hour of the night, at the Scaean Gates!"

CHAPTER XXIII

In the Vault.

THE SCAEAN GATES, WHICH WERE SITUATED ALMOST DI-
rectly beneath the towers of the same name, only a little
to the north, were the most important of the series that
pierced the walls of Troy on every side. Pointing eastward,
toward the Scamander, they were used more than all the others
combined.

The wall was thicker at this point than anywhere else, and
thus the arch through which chariots and wagons passed, as
well as those afoot, formed a damp and gloomy passage. Great
double iron gates were placed in the middle, and wooden ones
further in; on each side of these gates, however, was a narrow
passage which was always left open. This for the convenience
of the guard, that they need not swing open the heavy gates
of iron if one wished to pass through after night.

At each side of these narrow passages, built into the wall
itself, was an immense cavern-like apartment used for storing
the public grain at harvesttime.

Since the beginning of the siege the gates had been heavily
guarded day and night. The guard had never numbered less

than a score, and after the death of Hector was increased to fifty. They were stationed in pairs at the large entrance and each of the smaller ones, while the others remained in a tent close at hand to relieve them at intervals.

On the night of these events the guard had been stationed as usual. With this difference: the pair at the left passage and that at the middle entrance were common soldiers; the other pair, that stationed at the passage on the right, were Paris and myself.

This had been arranged by the authority of Paris with the captain of the guard.

Paris had obeyed me in everything with the blind obedience of a good soldier, because, forsooth, he thought me sent by Apollo! Even when I told him to discard his own arrows and take the two I gave him in their place, he offered no objection. His bow, which had been constructed by Pandarus himself and was the finest in Troy, was hidden under his cloak.

I stood at the entrance to the narrow passage; Paris paced impatiently up and down its length. We had arrived but a short while before, and had just been given our station by the captain of the guard. We had chosen the passage on the right because anyone going without was forced to use it.

It was a moonless night; the only thing that saved us from total darkness was the cluster of torches placed over the middle entrance, and their light was just strong enough to accentuate the universal blackness. High above our heads loomed the lofty wall, gloomy, indistinct. The passage itself was dark as the shades below; you could not see your hand before your face.

"We are much too early," said Paris fretfully, stopping in front of me. He had made this observation at least twenty times before.

"Better that than too late," I retorted, also as before.

"But where is the sense? I tell you, Idaeus, this will end in nothing.

"Did Apollo not appear to you?"

"Yes. That is so. But yet—you know my weakness—I am prone to fantasy. And I cannot imagine any conceivable thing that would bring Achilles to the very gates of the city. Even *he* would not dare!''

''I have told you 'tis a woman.''

''I cannot believe it. Would he risk so much for a wench? I know of no woman in Troy could so attract him.''

''Yet there is one.''

''Who is it?''

This question also Paris had asked me more than twenty times. Of course, I dared not tell him. ''You may not know that,'' I replied. ''I have promised not to betray her; would you have me break my word?''

''Is it Helen?''

''I have told you no.''

''Is it your Hecamed?''

''No. Do not ask me more. I will not answer.''

With which he was perforce content.

Seeing that there still remained some time before the middle hour, I proposed that we make a tour of exploration. To this Paris readily agreed. Signaling the captain of the guard to tell him to station others at the entrance during our absence, we made our way down the passage.

Emerging at the further end, we found ourselves at the edge of the plain outside the walls. There was nothing to be seen there, and, re-entering the passage to a point near its center, we turned into a narrow lane which led to the vault of which I have already spoken. It was blacker there than any night, and a damp evil atmosphere surrounded us. I returned to the guard tent for a lantern.

Guided by its light, we found that there was not one vault, but many. Joined together by narrow, low-roofed lanes, they stretched away beneath the walls in an unbroken series. They were all empty, foul and soaking with moisture. We were glad to get back in the open air as soon as possible.

''Do you suppose,'' asked Paris as we again reached the entrance, ''that we will be led far into the plain?''

''Probably to the tomb of Ilus.''

''But do you not think it possible they use those vaults as a meeting place?''

The thought had not occurred to me. "Hardly likely," I observed. "And yet—well, we shall see. Is your bow safe?"

Paris nodded, patting his cloak.

"And the arrows?"

"Yes."

"That is well. We shall keep this lantern; here, help me fasten it under my mantle."

We took our soldiers' lances—for not to have carried them would have excited suspicion—and prepared to wait. The hum of the city had ceased long before; all Troy was sleeping. Nothing came from the blackness but silence, broken now and then by a call from one wall sentry to another. A little to the south the massive indistinct form of the Scaean Towers sought the sky. All else was an undefined blur; even the Temple of Zeus, which we knew to be directly across the square, was nothing but a hazy blotch.

The monotony of our vigil was interrupted twice; first by a Persian merchant, who knocked for admittance of his chariot, saying that he had come from Thrace. The captain of the guard examined his credentials, which consisted of a tiny scrap of parchment signed by Ramnus of Thrace; the iron gates were swung open, and the Persian entered with his chariot, disappearing into the black mouth of one of the side streets.

The second interruption came when a man dressed in full armor approached and whispered in my ear the word:

"Thamyris."

That was the password the captain had given for the night. We stood aside to give the man a path; my thought was that he was probably some warrior who had been detailed by Æneas to make a night tour along the walls.

By then the middle hour of night was near. We began to be impatient, especially Paris, who paced up and down in increasing agitation as the time grew shorter, muttering under his breath. "If he does not come—but I have the word of Apollo—it must be—is my arm steady?"

Suddenly I saw a form approaching through the darkness, making straight for the entrance of the passage where we stood. "Polyxena!" I thought, and my heart stopped beating.

But it soon appeared that I was mistaken, for as the figure came closer I could see it was that of a man, dressed in a short mantle with a black military chlamys over his shoulders and a pointed Phrygian cap on his head.

Reaching us, he halted to pronounce the word in a low tone: "Thamyris."

I nodded and stepped aside; he moved forward into the passage.

As he did so something caught my eye, or perhaps it was my ear—I cannot tell. The gait, the manner of holding the shoulders; it could not have been any feature or outline of the face, for it was covered with the cap, not to speak of the darkness.

Whatever it was, something whispered to me:

"That is Polyxena, dressed in the garb of a soldier."

This thought, or series of thoughts, was not instantaneous; some precious seconds had passed. I sprang silently forward, seizing Paris by the arm. I did not dare even to whisper, but luckily he understood me. Together we entered the passage and crept cautiously down its length.

Soon we were at the further end, and one glance showed us that the plain was empty! To be sure, we could not see far in the darkness, but there had not been time enough for the nocturnal pedestrian to have got beyond our line of vision.

For a single moment I was nonplussed; then in swift decision I turned and re-entered the passage, followed by Paris. At the mouth of the narrow lane leading to the vaults I stopped and placed my lips against his ear to breathe:

"Not a sound. Not a whisper. On your life!"

Then we entered the lane.

It was ticklish work, for the least sound would have meant an alarm. We had covered our feet with sandals of soft silk, but even the rustle of our mantles, the very sound of our breathing, smote on my ear as the call of trumpets. It was my nerves, I suppose, for I was quivering and tense as a drawn bow-string.

We went forward slowly, cautiously, stopping every few

steps to listen. There was not a sound. In this manner we crossed the first vault and passed through the lane into the second. Still no sign.

But as we reached the mouth of the third vault I heard the low murmur of voices.

My fingers closed on Paris's arm; he nudged me to show that he also had heard. It seemed then that we moved not at all, so warily did we advance, and it was a long time before we reached the further wall and entered the passage leading to the fourth vault.

As we did so the murmur of voices became considerably louder; a little further, and the words were audible.

"But do you not grieve for Briseis?"

"I grieve only that you are not mine, to be with me always."

They were the voices of Polyxena and Achilles.

A thrill of intense excitement ran through me from head to foot; I felt the body of Paris, crouched close by mine, stiffen like a panther preparing to spring. This was a contingency I had not thought of; that Paris would recognize Polyxena by her voice. But there was no time then for regrets.

Suddenly I felt the form of Paris turn about, and his lips were placed against my ear. Before he had time to whisper a word I clasped my hand firmly over his mouth. A warning to Achilles at that moment might prove fatal.

Grasping my companion's arm firmly, I began again to move forward through the lane. He would have gone more swiftly, but I held him back. We were on our hands and knees, crawling like snails; I was dimly aware of the fact that the ground was damp and slippery beneath us, and that there was an odor of filthy slime. Once I felt the lantern, inside my mantle, slip from its fastening, but I caught it before it reached the ground. Paris had taken his bow and arrows from beneath his cloak and carried them in his hand.

The voices had continued to sound at intervals, and as we reached the end of the lane they became quite distinct; emerging suddenly into the vault, it seemed the speakers were so close to us I could put out my hand and touch them: I crouched back against the wall, pulling Paris with me.

"Only once have I seen you," Achilles was saying, "only once have I looked on your face as I held you in my arms. That I could dispel this accursed darkness!"

The voice of Polyxena came:

"Is it not enough to be with me?"

"No. Admiring your beauty as I do, how could that be?"

"But still—it is something."

We heard the rustle of garments and the sound of a kiss before the Greek spoke:

"I would have you with me always—always. For you I will batter down the walls of Troy; I will carry you in my chariot to my tent."

"I shall be waiting for you." Polyxena's voice sank to a murmur.

I felt the form of Paris suddenly stir beside me. I forced him back with a heavy hand on his shoulder. But, knowing his impetuosity, I was aware that I must act soon, or he would leap in the dark. I thrust my hand noiselessly inside my mantle and grasped the handle of the lantern.

"Once more—" it was Achilles's voice—"will you not come with me now? Will you not make me happy?"

"No, I cannot! Do not ask me." Polyxena's words were soft with tears. "It would break my father's heart; all Troy, all my friends, my brothers, my sisters, would loath and execrate me. But when you are once inside the city—"

"Yes; when I am inside the city—"

"I will be yours. Yours! And, oh, come—come soon!"

At that, maddened beyond control by these treacherous words, Paris leaped to his feet before I could restrain him and roared like a lion:

"Polyxena!"

The next instant I also was on my feet, drawing the lantern from underneath my mantle.

Feeble as its rays were, the cavern seemed to be flooded with light in comparison with the pitch darkness that had enveloped us. In one glance I saw Polyxena and Achilles standing side by side not ten paces away, startled into dumbness by the cry of Paris, who stood just in front of me with his feet set wide apart, drawing his bow to which he had fitted an arrow.

There was a sharp twang of the string. The arrow whistled through the air. But it went wide of its mark and struck the wall some distance away, so unsteady was Paris in his rage. The next instant Achilles bounded at us like a lion, drawing his sword.

Paris leaped aside, slipping on the damp floor of the vault. Whirling like a flash, the Greek was upon me.

More by luck than skill, I succeeded in dodging under the blow, and the sword passed harmlessly over my head; but the violence of his rush knocked me to the ground. I tumbled, sprawling on my back. The lantern flew from my hand, but landed upright and was not extinguished.

I got back to my knees in time to see Achilles turn on Paris. The son of Priam was fitting his second arrow to the string, but it appeared that the Greek would be upon him before he could send it. I sprang to my feet and hurled myself furiously at Achilles; my hand caught the end of his chlamys and pulled him backward.

He turned with a roar and made for me with uplifted sword.

Paris was barely in time. Just as I gave myself up for lost I heard the second arrow whiz through the air. The aim was not very good, but it was good enough. The point of the arrow imbedded itself in Achilles's heel; for an instant he halted; I leaped out of his path.

Reaching down to extract the arrow, he started for us again; we had retreated to the further end of the vault. He did not come far. Halfway across he stopped suddenly, threw his hands straight above his head, and then sank to the floor, bellowing fearfully and roaring curses.

I ran to his side, wrested the sword from his hand and stood above him as he lay twisting and writhing in agony. Indeed, the juice of Polydorus was potent!

"Plunge it into his black heart!" yelled Paris. "No," he added quickly, running forward, "let him suffer! You Grecian dog! Your words were true indeed—you will soon be inside the city! Hector, may your shade commend me!''

It was soon over. There was no reply from Achilles. A series of convulsive shudders shook his frame and frightful moans came from his lips, while I stood above him in silence and the son of Priam hurled taunts and insults. Soon the moans ceased; suddenly he raised himself half to his elbows, then sank back onto the ground and lay still.

Paris still raged, gloating over his fallen foe. I stooped over the body to listen at his breast; there was no movement. As I straightened up a voice suddenly sounded behind us:

''Son of Thetis! Aï! Aï! Aï!''

The next instant Polyxena rushed past me and threw herself prostrate across the form of the dead Greek, sobbing wildly and kissing his face and hair.

''Akh!'' roared Paris in indescribable fury. ''Polyxena! *You!*'' He turned on me, trembling with rage:

''Give me the sword! 'Tis fitting she should die on his foul carcass!''

''Yes!'' screamed Polyxena. ''You murderer! Kill me, too, that I may join him!''

There began a tussle between Paris and me, on his part to gain possession of the sword, on mine to keep it. His hands closed over the blade as he tugged and pulled; blood streamed to the floor.

''Would you murder your sister?'' I cried, jerking back with such force that the weapon slipped through his fingers.

He was beside himself; ''bloodcrazy,'' we called it in Troy. For an instant he glared at me, ready to fly at my throat; then, as though struck by a sudden thought, he turned and cast his eye around over the ground. With a cry of exultation he sprang forward, stooped over and rose quickly. In his hand was the arrow that had entered the heel of Achilles.

''You traitorous whelp,'' he cried, raising the arrow and rushing on Polyxena. ''If death is your wish, you shall have it!''

I reached him barely in time, gripping his shoulder and hurling him back. He fell sprawling. "In the name of Apollo," I thundered, "will you come to your senses?"

But it was like trying to argue with a wild animal. He scrambled to his feet and came at me, brandishing the deadly arrow. Thrice he lunged, and each time the point of poison missed me by the breadth of a hair. I saw that if I would avoid the fate of Achilles I must adopt sterner measures. He lunged again. Stepping nimbly aside so that the arrow passed just over my shoulder, I raised my arm and brought the heavy sword down on his head with all the strength that was in me.

He dropped like a log, with his skull cloven in two clear to his chin.

I took a step backward. The sword dropped from my nerveless fingers. "Great Zeus!" I groaned. "Is this thy penalty?"

Then I turned to Polyxena.

She still lay across the body of Achilles, sobbing and moaning; her fingers were wound in his golden hair; her face lay against his. Thrice I called her name, but she gave no heed.

I grasped her by the shoulder and hauled her to her feet. She kept her face turned to the body on the floor, wailing and moaning. There was no time for gentle persuasion. I shook her so roughly that her hair flew about her face and her teeth rattled.

"Come," I cried, "there is no more to be done here!"

She glared at me fiercely, crying: "Let me go; I will not leave him!"

"Then I will leave you! Do you know that your brother also is slain?" I pointed to the body of Paris; she glanced at it, shuddering.

"Come, Polyxena; come to your senses. Would you have all Troy know your infamy? Would you have your father's curses on your head? There is yet time to save your name from dishonor. For the sake of Hecuba, your mother; of your sister Cassandra—"

I picked up the Phrygian cap from where it had fallen on the ground and pulled it over her head; then, taking her by the arm, led the way from the vault.

At the mouth of the lane we glanced back; the lantern's

feeble gleams barely disclosed the two still forms lying in the center. Polyxena jerked away from my grasp, ran back to the Greek, stooped over and placed a kiss on his forehead.

"My love!" she sighed piteously. Then she rejoined me, saying firmly:

"I will follow you."

At the next vault we found ourselves in darkness, but I could not make myself go back for the lantern. We groped our way forward. Through another vault, and another; at length we were in the outer passage.

"Straighten yourself; walk firmly," I whispered to Polyxena, for she was leaning heavily on my arm. "Be brave; cease your moans; soon you will be safe."

The captain of the guard met us at the main entrance to the gates.

"Well, were you successful?" he asked jovially. He had known nothing of the nature of the adventure that had brought the kesten Idaeus and Paris, son of Priam, to the Scaean Gates.

I spoke in a loud and distinct tone:

"Yes. It has been successful, and yet disastrous. I have a task for you, captain. Take your men and go to the fifth vault in the passage on the right. Achilles has slain Paris. I have slain Achilles. Their bodies are there. Good night!"

And before the astonished captain could fully grasp the meaning of my words or open his mouth to reply to them, Polyxena and I had turned swiftly and disappeared into the night.

CHAPTER XXIV

※

THE WOODEN HORSE.

THUS CAME ABOUT THE REJOICING OF TROY. IT BEGAN
with the sun of the following morning. Hector was all
but forgotten; the sufferings of the siege were laughed
at; Priam and Hecuba were once more seen to smile. The city
was bathed in joy. The very birds in the trees seemed to twit-
ter:

"Achilles is dead!"

No one knew exactly how it happened. A thousand stories
raced through the streets of the city. The only true source of
information was myself, and I would say but little. "Paris slew
Achilles with an arrow in the heel. Achilles clove Paris's head
with a sword." When anyone pressed me for details—even
Priam himself—I answered that the darkness of the vault and
the excitement of the action had kept all details from me.

When I was asked how Achilles came to the Scaean Gates,
and for what, I replied that that knowledge was buried in the
breasts of the slain.

I did not forget having told the captain that I myself had
slain Achilles, but I decided not to stick by that statement. In

the first place, it was a dangerous honor, for it would have brought on my head the vengeance of all the Greeks; Paris, being dead, could carry the glory with more safety.

Not to mention the fact that he deserved it.

As for Polyxena, she was safe. I had taken her in with me at the main entrance of the palace, and she had succeeded in reaching her own apartments without being detected. There she remained all of the following day, refusing admittance even to Queen Hecuba, her mother. Hecamed tried many times to see her, in vain. In the great excitement over the death of Achilles her behavior attracted little attention; King Priam dismissed it with the observation that she was probably having another of her tantrums.

No one went to the field. The palace was crowded with warriors and councilors, their faces lit up with smiles of relief and joy. Some—especially Æneas and Agavus—were not a little touched with envy that they had missed the glory, but even they showered congratulations upon me. I was the man of the hour.

We could imagine, though we could not see, the consternation of the Greeks. After a long absence, during which they had suffered defeat after defeat, Achilles had returned to the field. Immediately victory had perched on their banners. Hector had fallen. It thus appeared that Achilles was the only man who could bring them success; and Achilles was dead. Certain, they were in the depths of despair.

Four days the citizens labored on the construction of a funeral pile for Paris, and throughout those four days the body of Achilles was displayed in a public square, while insult and contumely were heaped upon it. No man of Troy passed the place without spitting contemptuously into the dirt; the women and children danced about the corpse, singing ballads.

On the fifth day everyone gathered in Doreon Square for the funeral of Paris. It was an occasion of joy rather than sorrow, for he had died far more gloriously than he had lived. There was no Andromache to mourn him; Helen was as unmoved as though he had been some common slave, and he had never been a favorite of Priam or Hecuba.

But we rejoiced to do him honor. Had not his hand, guided by Apollo, saved Troy? The story of his dream was all over the city; evidently he had told it to others besides myself.

On the following morning the warriors prepared to take the field with light hearts. Æneas was to lead; second in command was Hyrtacides of Arisbe, for Evenus was no more. Freshened by their five days of rest and newly heartened by the death of their greatest foe, the troops shouted and sang as they marched through the streets toward the gates.

Priam and Hecuba appeared again on the Scaean Towers, together with all the members of the royal household. Andromache was absent, but her little son, Astyanax, the offspring of Hector, came with his aunt Cassandra. I had once more begged permission of Priam to go to the field, but he had refused; accordingly, I took Hecamed to the Towers.

Emerging from the Passage of the Seven Pillars, we found ourselves face to face with Polyxena. It was the first time she had left the palace since that fateful night five days before. Hecamed advanced to her with outstretched hand, exclaiming eagerly:

"Polyxena! I am so glad to see you!"

Whereupon the daughter of Priam swept us both with a glance of scorn and hatred, turned her back and walked away. This was her gratitude for my having preserved her from odium and shame, perhaps from death itself. There may be something to be said on her side of the matter, but surely nothing strong enough to warrant a public insult.

Luckily it passed unobserved. Hecamed and I moved on to the main part of the Towers. Hailed by Cassandra, she left me to join her at one of the tables against the wall, where she began playing with little Astyanax; I proceeded to the eastern parapet, and, after making my obeisance to Priam, entered into conversation with Antenor and Hicetaon, who stood nearby.

Soon the sound of shouts came from below. Looking over the edge of the parapet, we saw the first of the soldiers, led by Æneas, emerge from the gates. He stood erect in his chariot, encased in shining armor; the rays of the sun, reflected from his brazen shield, dazzled our eyes.

''He is the hope of Troy,'' observed Antenor at my side.

''And now that Achilles is gone, he will bring us victory,'' put in Hicetaon.

But the field was not destined to see bloodshed that day. Æneas had entered the plain and Hyrtacides had emerged from the gate, when a herald was observed suddenly to point excitedly towards the east, at the same time shouting something that did not reach us on the Towers. Turning our eyes in the direction indicated, we saw a Grecian chariot approaching at top speed across the plain.

It was already some distance this side of the field; we would have observed it much sooner from the Towers if our attention had not been bestowed exclusively on the soldiers below. Drawn by four white horses and followed by a trail of dust, it came forward like a whirlwind, headed straight for Æneas where he stood in his chariot at the head of the troops.

Those on the Towers ran excitedly to the parapet. Exclamations were heard on all sides:

''It is Ajax!''

''Nay, 'tis Menelaus; he is smaller than Ajax.''

''Ulysses! By Zeus, 'tis Ulysses!''

''What can he want?''

There was a chorus of cries on all sides:

''He has come for the body of Achilles!''

The chariot of the Greek had come to a stop not ten paces from that of Æneas. The Greek descended, and it was then seen by all that it was indeed Ulysses himself. Æneas also had leaped to the ground; the Greek and the Trojan met with a formal salute, and Ulysses began speaking, but in a voice so low that its sound did not reach us on the Towers.

This for a short moment, then the two warriors turned and started toward the gates side by side. The troops made way for their entrance.

We were in a fever of excitement, for though we thought we knew his errand—to ask for the body of Achilles—still the appearance of the renowned Ulysses within the walls of Troy was a memorable event. Besides, we were consumed with curiosity to know how Priam would answer his request.

There was a long wait—it took some time to climb to the top of the Scaean Towers—and then we saw them advancing down the Passage of the Seven Pillars. At the door Æneas stepped aside to allow Ulysses to enter first. Running the gantlet of a hundred pair of curious eyes, the haughty Greek crossed the platform and stopped before the throne of Priam.

"O king," he began, "you see before you Ulysses of Ithaca, ambassador of the Greeks, who comes thus alone to crave your ear."

Priam wore a heavy frown; he glared at the visitor with cold eyes.

"I can guess your purpose," he said. "It were as well not spoken."

"But you have not heard me," replied the Greek with an appearance of surprise. "Is my errand known?"

"I say I can guess it."

"Still, may I speak?"

"If it is your desire. What would you?"

Ulysses cleared his throat and took a step forward. "Now, O king," he began, "I am sent by Agamemnon and the Grecian princes in council. These are the words:

"Our attack on the kingdom and city of Troy was begun to wrest from Paris the person of Argive Helen, whom he wrongfully stole from Menelaus of Sparta, her rightful husband. Now that Paris is dead, we are revenged on him; our purpose in that is achieved. The honors of the field weigh equal on either side; many of our soldiers have fallen, so have yours. Achilles is no more; Hector is slain. Diomed and Antilochus have perished; Evenus and Troilus have fed the pyre. Helenus has gone—"

Priam interrupted the orator:

"Have you come, Ulysses, to remind us of our grief or to boast of your victories?"

"Nay," returned the Greek; "do I not also name the Acheans who have fallen? To prove our equality is my purpose; more is not needed. Know that my errand is one of friendship. In few, the men of Greece pine for their wives, their sons, their hills and valleys, their vineyards, their fields of grain. The hardships of war weigh more heavily on us than on the men of Troy, absent as we are from our homes. My purpose, O king, is to conclude an honorable peace with you. Our intention is to depart for our own shores.''

At these astounding words Priam bent forward eagerly; the councilors pressed forward; a murmur of excitement ran over the throng. Ulysses continued:

''To speak frankly, what hope to scale the walls of Troy without Achilles to lead us? If that is to acknowledge defeat, we do acknowledge it. But we would have the peace honorable. A present from you to Agamemnon would betoken your respect and good will; on our part, we have labored for five days on the construction of a gift suitable to great Troy. We await your answer.''

As Ulysses finished and made his obeisance the crowd surged forward toward the throne with a great shout of joy. Æneas stepped up to speak in a low tone to Priam; his words could not be heard above the clamor. Three or four were seen to dash excitedly toward the Passage of the Seven Pillars, each wishing to be the first to carry the glad news to the thronged streets below. All was confusion; everyone laughed and talked at the same time.

Hecuba alone was sorrowful. ''Alas! my Hector,'' she sighed, ''if this had only come sooner!'' Observations were heard on all sides:

''The Greeks have had enough.''

''They find they can do nothing without Achilles.''

''Ulysses himself comes to sue for peace! They must be in a bad way indeed.''

And so on, ad infinitum; Ulysses must have heard many of the disparaging remarks, but he gave no sign.

Priam, old as he was, had not forgotten the diplomatic tricks for which he had formerly been famous. No doubt his heart was thumping with relief and joy, but there was no appearance of it in his face as he listened gravely to the words of Æneas. At length Æneas finished; Priam rose to his feet, stretching forth his hand, and instantly silence took the place of clamor. All gazed breathlessly at the king, awaiting his answer.

''Ulysses,'' said Priam, looking sternly at the Greek, ''it is no matter of wonder that the Achaeans seek peace. But though warlike, the men of Troy are not too fond of war. Methinks I could answer for them now, but I shall consult my advisers in council. Antenor, Æneas, Hicetaon, Panthous, Ucalegon, Lampus, repair with your companions to the council chamber; Idaeus—where is my kesten?—Idaeus, do you go also. I will attend you there. Polites, conduct Ulysses to the palace; entertain him with feast and dance while we deliberate.''

A murmur of disapproval came from the crowd; it was easy to see this delay did not please them. If honorable peace was offered, why not accept at once? But Priam silenced them with a glance, motioning to his slaves to assist him from the throne.

With war chariots as conveyances, we returned to the palace. The streets were filled; all faces beamed; even Ulysses was greeted with cheers on all sides. This I thought most unpolitic, for it was not wise to allow the Greek to perceive our desire for peace. But he who expects wisdom from the people will ever be disappointed.

The atmosphere of the council chamber on that day was free from the gravity and anxiety that had lain over us for so many weary months. One glance at the faces of the councilors was sufficient to know their opinions; without exception they glowed with satisfaction and beamed with joy.

The first question that arose was whether to accept the proposal of peace. On this there was no debate; everyone was unanimous for the affirmative. That settled, Priam introduced the subject of a present to the Greeks, observing that since this was a great and unusual occasion the selection must be no ordinary one.

Instantly a dispute arose. Panthous suggested the golden vases of Euryalus; Antenor retorted that the Greeks would probably think they were funeral urns and take it for an insult.

Antenor suggested the corpse of Achilles, but everyone laughed at that.

Proposals followed from all sides: twelve steeds of Thrace; the famous tapestry cloaks of Hector; a hundred talents of fine gold; the person of Helen.

Dissension was growing apace, when suddenly Hicetaon

raised his voice with the remark that it might be well to ascertain what gift the Greeks intended to proffer before we decided on our own. According to Ulysses, it had taken them five days to construct it, working day and night; it must indeed be something original.

This suggestion met with the approval of all, and a herald was despatched to the chamber where Ulysses sat with Polites, to ask him the nature of the Grecian gift. We awaited his return in silence.

Soon he reappeared. "The gift of the Greeks," he reported to Priam, "is a great horse of wood, twenty cubits high."

We looked at one another in surprise, wondering where the Achaeans had got hold of an idea so strange.

"An odd fancy," observed Panthous, "probably with reference to the steeds of Thessaly captured by Diomed."

"More likely they mean to intimate that Troy is sadly in need of horses," put in Hicetaon sarcastically.

Æneas arose.

"O king," he said, addressing Priam, "I like not this contrivance of the Greeks. A more usual gift would please me more; I like it not."

"You are ever suspicious," frowned Priam. "What harm can you suspect in this?"

"I know not. But—in short—I would advise that we refuse this strange gift. If for no other reason, because it is the wily Ulysses who offers it. You know his reputation; he needs to be watched with three eyes."

But the objection of Æneas was laughed away. Even Antenor scoffed at him. "If you fear a horse of wood," Priam observed, "what would you say to a man of flesh? The Greeks would jeer at us. Their gift is an ingenious one, intended to please us: it is not meet we should insult them by a refusal."

Whereupon we resumed the former discussion. There is no need to report the details of the tiresome debate, which lasted till the middle of the day; it is enough to say that our final decision rested on the tapestry cloaks of Hector and a hundred talents of fine gold.

This decision having been concurred in by all, though

Æneas held to his suspicion, a herald was sent for Ulysses. He received the news of our acceptance with an impassive countenance, saying that the wooden horse would be delivered that same day at the Scaean Gates.

We escorted him to his chariot; slaves followed with the tapestry cloaks of Hector and the hundred talents of fine gold. These were heaped about the feet of the Greek in the quadriga; the driver sprang to his seat, and, surrounded by two score soldiers as a guard of honor, Ulysses departed for the camp.

Thus did peace come to Troy. A short-lived peace indeed; a false calm before a devastating storm; but we did not know that then. Women and children marched through the streets singing ballads and hymns; soldiers embraced their wives and sons with tears of joy; arrangements were set on foot for a monster feast and festival to be celebrated on the third day.

Sorrowful faces there were indeed, for many were gone who would never return; peace itself cannot remedy the past, nor do souls return either from the shades below or the fields of Elysium. But this note of sadness only served to accentuate the general rejoicing.

Late in the afternoon I set off with Hecamed for the Scaean Towers, together with all the royal household, the councilors, and the warriors. Æneas, seeing me descend the steps of the palace, sent me an invitation to ride in his chariot. I accepted gladly, leaving Hecamed to follow with Cassandra and Andromache in one of the palace wagons.

Our progress through the streets was slow. On all sides Æneas and I were recognized; it was easy to see that he took the cheers and acclamations for himself, though it is probable that most came from the appreciation of my part in the death of Achilles; nor had the people forgotten that it was I who drove Priam to the Grecian camp to rescue the body of Hector.

But, petty jealousies aside, we arrived at the Towers to find a great crowd already collected there, for it was then toward the end of the day. More were arriving every moment. Advancing to the eastern parapet, Æneas and I saw that what we had come to see was at that moment advancing across the plain toward the gates of the city.

It was the wooden horse, pushed along by two hundred soldiers, led by a warrior in a chariot. Even from the height of the Towers it appeared to be immense; Ulysses's estimate of twenty cubits seemed short of the fact. Great straps of leather were fastened in front; half of the soldiers tugged lustily at these, while the other half pushed from behind.

Excitement on the Towers ran high, not so much at the appearance of this strange gift as at the peace it betokened, though curiosity was not absent. The arrival of Priam and Hecuba created but a small stir, though there was some whispering when it was seen that they were accompanied by Andromache, Cassandra, Hecamed, Polyxena, Agavus—in short, all the royal household—followed them.

Soon the wooden horse was almost directly beneath us. Its appearance was ludicrous enough. Its legs were about twice too long for its body; its tail, also of wood, stretched out behind like a handle on a water-box; thirdly—but if I were to enumerate all its defects and oddities I should never end. I turned to Æneas to observe that it was a good thing Ulysses had told us it was a horse, for we should never have guessed it ourselves.

Wheeling the thing to a position not ten paces away from the gates, the soldiers fell back at the command of their leader, who, standing in his chariot, raised his voice to the Towers:

"Great Priam, I bring the gift of the Greeks. It is our farewell; even now the anchors of our ships are lifted; our tents are folded. May you and Troy forever enjoy peace and happiness. Farewell!"

In reply Priam merely nodded.

The Greek wheeled his chariot about; the soldiers fell into line. The next moment they were marching swiftly across the plain toward the Grecian camp. Straining our eyes eastward, we saw that he had spoken truth; the tents of the Greeks were not to be seen.

Priam turned to a herald.

"Go below to the captain of the guard. Tell him to open the gates and bring the wooden horse within. It is to be placed in Doreon Square on the spot where was erected the pile of Hector. Go.''

The herald turned to depart. As he did so a cry came from the rear of the throne:

"Stop!"

It was the voice of Cassandra. She came forth and stood before the king with outstretched hands:

"Father, hear me, I beseech you! I can hold my peace no longer."

No doubt Priam understood her intention, for before answering her he nodded to the herald to proceed on his mission. When he had been obeyed the king turned to Cassandra:

"Now, daughter, I will hear you."

"Then call back your herald!"

"That I will not do. Speak!"

Cassandra took a step forward.

"You know I am endowed by Apollo with the gift of prophecy," she began in a voice of entreaty.

"You have said so many times," Priam smiled, and a ripple of mirth ran over the assembly. Cassandra's face turned red with mortification, but she continued firmly:

"If I have said so, have I not also offered proof? But of the past no more; I warn you, heed my words."

"I remember you predicted that Troy would fall before the Greeks," Priam interrupted. "And now—their tents are folded!"

"I care not," Cassandra replied stubbornly. "My office comes from Apollo and I speak the words of the God. If the gift of the Greeks"—she pointed below to where the wooden horse was being pushed through the gates—"is allowed to enter Troy will fall, and you and yours will perish."

"But what fear, since it drags no chariot?"

The crowd laughed at the king's excellent joke; like a flash Cassandra turned on them.

"You gaping crew!" she cried, while her eyes filled with tears of rage. "You shall remember my words when the sword of the Greek is at your throats!"

Silence followed, and I, for one, felt a thrill of premonition run through me, so strange were her tones. But it soon passed away, when Cassandra moved again to the rear of the throne and those about me began to crowd toward the north wall to witness the entry of the wooden horse.

By then it was through the gates and well across the open square before them, half dragged, half pushed, by the willing hands of a thousand soldiers and citizens. We waved our mantles at them, calling ironical words of encouragement; they laughed back at us and pushed harder than before. Soon they had reached the entrance of a street and started toward the place Priam had designated it should be set.

Suddenly a mighty shout came from someone on the eastern parapet:

"The Greeks are departing!"

We rushed across and strained our eyes toward the Scamander. It was true. The great fleet that had lain so long at anchor was slowly moving down the river. The fluttering sails appeared in the distance like an immense flock of birds with gigantic wings. The Greeks were departing for their own shores.

It would seem that until that moment we had retained a doubt of the genuineness of their declared intention to end the war, for the sight of the moving ships aroused us to a sudden enthusiasm beyond any Troy had known.

The scene that took place on the Towers was indescribable. Priam and Hecuba, bathed in tears, embraced each other; women jumped about as though they had suddenly lost their senses, flinging their mantles high in the air, caring nothing if strange eyes saw their undergarments; men slapped one another on the back, shouting and dancing in glee. From the city beneath there ascended a mighty roar. The cry was passed from street to street:

"The Greeks are departing!"

But I noticed that Cassandra sat in a corner regarding the merrymakers with a face of gloomy sadness, and Æneas stood apart, frowning off into space.

A little later people began to leave the Towers, for it was nearly night. Jovial salutes and farewells were exchanged on every side; even Andromache smiled as she accepted the offer of Hicetaon to conduct her to the palace. A meeting was arranged for the following day to consider the details of the feast and festival of celebration.

Hecamed and I decided to walk to the palace, for the evening air was soft and balmy; this notwithstanding the fact that we received many offers of chariots. Descending the winding stairs and pushing our way through the throng about the gates, we found ourselves in one of the narrow streets flanking Doreon Square.

At Hecamed's suggestion we turned aside to take a look at the wooden horse. There it stood, high above our heads, hugely grotesque in the twilight, with its sprawling legs and tail sticking straight out. It was certainly a monstrosity.

"I wonder," observed Hecamed curiously, as we turned to go, "if it is empty?"

If only someone in Troy had been curious enough, or wise enough, to discover the answer to that question before it was too late!

CHAPTER XXV

✥

CONCLUSION.

AT THIS DISTANCE OF TIME, SURROUNDED BY HAPPINESS and security, I wonder at the folly of Troy. Even Æneas, who had warned the council against the strange gift offered by the crafty Ulysses, allowed all guards to be taken from the walls, and himself lay by the side of his Creüsa to enjoy the first good night's sleep he had known in months.

Everything is known to me now—to me with the rest of the world; how forty Greeks, commanded by Ulysses, were secreted in the belly of the wooden horse; how they came forth in the dead of night and made their way to the Scaean Gates; how they overpowered the small guard they found there and opened the barriers for the whole Grecian army, which had anchored a short distance down the river and stolen back under cover of the darkness.

All this, I say, I know now; but all I knew then was that after I had been soundly asleep for some time I was awakened by the voice of Hecamed at my side:

"Idaeus! Get up! Someone is pounding on the door!"

I sat up, rubbing my eyes. "What do you want? What is it?" I muttered sleepily.

Then the pounding reached my ears and I leaped out of bed. "What are you trying to do, break the door down?" I shouted angrily, slipping on my chiton; for whoever the intruder was, he appeared to be trying to kick in the panels with his boots.

As I ran down the hall the sound of voices came to me from the corridor without. A thrill ran through me at the tones. "What is it?" I shouted through the door. In reply I heard only two words:

"The Greeks—the Greeks—the Greeks—"

I opened the door. A herald faced me.

"The Greeks—we are doomed!" he said, and disappeared.

I caught a glimpse of other forms flying down the corridor, but I did not stop to inquire further.

In two moments Hecamed had thrown on her himation and sandals and was helping me with my armor. Thank the Gods I stopped to put it on! She hastened to the rear to call Thersin; an instant later he went flying past me and through the door. That was the last I ever saw of him. Hecamed and I followed.

In the corridor we found men and women, half-clothed, flying toward the great staircase. Their hair streamed behind them; their faces were white with fear; they were screaming in tones of panic:

"The Greeks are coming!"

For the most part they appeared to be slaves. The only one I recognized was Agavus, son of Priam. Him I caught by the arm, demanding to know the cause of the alarm.

"I know not—let me go!" he shouted, and bounded toward the stairway like a scared rabbit.

I turned to Hecamed:

"Let us see. It is probably nothing."

A moment later we were at the entrance without. A single glance showed us that it was a great deal more than nothing.

The square in front of the palace was filled with a struggling mass; the light from the torches on the portals was too dim to distinguish anything clearly. But what made me halt, while my face turned white, was the dreadful din and clamor that came from all over the city.

Men and women were rushing past us through the entrance, only to turn again when they caught sight of the struggle in the square. Some turned once more and darted off to one side or another in the darkness of the palace grounds.

For a single instant I was seized with panic. The sudden transition from peaceful sleep to this scene of conflict, the glare of the torches, the screams of women and the shouts of men, struck me with dumb fear. I grasped Hecamed by the arm, thinking, like the others, to escape in the darkness.

But only for a moment. The next I had drawn my sword from its scabbard and turned to Hecamed:

"Go back to our rooms. Await me there. Stir not till I come for you."

She clung to me, trembling violently. "Idaeus—do not leave me—you will be killed—"

"Probably. So will everyone else." And I shoved her back within the entrance. "Obey me!" Then I turned and started for the square.

As I got closer it was a fearful sight that met my eyes. Some three or four hundred Trojans, half-naked and armed only with lances and darts, were holding back twice their number of Greeks, whose brazen armor glistened in the light of the torches. Seeing that it would be folly to enter so unequal a combat, I drew back. Then, struck by a sudden thought, I ran forward and hurled myself straight into the fighting throng.

I gained the foot of a column in the ornamental wall that surrounded the palace. Somehow I mounted the column to its very top. Greek darts and javelins came at me from below; one or two landed, but grazed harmlessly off my armor. I bawled at the top of my lungs:

"Trojans, fall back! To the entrance of the palace!"

Some heard me above the din, and understood. The palace entrance, being somewhat narrow, could be defended; here in the open square they would all be butchered. I leaped from the column and ran for the entrance, followed by twoscore Trojans. Others, observing the movement, joined us. The

Greeks rushed after them with yells of triumph, thinking we retreated.

They soon discovered their mistake. Dashing headlong up the steps, they met our lances in their faces; I saw one Trojan, a huge fellow, pick up a Greek in full armor and hurl him clattering down the steps, which were soon half covered with the bodies of their dead.

But a minute of that and they learnt caution; retreating towards the square, they sent their javelins through the air at us. We took refuge as far as possible behind the columns.

Suddenly I heard a voice behind me:

"Well done, Idaeus!"

I turned. "Æneas!" I exclaimed.

"Yes. I saw you from the rear."

"But how did you come—"

"Through the door of Amphibus."

"What—how did the Greeks—"

"The wooden horse. They were concealed in its belly—they opened the gates—the others came—'twas a trick of Ulysses—"

"But you—your wife—your son—"

"I was surprised in bed. They are all over the city. My wife is killed. My son is in the palace. My home is burned."

It was then, glancing out, I saw the first sign of fire—a dull red glow off to the east, towards the Scaean Gates.

That glow was destined to spread.

"I escaped somehow," Æneas was saying. "We must save Priam and Hecuba. Have you seen them?"

"No."

"Go. Search for them and take them to the red chamber in the rear; it can best be defended. I will take your place here."

"But if they should refuse—"

"Go! Haul them forth!"

With one glance backward at the Greeks, who, with constantly arriving reinforcements, were hurling stones and javelins at the entrance, I turned and ran within the palace.

Slaves—mostly women—were running about distracted in every direction, shrieking and tearing their hair. One stood directly in my path at the end of the corridor; I rushed past, knocking her against the wall in my frenzy. Her curses followed me.

I reached the apartments of the king. The antechamber was empty. At the entrance of the next room I stopped short at the sight that met my eyes.

Priam stood in the middle of the floor, buckling on his armor, so heavy that his withered old arms could scarcely lift it. Brave old man! At his feet knelt Hecuba and their daughters Cassandra, Polyxena, and Andromache. They were wringing their hands in terror and beseeching him not to go.

"Shall I sit like a woman while my palace is attacked?" he roared. "Cassandra! Andromache! Well, if you will not help me—" He tried in vain to put the massive shield in place.

"Idaeus!" he cried, catching sight of me.

I ran forward. "Yes. I am sent by Æneas. You are to go to the red chamber; we can defend you there." I jerked the women to their feet and pushed them towards the door, then took Priam's arm. "To the red chamber!" I shouted.

He would not go; I pulled him along; the queen and princesses followed. Priam bellowed that I should pay dearly for touching his person. I picked him up and carried him down the corridors and stairs at a run.

We found several already gathered in the red chamber; some of Hecuba's and Cassandra's waiting-women, Agavus and Polites, sons of Priam, Ascanius, the little son of Æneas, and a crowd of slaves. I instructed Agavus to watch over Priam and see that no one ventured out of the chamber. Then, with Polites at my side, I started for the entrance without.

Suddenly I halted. Should I go to my rooms for Hecamed and bring her too to the red chamber? I decided that she was as safe where she was.

We found Æneas and his men holding their own at the entrance, but the square without was overflowing with Greeks and more were arriving every moment. Javelins and stones were flying at us in a storm. We returned them, but as the Greeks were in full armor we could hope to do little damage. The dull glow I had noticed in the direction of the Scaean

Gates had increased in brilliance and was approaching across the city; as I looked a tongue of flame shot high into the air in the neighborhood of the Temple of Mulciber.

Suddenly a figure detached itself from the mass of Greeks in the square and approached the palace. Trojan darts and lances fell thick about him, but he heeded them not. As he came within the light of the torches we saw that it was Ulysses.

"Ho! Æneas," he called, "will you try your strength, you hider behind pillars?"

Æneas roared at him:

"You lying knave! Before you enter this palace you shall pay for your treachery!"

Ulysses laughed mockingly, then turned to the Greeks:

"Ajax! Men of Ithaca! Forward!"

The next moment a thousand hurled themselves at the entrance.

"Hold your shafts!" commanded Æneas. "Wait till they reach the top!"

The Greeks, led by Ajax, met our lances in their faces. We made no attempt to pierce their armor, merely pushing them back down the steps against their comrades. They tumbled in heaps, rolling to the bottom. Æneas himself met Ajax; his sword struck the Greek in the crevice between his gorget and helm; he toppled backward.

Again they rushed, and were again repelled. Many Trojans had fallen, unprotected against the enemy's javelins. Still there were more than enough to defend the steps; I believe Æneas, Polites, and myself could have held them alone for hours.

A dozen Greeks reached the landing, but they soon fell never to rise more. Again and again they rushed up the steps, leaving dead behind them at every attack. The steps were cluttered with the corpses; they sprang upon the carcasses of their comrades and dashed at us, led by Ajax.

"What folly!" muttered Æneas, thrusting out with his sword. "Where is Ulysses? I would die gladly if I could first pierce his lying throat!"

At that instant, as though in answer to his question, a great cry came from within the palace. The next moment Agavus rushed out to us with blanched face and staring eyes.

"They have entered from the rear!" he shouted. "We are lost!"

Calling to Polites to hold the steps with his men, Æneas and I turned and ran into the palace. Up a flight of stairs, down a corridor, and we found ourselves at the entrance of the red chamber.

We halted with a cry of horror and rage at the sight that met our eyes. Ulysses, at the head of twoscore Greeks, had just reached the door. On the threshold stood King Priam, holding aloft a huge battle-sword; his grim old face was filled with the resolution of despair and with a frightful courage. The sword descended, glancing harmlessly off the helm of Ulysses.

The Greek laughed aloud and lunged forward with his own sword. The old king fell to the floor without a sound, with the blade buried in his breast.

Æneas sprang forward with a scream of fury; I followed. The Greeks blocked the door, and more came running down the hall. Fighting like madmen, we cut our way through. We crossed the threshold in time to see Ulysses lift Queen Hecuba from the floor by her hair and sever her head from her body with one stroke of his sword.

The next moment the room was filled with Greeks. Andromache, Cassandra, and Polyxena were carried off, shrieking and wailing. Æneas fought his way through the mass to where his little son Ascanius crouched in a corner, lifted him to his shoulders and turned like a lion at bay. The boy held on with his arms around his father's neck. Æneas was calling to me that no more was to be done except to save ourselves, if that were possible.

I saw him strike Ulysses and two others to the floor with one sweep of his sword.

I fought wildly, blindly, to reach the door. Those who stood in my way were naught but common soldiers; there was no room for the play of their long javelins, and I cut them down with my sword. They threw themselves on my shoulders and clung all over me, but somehow I kept my feet. With one great plunge I shook myself free and stumbled through the door.

I raced through the corridors; a few tried to stop me, but I felled them with my sword. I saw Aethra and Clymene, Helen's waiting-women, in the arms of Greek soldiers; no doubt Helen herself had long since been torn from her bed by Menelaus.

Reaching the upper corridor, I saw that it had not yet been invaded. With a prayer of hope and thankfulness in my heart, I ran to the further end and entered my own rooms.

"Hecamed!" I cried.

Then I saw her kneeling in the middle of the floor with her hands upraised to heaven.

"I thought you had been killed," she moaned. "I wanted to fly—"

I had already decided what to do; indeed, there was only one possible means of escape. Running to the kitchen, I secured two pieces of whitleather, each some twenty cubits in length, and fastened them securely together. Then I went to Hecamed's room, the window of which looked out on the gardens at the rear of the palace.

Together we dragged a heavy marble bench to the window and placed it in a position so that its ends came squarely against the jamb on either side. I tied one end of the leather rope to the top of the bench and dropped the other end out of the window.

I turned to Hecamed:

"Can you descend that?"

For answer she clambered onto the sill.

"When you are at the bottom," I instructed her, "shake the rope; I will follow. Do not call; do not even whisper."

"Yes." She grasped the leather with her hands, twisted her foot in it further down, and began to descend. I leaned out of the window to watch her. Once she slipped—I suppressed a cry of horror—but she caught herself and finally reached the ground in safety.

There was no need to shake the rope; the light of the burning buildings on the other side of the palace grounds disclosed her plainly to view.

In another moment I was on the ground beside her, sword in hand.

Our only hope was to reach the Pylian Gates at the western end of the city. Even that hope appeared slim indeed, but it was the only chance.

Turning sharply to the left, we proceeded to the end of the palace grounds, passing the lodgings of Hector and Paris in the rear, besides the other outlying buildings.

Reaching the public streets, we gave ourselves up for lost. A dreadful din and clamor smote our ears from every side; in whatever direction we looked we saw leaping flames and indescribable panic and confusion. The streets were filled with Greek soldiers, drunk with victory, striking down men and children and bearing off women. Many, satiated with blood, were already looting the homes and shops and piling their booty in the streets, preparatory to firing the buildings.

Stopping only a moment to get breath, Hecamed and I plunged side by side into the mouth of the first street to the west.

No single detail of that fearful journey across Troy remains in my mind; I have only an impression of an indistinct and horrible nightmare. We saw men torn from the arms of their wives and struck down before their eyes; we saw children and babes slaughtered on their mothers' necks; we saw many nameless and terrible deeds.

Often we ourselves were attacked; we escaped only by a miracle, though my sword was never long idle. In the eastern part of the city we would have been cut down before advancing a hundred paces; here in the west were none but common soldiers, the overflow from those about the palace.

At length we reached the Pylian Gates. They were swinging wide open; the guard had disappeared, though the Greeks had not yet come so far. Trojan fathers and mothers, carrying their children on their backs and their household goods in their hands, were fleeing forth into the fields. Hecamed and I joined them.

As we passed through the gates Hecamed stopped suddenly to stoop over a little fellow—a boy about seven years of age—who stood directly in our path. He gazed up at her with wide-open, curious eyes.

"Where is your mother?" asked Hecamed, for he appeared to be alone.

The boy replied simply, without any trace of emotion:

"Dead."

"And your father?"

"He is dead, too."

"Are you alone?"

"Yes."

"How did you come here?"

"I ran."

"What is your name?"

"Pieranthus, son of Aleus."

"Will you come with me?"

For answer he put out his hand. She took it, and the next moment we had passed through the gates.

Others around us were turning to right or left, avoiding the steep hills directly west of the city. This appeared to me to be foolish, for the Greeks would surely arrive at the gates before long, and to pursue the fugitives over the plains would be an easy matter. So I started for the hills, followed by Hecamed and the boy.

For a long time we toiled upward, clinging to roots and bushes and sometimes crawling on our hands and knees. Our clothing was torn, our faces were scratched and our limbs were wearied, but we struggled on. At length, reaching the flat eminence known as Sarpedon's Rock, we stopped to get our breath and take a last look at Troy.

It was not Troy we saw, but a roaring furnace of fire. The flames leaped and sprawled high in the heavens. The beautiful city was doomed, but never had it appeared so terribly beautiful as at the moment of its destruction.

Across the plain and up the hills there came faintly to our ears the sound of its death cry.... My eyes filled with tears;

Hecamed's hand touched my arms tremulously. . . . We turned to go.

And somehow, bleeding, exhausted, but safe at last, we reached Mount Ida, where Aenone found us.

Here, in these lovely groves, with Hecamed and the boy Pieranthus at my side, I lead a solitary but happy existence. How the members of the fashionable Trojan society, if they were not in their graves, would laugh at their fellow-member Idaeus wearing the garb and performing the duties of a lowly shepherd!

But I was ever given to philosophic thoughts, and I derive much pleasure from my lonely meditations on the flowery banks of the silver river.

Now and then, when Aenone has a visitor, news comes from the great world. I hear that Cassandra resides at the home of Agamemnon; that Andromache is the wife of Neoptolemus, son of Achilles; that Polyxena was burned to death by the Greeks; that Helen was taken back to Sparta by Menelaus: that Æneas, after many perilous wanderings over the face of the earth, has finally reached the court of Queen Dido at Carthage, where he is looked upon with great favor.

Thus do I conclude that of all those who escaped with their lives on that fateful night, Hecamed and Idaeus are the most blessed and happy. We are thinking of making a visit to Tenedos in the spring, but before I venture so far from Mount Ida I shall certainly inquire whether any Greeks are loitering about in that neighborhood.

As for Pieranthus, I have come to the conclusion that his father was assuredly a warrior. All day long he marches up and down the flowery meads with a stick in his hand, making ferocious thrusts at the trunks of trees and crying out in his shrill, boyish tones:

"The Greeks are coming!"